TOURO COLLEGE LIBRARY
Kings Hwy

WITHDRAWN

"David Perkins's *Making Learning Whole* is a highly creative book that gives us ways of achieving more—much more—from our schools. The book presents a fascinating rethinking about how education might take place—and already does for the fortunate few with the most insightful teachers. Perkins teaches us that what those rare teachers do can be learned by new teachers and promoted by thoughtful principals. The result is a practical guide for thinking about how to make our schools exciting for teachers and students, and more productive than ever. This book ought to be read by everyone who is concerned about improving curriculum and instruction."

—David C. Berliner, Regents' Professor,
Mary Lou Fulton College of Education, Arizona State University

"Only David Perkins, the inimitable master of the metaphor, can so patently explicate practical steps to transforming education. This book is essential reading for educators at all levels."

—Rod Rock, director of Instructional Services,
Saginaw (Michigan) Intermediate School District

"David Perkins goes straight to the heart of the matter. His seven principles of teaching vividly explain how to organize learning in ways that allow people to *do* important things with what they know—which is, after all, the point. Every educator should read this book, and so should policymakers whose work influences whether and how we can finally make school learning whole."

—Linda Darling-Hammond, Charles E.
Ducommun Professor of Education, Stanford University

"David Perkins brings one of the most creative and energetic minds in education to generate a coherent whole from the seeming cacophony of proposals to fix our schools. He shows in this book how a potent metaphor can shape and order seven potent teaching/learning principles for everyday practice, in an engaging and often entertaining narrative that will be of enormous practical importance to teachers, administrators, policymakers, and college and university instructors."

—Kieran Egan, faculty of Education, Simon Fraser University;
Director, IERG (Imaginative Education Research Group)

WITHDRAWN

"A must-read for those serious about transforming education to prepare our youth for success in a rapidly changing world."

—Dr. Jayne H. Mohr, Associate Superintendent,
Traverse City (Michigan) Area Public Schools

"If educators, education scholars, and students want to delve into a refreshingly clear, overarching, and bold treatment of school-based learning, this is the book they are likely to enjoy and greatly benefit from. David Perkins, the well-known Harvard innovative intellectual, summarized years of synthesizing observations, reflections, and the accumulation of serious research, cutting through the Gordian Knot of learning theories, to yield this very well-written book, filled with penetrating wisdom—a must for all those interested in learning."

—Gavriel Salomon, recipient of the Israel Award for
Scientific Achievements in Educational Research, Haifa University, Israel

"School administrators and policymakers need sturdy yet flexible ways to understand the complex and interdependent issues surrounding equitable learning. David Perkins provides such a framework through engaging metaphor and easily accessible prose. In Alameda County, we've benefited from his ideas for over five years in our work to engage the creativity of students, teachers, administrators, artists, families, and community members in making good on America's promise of a high-quality education for every child.

We are fortunate to have found a scholar who speaks clearly and directly to practitioners about innovative theory and solid research. Such tools give us the support we need to develop and implement meaningful and relevant pedagogical strategies to grow the hearts and minds of the next generation of workers and citizens."

—Sheila Jordan, superintendent, Alameda County Office
of Education (California)

"David Perkins is one of the great teachers of our time. In this insight-filled book, you can learn how he achieves his educational goals and how you can achieve yours as well."

—Howard Gardner, Hobbs Professor of Cognition and
Education, Harvard Graduate School of Education;
author of *Five Minds for the Future*

Making Learning Whole

HOW SEVEN PRINCIPLES OF TEACHING CAN TRANSFORM EDUCATION

TOURO COLLEGE LIBRARY
Kings Hwy

David N. Perkins

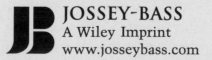 JOSSEY-BASS
A Wiley Imprint
www.josseybass.com

KH

Copyright © 2009 by David N. Perkins. All rights reserved.

Published by Jossey-Bass
A Wiley Imprint
989 Market Street, San Francisco, CA 94103-1741—www.josseybass.com

No part of this publication may be reproduced, stored in a retrieval system, or transmitted in any form or by any means, electronic, mechanical, photocopying, recording, scanning, or otherwise, except as permitted under Section 107 or 108 of the 1976 United States Copyright Act, without either the prior written permission of the publisher, or authorization through payment of the appropriate per-copy fee to the Copyright Clearance Center, Inc., 222 Rosewood Drive, Danvers, MA 01923, 978-750-8400, fax 978-646-8600, or on the Web at www.copyright.com. Requests to the publisher for permission should be addressed to the Permissions Department, John Wiley & Sons, Inc., 111 River Street, Hoboken, NJ 07030, 201-748-6011, fax 201-748-6008, or online at www.wiley.com/go/permissions.

Readers should be aware that Internet Web sites offered as citations and/or sources for further information may have changed or disappeared between the time this was written and when it is read.

Limit of Liability/Disclaimer of Warranty: While the publisher and author have used their best efforts in preparing this book, they make no representations or warranties with respect to the accuracy or completeness of the contents of this book and specifically disclaim any implied warranties of merchantability or fitness for a particular purpose. No warranty may be created or extended by sales representatives or written sales materials. The advice and strategies contained herein may not be suitable for your situation. You should consult with a professional where appropriate. Neither the publisher nor author shall be liable for any loss of profit or any other commercial damages, including but not limited to special, incidental, consequential, or other damages.

Jossey-Bass books and products are available through most bookstores. To contact Jossey-Bass directly call our Customer Care Department within the U.S. at 800-956-7739, outside the U.S. at 317-572-3986, or fax 317-572-4002.

Jossey-Bass also publishes its books in a variety of electronic formats. Some content that appears in print may not be available in electronic books.

Library of Congress Cataloging-in-Publication Data
Perkins, David N.
　　Making learning whole: how seven principles of teaching can transform education/David N. Perkins.
　　　　p.　cm.
Includes bibliographical references and index.
　　ISBN 978-0-470-38452-7 (cloth)
　　　　1. Learning.　2. Effective teaching.　I. Title.
LB1060.P448　2009
371.102—dc22

2008036106

Printed in the United States of America
FIRST EDITION

HB Printing　　　　10　9　8　7　6　5　4　3　2

8/28/09

CONTENTS

To my father, who taught me how to play baseball and much more; and to my mother, who taught me how to be stoic and much more. I never achieved excellence in either one, but the lessons were important anyway.

ACKNOWLEDGMENTS

A familiar saying recommends turning a problem into an opportunity. I suppose this book is an example of that, because its origins reflect what has been a perennial problem for me. These pages come from my own struggles to share ideas about learning with students at my home institution as well as teachers, educational administrators, mentors, organizational leaders, and even occasionally parents in a variety of settings. As I've pursued this mission over the years, I've striven to tell the whole story in a clear way.

The challenge is not one of arctic sparsity but rain forest abundance. There are too many ideas about learning that merit attention, too many from practical experience and too many from the research literature, ideas about human motivation, mastering difficult concepts, acquiring broad literacies, learning in groups, self-regulated learning, developing problem-solving and decision-making skills, and on and on. I've often felt frustrated about how to sort and bundle them into a coherent view that affords practical leverage. Until I sat down to write this book. The story told here certainly is not perfect, but I think at least it's an improvement on my scattered notes.

A little bit of digital archaeology in my computer files revealed this book's birthday: about four years ago. But for sure, the baby was not born walking and talking. First there was the basic notion of learning by wholes and the metaphor of "playing the whole game," with a few other concepts bundled loosely around it. Gradually the metaphor of the game expanded to "make the game worth playing," "uncover the hidden game," and other principles, eventually seven in all. Opportunities to share the story in various settings helped to expand and refine it. With considerably more thought and callused typing fingers, the results are before you today. I hope that you find them useful.

All this required a great deal of help. Appreciation goes to Piero Buscaglia, my administrative assistant at the Harvard Graduate School of Education, who assisted with reference work and some syntheses of relevant research. Thanks also to Lisa Frontado, my administrative assistant before Piero, who made similar contributions to the earlier stages. My wife and my youngest son, Tom, were victims of my efforts to try out possible titles and phrases for key concepts, so thanks to them as well.

Appreciation is also due to many colleagues at the Harvard Graduate School of Education with whom I've had conversations and collaborations over the years that feed into this volume, and to the sponsors of related research. Perhaps it is best here simply to recognize five principal lines of work. One is research on thinking and learning dispositions, where my principal colleagues over time have been Ron Ritchhart and Shari Tishman, with current sponsors Bialik College of Melbourne and the Abe and Vera Dorevitch Foundation, and earlier Peder Wallenberg and the Stiftelsen Carpe Vitam Foundation, and before that the MacArthur Foundation. Then there is research on teaching for understanding sponsored by the Spencer Foundation, with principal colleagues Howard Gardner, Vito Perrone, and Martha Stone Wiske. My principal colleagues for research on organizational learning and development have been Daniel Wilson and earlier Chris Unger, with current support by several corporate, nonprofit, and government affiliates and earlier by La Universidad de Bogotá Jorge Tadeo Lozano. Research on causality and understanding science, which began as a collaboration between Tina Grotzer and myself, has been taken much further by Tina, all with support from the National

Science Foundation. Finally, there is WIDE World, an initiative on widescale online teacher development, where my principal colleagues have been Martha Stone Wiske and David Zarowin, with invaluable support and counsel from Al and Kate Merck. I have learned from them all and from many others as well, and I have tried to identify specific contributions by appropriate references throughout the following pages.

Thanks are due to two academic institutions as well. Much of this book was completed during my sabbatical in calendar year 2007 from the Harvard Graduate School of Education, sabbaticals being one of the genuine and productive privileges of the academic life. Almost half of that was spent at the Center for Advanced Study in the Behavioral Sciences at Stanford, where I was a fellow in spring 2007, joining a number of other scholars, most of them on sabbatical as well, for a mix of lively conversations and individual work.

Moving closer to the process of bringing these words to the world, I also want to thank my agent of many years, Faith Hamlin, and the firm of which she is a member, Sanford J. Greenburger Associates. Faith has long provided not only assistance in placing my writings but substantial counsel about content, organization, titles, and related matters. In the same breath, let me thank my editor at Jossey-Bass, Kate Bradford, for her close reading and helpful feedback toward the final version, as well as her confidence in the project in the first place.

So now, let the games begin . . .

Making Learning Whole

Introduction:
A Whole New Ball Game

BASEBALL FOR ME WAS A TRIUMPH OF MEDIOCRITY. I WASN'T ESPECIALLY GOOD at it, but I wasn't awful either. This was an achievement because I didn't show much talent for sports in general. I was not bad at batting. A hit got this chunky child chugging around the bases, sometimes picked off but sometimes scoring. Perpetually assigned to the outfield because of my incompetence at catching, I would reliably miss the flies that came my way.

Maybe this mediocrity sounds dismal, but I was pleased with what I could do. I enjoyed playing baseball as one of a dozen ways I could spend a couple of hours on a summer afternoon. Moreover, in the years since those days I've come to an odd conclusion about those early learning experiences: The results were only so-so but the process was pretty good.

So what was the process? I remember my father teaching me to bat in our backyard. He showed me how to place my feet, how to hold the bat, how to swing. Keep your eye on the ball, he said—the familiar incantation! He pitched with a gentle underhand as I tried to get the hang of it all.

One summer I participated in Little League baseball. I didn't like the formality and elaborateness of it. Most people were taking the whole thing as seriously as a military campaign. Still, I did it: practiced catching, practiced batting, ran the bases, stood in the field, missed the flies. With more fondness, I remember casual games in anybody's backyard, seven or eight kids, just two bases or maybe one, not bothering with nine innings, sometimes not even bothering to keep score, simply playing.

So why would I say the process was pretty good? In a gut sense it was pretty good because I enjoyed playing and learning. In a more analytical sense, it was pretty good because from the beginning I built up a feel for the whole game. I knew what hitting the ball or missing the ball got you. I knew about scoring runs and keeping score. I knew what I had to do to do well, even though I only pulled it off part of the time. I saw how it fit together.

All this sounds very ordinary, but I'm simply stunned when I think how rarely formal learning gives us a chance to learn the whole game from early on. When I and my buddies studied basic arithmetic, we had no real idea what the whole game of mathematics was about. (Maybe you're thinking: Well, how could you? You were just kids and mathematics is an elaborate technical discipline. But I'm not so sure that the basic shape of doing mathematics requires calculus or algebra or even fractions.) Or I think about learning the facts of the Civil War, without getting much of the sense of how anyone found out these facts or what one might do with them—say, compare them with other civil wars in other times and other nations. (Maybe you're thinking: Well, how else could one make a start for youngsters who don't know very much history to begin with. But I'm not so sure that one has to start in such a piecemeal manner.)

Put it this way: When I was playing baseball, most of the time I wasn't playing full-scale, four bases, nine innings. But I was playing a perfectly suitable junior version of the game. A junior version was just right for my size and stamina and the number of kids in the neighborhood. But when I was studying those shards of math and history, I wasn't playing a junior version of anything. It was kind of like batting practice without knowing the whole game. Why would anyone want to do that?

Of course, there was also a lot wrong with the way I learned baseball. For one thing, baseball wasn't a campaign for me, just a pastime, and really serious learning of almost anything has to be something of a campaign. Even so, those sunny afternoons with the smell of grass and a bit of sweat and a cheap leather glove on my hand still linger in my mind. And today I wonder: Maybe learning most things should be more like learning how to play baseball.

Approaching Complexity

Some learning comes easy. You walk into a new shopping mall and quickly and almost automatically get oriented to the major landmarks: the bookstore, the department store, the electronics store, the food court. We soak up first languages quite spontaneously. The time-on-task is enormous, but the process is so programmed into human nature and so socially supported and so woven into the activities of everyday life that it happens with little deliberate attention.

However, much of what we need to learn poses significant challenges. Baseball is a complicated game, not at all like walking into a shopping mall and almost automatically getting oriented. So is basic arithmetic or algebra, reading, understanding literature, scientific inquiry and the scientific worldview, historical understanding and its relevance to current times. Also challenging are less academic areas, such as management and leadership, sustaining good relationships with other people, and social responsibility.

In all these cases education formal or informal faces its most fundamental and general problem: approaching complexity. Education aims to help people learn what they cannot simply pick up as they go along. Education always has to ask what can be done to make challenging knowledge and practices accessible.

This question becomes particularly acute in formal settings of learning such as schools and universities, with large numbers of people and vast amounts of content. Here are the two most popular answers to approaching complexity:

1. *Elements first.* Ramp into complexity gradually by learning elements now and putting them together later.

2. *Learning about.* Learn about something to start with, rather than learning to do it.

Let's look at them in turn.

Approaching complexity by way of elements has enormous appeal. Starting with elements first works quite well for producing cars on an assembly line out of drivetrains, engines, and tires. It works quite well for fashioning prefabricated houses out of walls and windows and roofs. The logic of assembly is so natural that one finds elements first in almost any niche of learning from kindergarten to corporate training. Students study elements of arithmetic such as addition, subtraction, multiplication, and division, with the promise that eventually they will have a chance to put them together to solve meaningful problems. Students study the elements of grammar with the idea that the knowledge will later coalesce into comprehensive, compelling, and of course correct written and oral communications.

The problem is that elements don't make much sense in the absence of the whole game, and the whole game only shows up much later if at all. For instance, very little that schools ask youngsters to do around arithmetic is a good example of how arithmetic gets used in everyday life, and there is hardly anything early on worth calling mathematical thinking. Or take writing: I remember discovering with alarm that my youngest son had learned all the elements of writing, but his teachers rarely asked him or any of the other students in his classes to do much extended writing. So troubling is this trend of approaching things through elements with the whole game nowhere in sight or a minimal presence that I like to name it as a disease: *elementitis.*

I remember sharing some of these ideas with a group once, and a lady put up her hand with an interesting puzzle: "I have two daughters who are very different from one another. One likes just to dive in, but the other one likes to take things a piece at a time and feel well prepared before attempting 'the whole game.' Isn't that okay?"

Sure it is. *Elementitis* does not mean learning a few elements and putting them together into the whole game right away. Elements first can be a good short-term strategy. *Elementitis* means week after week, even year after year of focusing on elements with very little of the whole game ever played.

It would be comforting to think of *elementitis* as a rare disease. Not so. Common experience testifies to its common character. So does hard evidence. In *The Right to Learn,* Stanford educator Linda Darling-Hammond logs how narrow curriculum standards, bloated textbooks, and the pressure for coverage have led to a piecemeal curriculum. Every conceivable topic gets its fifteen minutes of fame. In a 2007 *Educational Researcher* synthesis of multiple sources, Wayne Au reports how the influence of the U.S. No Child Left Behind policy has both narrowed and fractured the curriculum. What's not relevant to the test gets dumped and what is relevant gets chopped up into test-sized bites. This doesn't have to happen. Some schools manage the challenges of No Child Left Behind better, and some states test in more meaningful ways. It doesn't have to happen . . . but it's the trend.

Harvard psychologist Ellen Langer would characterize such education as *mindless*. For decades, Langer has sustained a rich line of research on mindfulness and mindlessness, demonstrating that in many ordinary circumstances people fall into blind and narrow patterns of thought and behavior, muddling up situations where they could proceed more thoughtfully. However, people can cultivate a more mindful flexible stance, open to new information and aware of multiple perspectives. In *The Power of Mindful Learning,* Langer warns of the general trend in education toward mindless patterns of learning and shows how it need not be that way. One particular hazard akin to *elementitis* is the idea that the basics must be mastered so well that they become second nature. Another is a culture of deferred gratification, with the rewards of actually "playing the game" always coming later.

Now let's consider the other almost universal strategy for approaching complexity, learning *about* something toward learning to do it. Reading and mathematics generally escape this, since students certainly learn to do, but learning *about* dominates early learning in disciplines such as history and science. Typical history instruction has been characterized as learning "other people's facts." It's acquiring information about a particular version of history, with very little thoughtful interpretation or critical perspective. One might equally well describe the typical study of science as learning "someone else's theories." Students become familiar with Newton's laws or the steps involved in mitosis to the point where they can perform well on the quiz or the problems at the end of the chapter. However, a huge body of research on science understanding demonstrates that learners show very limited understanding, bedeviled by a range of misconceptions about what the ideas really mean.

A certain amount of learning *about*, just like a certain amount of elements first, is fine. The problem is overdoing it. The problem is endless learning about something without ever getting better at doing it. So, to parallel *elementitis*, I like to call endless learning about *aboutitis*. Yes, it lets learners acquire some information about the French Revolution and the American Revolution, mitosis and meiosis, the positions of the planets, continental drift, and the tensions of race and status in *Othello*. But this only provides a kind of an informational backdrop rather than an empowering and enlightening body of understanding.

Nor is the problem of *aboutitis* limited to the earlier years of education. Professional education suffers enormously from *aboutitis*, including teacher education, where teachers sit through innumerable sessions concerning learning theory and classroom dynamics with a shockingly small percentage of their time spent playing the game of teaching in various practice roles in schools.

In case *elementitis* and *aboutitis* seem too harsh a characterization of the norms of formal learning, let me acknowledge that even *elementitis* and *aboutitis* can do good up to a point. In less-developed countries starting from hardly anything, traditional straightforward teaching can have quite an impact. Teachers with some measure of teacher education, textbooks in the classrooms, acquisition of basic literacy and numeracy, and general knowledge of the subject matters—all these can be important. The complaint about *elementitis* and *aboutitis* is not that they don't accomplish anything but that we could accomplish so much more.

The natural question is how? The problem of approaching complexity is very real. What option is there besides either taking something complicated element by element and putting it together much later or only learning about it for quite a while? What else can one do?

An attractive answer is already at hand. It's the notion of the junior version. Remember those simpler versions of baseball that my buddies and I played in backyards on summer afternoons: not element by element, not information about, but engaging junior versions. This is a fundamentally different way of conceptualizing how to approach complexity, and a fundamentally more powerful one. It lets learners in on the big picture, so that the challenges along the way become meaningful. And it gives learners a chance to develop the largely tacit knowledge involved in active engagement, the kind of knowledge we point to when we speak of having a sense of the game or getting the hang of the game.

It suggests a different way of thinking about teaching and learning. More on junior versions later, but let's jump in. Let's look at the entire concept in summary form.

Seven Principles of Learning

So, what if learning most things could be more like learning how to play baseball, or other activities we usually learn as wholes? Learning most other sports works the same way. Most games such as bridge or checkers or chess or backgammon are learned as wholes. And so are the arts: From the start, one spends much of the time crafting whole drawings or paintings or poems. Likewise with musical performance: From the very beginning, one sings entire songs and plays entire pieces. So let me try to outline a general way of thinking about good learning that follows the spirit of learning how to play baseball or play an instrument or paint a landscape.

By "general" I mean something that can work in just about any place and for just about anyone at all. I'm not only speaking of classrooms or church groups or on-the-job learning. And it can be applied to pretty much anything you might imagine—the theory of relativity, skating, calculus, making and keeping friends, business management, the poetry of T. S. Eliot, speaking Mandarin, making beds or making quilts. It really doesn't matter, because the big principles are the same.

In the spirit of learning the whole game, we can call this broad view *learning by wholes* and divide it into seven principles. I will list these principles here, go over each of them briefly in this chapter, and then explore them more fully in the later chapters.

THE SEVEN PRINCIPLES OF LEARNING BY WHOLES

1. Play the whole game.
2. Make the game worth playing.
3. Work on the hard parts.
4. Play out of town.
5. Uncover the hidden game.
6. Learn from the team . . . and the other teams.
7. Learn the game of learning.

---

1. Play the Whole Game

Another thing my father taught me besides how to hold a bat was how to play checkers. We began with the whole game, and I won the first game I ever played. He explained the rules briefly, reminded me of them as we went along, let me take my time, and amazingly, I captured all his pieces!

A little too amazingly even for the young and naïve kid I was. "Did you let me win?" "Yes," my father confessed, honest to a fault as always.

"Don't do that!" I complained. "Okay," my father responded. He was a man with considerable quiet pride, and he could understand my pride too. From then on for two or three years, before the habit fell away as these things do, the two of us would play from time to time, but I never ever beat him again! Still, I got considerably better and I had fun anyway. I enjoyed the process of learning the whole game, whether I won or not.

We can ask ourselves when we begin to learn anything, do we engage some accessible version of the whole game early and often? When we do, we get what might be called a "threshold experience," a learning experience that gets us past initial disorientation and into the game. From there it's easier to move forward in a meaningful motivated way.

Much of formal education is short on threshold experiences. It feels like learning the pieces of a picture puzzle that never gets put together, or learning about the puzzle without being able to touch the pieces. In contrast, getting some version of a whole game close to the beginning makes sense because it gives the enterprise more meaning. You may not do it very well, but at least you know what you're doing and why you're doing it.

2. Make the Game Worth Playing

Schools and other settings of learning ask us to do many things that aren't all that enthralling. We feel as though we are playing the school game and not the *real* game. We learn the ritual of inverting and multiplying to divide fractions, a numerical somersault with mysterious motives that hardly anyone understands . . . it's just what you do. Or we memorize the dates of the presidents or the wives of Henry VIII, or we practice crafting paragraphs with good topic sentences.

Now and again some pushy student asks the deflating question, "Why are we studying this?" The answer forthcoming from the teacher or maybe anticipated by the text pretty much has to be something like this: "You'll need to know it later." "You need it for the test." "It's on the objectives for this unit."

So what makes a game seem worth playing? In fact, we've already seen one of the simplest contributing factors: Play the *whole* game. Inverting and multiplying, memorizing names and dates, practicing paragraph structure, these are bits and pieces that make sense in the context of the whole game. But they don't make sense unless the whole game of mathematical thinking or historical understanding or discursive and expressive writing gets played often enough in a junior way to make it familiar. Playing the whole game clarifies what makes the game worth playing, because you see right away how things fit together.

To be sure, some whole games are not all that interesting to most learners and no one is going to be interested in everything. Even so, whole games help, and artful teachers use many other ways to connect learners with what's interesting about a topic. The full importance of a topic is not always going to be apparent at once. Even so, there are many honest ways to preview the importance of something instead of just saying, "You'll need to know it later."

3. Work on the Hard Parts

My parents played bridge regularly with another couple for many years. Eventually I learned to play bridge also and tag-teamed into the game sometimes, or my wife and I played with my parents. Only then did I become aware that my parents weren't getting any better. They were doing and doing, but not learning by doing.

Think about something that you've done for a number of years. Very often, you will find that you're not getting any better at it. The missing ingredient is usually our third principle: Work on the hard parts. At the very beginning of learning something this isn't as important as getting oriented to the whole enterprise. However, as the learner settles into the pattern of activity, the hard parts start to emerge.

The hard parts have an annoying characteristic: They do not always get better just through playing the whole game. Real improvement depends on deconstructing the game, singling out the hard parts for special attention, practicing them on the side, developing strategies to deal with them better, and reintegrating them soon into the whole game. Batting practice!

Normal schooling includes significant work on the hard parts. That's good. But there's usually not enough of this kind of work, and it's not individually targeted. As I think back on my schooling, all the way from kindergarten through university, it's amazing how rarely I had the chance to revise anything to strengthen the hard parts.

Shortly after handing something in, I would get a few corrections back with comments like "95 percent," "70 percent," "nice point," "needs further evidence"—not enough information to diagnose effectively exactly what was hard about the hard parts and no chance to tune them up because we were already continuing on to the next topic.

4. Play Out of Town

Back to baseball: There's the home-field advantage phenomenon. When the Boston Red Sox get to play in Boston's Fenway Park, not only do they benefit from the support of an enthusiastic crowd, but also from familiarity with some very definite quirks of the stadium. You can talk about the home-field advantage for any sport, but it's particularly significant in baseball, where various stadiums around the country have their own idiosyncratic layouts.

The dark side of home-field advantage is the away disadvantage. When the Boston Red Sox play out of town, it's a problem, but it's also a learning opportunity. The new setting challenges the players to stretch and adapt their skills and insights. They can find out how best to capitalize on a different circumstance, and maybe generalize what they learn so that the next away-from-home stadium after that becomes a little less of an away disadvantage.

Does a different setting matter that much? Looking across sports, this varies a lot. For sports played indoors on highly standardized courts it matters least. In contrast, football commonly brings traveling teams to weather they are not used to, say, playing in a blizzard. In tennis, differences between grass, clay, and hard courts influence considerably who has the best chance in a tournament. The extreme team sport of adventure racing deliberately places small teams in wilderness areas unfamiliar to them. They need to figure out their own routes between designated stations to cover long distances over dangerous terrain as quickly as possible. A systematic study of adventure racing conducted by my colleague Daniel Wilson reveals the remarkably complex and tricky interactions among team members as they cope and learn in the midst of races. Adventure racers are *always* playing out of town!

Beyond sports, the same out-of-town phenomenon applies in various degrees to learning anything. The whole point of formal education is to prepare for other times and other places, not just to get better in the classroom. What we learn today is not for today but for the day after tomorrow. Sometimes the day after tomorrow is pretty much the same as today, but it very often isn't.

The trouble is, in formal education usually no one sends us out of town to play and broaden our experience. The ideas and algorithms in mathematics are very general, but in practice students focus on a few stereotyped exercises about trains or sailboats or buying apples. The ideas about good citizenship are very general, but in practice students focus on a couple of stories about voting or community service. Even the classroom across the hall may be too far away. One of my favorite quips about learning, remembered for many years, came from a high school science teacher bemoaning his students' troubles applying mathematics to science along these lines: "It's as though walking across the hall from the math room to the science room, the students forget their math."

Researchers call this the problem of *transfer of learning.* Playing out of town well is not something that happens automatically. Like other facets of learning, it's something we have to work on.

5. Uncover the Hidden Game

Look up "baseball hidden game" on the Internet and one of the first hits you will see is *The Hidden Game of Baseball,* a 1984 book by John Thorn and Pete Palmer. In most people's minds, baseball and math probably do not sit in the same category, but *The Hidden Game of Baseball* brings them together. It's a statistical perspective on baseball, why baseball games and whole seasons play out the way they do, and what smart strategy looks like.

What is true for baseball is true for just about any endeavor—literary criticism, making and sustaining friends, mathematical modeling, playing the stock market, making peace, making war, making art—there is always the hidden game. In fact "the" hidden game understates the matter. Any complicated and challenging activity always has multiple layers beneath the obvious. Baseball and physics both have their statistical sides, their strategic sides, and even their political sides. There is also a very interesting physics of baseball, although I'm not sure that there is a baseball of physics.

The hidden games are not only interesting but often important to doing well at the surface game. Coaches and managers have to pay attention to the statistical trends in batting and pitching and play the odds. In playing chess, it's essential to attend to broad strategic considerations such as control of the center. In learning science concepts, it's important to have some feel for the underlying principles of causality involved in various scientific theories. Often they are very different from everyday conceptions of causality. Without a sense of the hidden game, you are likely to misunderstand what's going on.

A great deal of learning proceeds as if there were no hidden games. But there always are. They need attention or the learners will always just be skating on the surface.

6. Learn from the Team . . . and the Other Teams

Do your own work! If there were Ten Commandments for the conduct of pupils, this is a pretty good candidate for the top of the list; good by the measure of common practice but odd by the measure of how society works. Hardly anything we do is done solo. No matter whether you are an athlete, a business person, a scientist, a trash collector, or a clerk, you are almost always coordinating with other people in a complex way. Human endeavor is deeply and intrinsically collective, except in schools.

That is why on this list of seven principles for learning we find "learn from the team . . . and the other teams." It's actually very hard to learn well from a single source, from a passive text or from a teacher who has many others to attend to besides yourself. Much better is a personal coach, but most individuals cannot afford that, nor can most societies afford to provide personal coaches for any process of wide-scale learning! And even that personal coach can only tell you about the art and craft of coordinating with others on whatever team you're on, not do it for you.

To be sure, some activities are more naturally solo than others. It's easy to make reading into a group activity but harder for writing, although it can be done. However, the principle of learning from the team and the other teams should be interpreted generously. The principle concerns not just activities that naturally have a group character, but also about learning from others engaged in the same pursuit—friends, partners, colleagues, rivals, enemies, paragons, mentors, even learners not as far along as oneself.

7. Learn the Game of Learning

Many people study a second language and some people get to a third language. Learning that third language is an interestingly different experience from working on the second. Learning any language beyond your mother tongue is very challenging, but hour per hour the third is usually not as daunting as the second. In learning your second language, you develop a better understanding of how grammars are organized, so it's easier to make sense of the grammar of the third language. The rhythms of memorizing vocabulary and syntactic structures have become familiar. You have learned something in addition to the second language itself, something about how to learn languages.

Learning to learn is a much more general phenomenon than learning to learn languages. Even nonhuman mammals learn to learn in a kind of a rudimentary way, getting used to and often engaged by the rhythms of the training process. Learning to learn has to do with many things: directing one's attention, choosing time and place, relating new ideas and skills to what you already know. Indeed, it has a lot to do with the previous six principles. The self-managed learner makes a point of practicing the hard parts, even when no coach or teacher imposes a regimen. The self-managed learner makes a point of playing out of town—connecting ideas and skills with other contexts—even when no coach or instructor sends the team out of town.

I can hardly think of anything more worth learning than learning to learn. It's like money in the bank at compound interest. Unfortunately, most settings of learning give very little direct attention to learning the game of learning.

A Matter of Order

Does the order of the seven principles have any special significance? The earlier principles are not more important than the later ones. Nor do we need to pay attention to the principles in their numerical order. For instance, sometimes a topic lends itself to uncovering some feature of the hidden game (#5) or learning from the team (#6) early on.

Play the whole game comes first because that is the central idea. *Learn the game of learning* comes last not because it's the last thing to address but because learning to learn is a superordinate agenda cutting across particular topics. In between, the order simply seemed to make a good narrative. If you'd like to think of the principles in a different sequence, by all means do so.

Yes, But . . .

I hope that all this makes sense. I hope it aligns with many good and bad and middling learning experiences in school and out of school that people remember. I hope that others besides me recall what it was like to learn to play baseball or some other sport or game they enjoyed, getting the hang of it without necessarily being very good at it early on. I hope that others besides me recall what it was like to develop a particular art or craft, getting the hang of it without necessarily being very good at it early on. I hope others besides me recall the empty *elementitis* of learning the pieces without the whole game and the not very interesting *aboutitis* of learning about something endlessly without ever getting to do it.

Even so, learning by wholes could seem like an idealistic undertaking, as far away from practical attainability as the top of the Matterhorn, so let's briefly counter some reservations.

One natural "Yes, but . . . ," stems from the fact that mathematics, history, and science are structured much more loosely than baseball, bridge, and badminton. These three B's are designed as games with rules, but what is it to play the "whole game" of mathematics, history, or science? What is it to play particular games within them, say seeking a mathematical proof, assembling and assessing historical evidence, or designing and running an experiment? *Part of my mission in the rest of the book is to convince you that the whole game metaphor points in useful directions.* Even though the academic disciplines have few strict rules, there are rules of thumb, guidelines, conventional practices, typical forms, widely used strategies, and the like that help to define the "game."

For another natural objection, some disciplines—mathematics again is a good example—seem like pyramids. You can't build the top of the pyramid before you put the bottom in place. You can't ascend to heights of understanding and creative problem solving until you establish some foundational facts and routines. There is no junior version of the game, this objection says. *Part of my mission in the rest of this book is to make the case that there is always a junior version.* While the pyramid has a certain reality, there are legitimate and energizing junior versions in the several disciplines for the beginning learner.

Let me add that we shouldn't just be interested in learning within the disciplines. There are many other types of learning that matter as much—for instance, skills and attitudes of leadership, human relations, moral decision making, and citizenship. As with academic disciplines, although there are not strict rules in such areas, there are certainly guidelines, conventions, strategies, and so on that help to frame what it is to "play the game."

However, there are many good sources about theories of learning and how they connect to education, for instance, Bransford, Brown, and Cocking's *How People Learn.* So one might wonder, "Do we really need another theory of learning? We already have such scholarly perspectives on learning as behaviorism, constructivism, and human development."

Good question . . . and some good news: Learning by wholes is not a theory of learning to rival others at all. Learning by wholes is a theory of teaching, or more broadly, educating. Learning is a much broader category than education. Learning happens incidentally all the time—in casual conversations, in the supermarket, on the street, playing shoot-'em-up video games, puzzling over stock market investments.

Education is choreography for learning, an effort to organize learning for greater timeliness, focus, effectiveness, and efficiency. That is where learning by wholes comes in.

Learning by wholes incorporates various learning theories to offer a design framework. Learning by wholes is an integrative approach for keeping in mind and keeping in action many key features of learning toward educating well. It's what is sometimes called a theory of action. *Part of my mission for the rest of the book is to show the learning science underneath each one of the seven principles of learning by wholes.*

Let's start now. Without reviewing much about behaviorism, constructivism, or any other view of learning, let me sketch very broadly how learning by wholes relates to them. Learning by wholes is not very behaviorist in tone, especially if we are talking about hard-core behaviorism, which denies the existence of minds and intentions. Learning by wholes treats learners as aware and active and capable of becoming more so.

However, learning by wholes does share with behaviorism the idea that things go better when feedback is immediate and informative and when the incentive structures around an endeavor are largely positive and not deeply threatening.

Learning by wholes is very constructivist, embracing the idea that learners always in some sense construct their own meanings from learning experiences. Indeed, learning by wholes is one way of putting meat on the rather sketchy bones of generic constructivism. Discovery and inquiry learning can be understood as particular spins on constructivism, and some examples in the pages to follow have the flavor of discovery or inquiry learning.

However, learning by wholes definitely does not say that all learning should be aggressively discovery oriented. What suits a particular topic is something of a judgment call. There are many occasions, including in most sports and games, when the best way to get started on something is to explain and demonstrate it clearly, ask learners to try it and try it again, and coach them through a process of improvement. This is a far cry from inviting them to figure it out for themselves with an occasional hint.

In very general terms, a developmental perspective on learning foregrounds how people's readiness for learning changes. In the course of years, children and adults develop broad cognitive capacities, views of knowledge, and ways of understanding that enable more powerful thinking and learning. A learner more advanced along a developmental trajectory can be much more "developmentally ready" to learn a particular idea or topic with understanding. Also, learners of the same physical age may not have the same developmental age. Well-designed learning accommodates different levels of readiness within the same group.

So how does learning by wholes fit in? Learning by wholes certainly urges sensitivity to developmental readiness as a general matter. Learning by wholes does not foreground one specific developmental model over others, because the field of human development is so complex, a whole story in itself. Some further ideas about development appear in the next chapter and toward the end of Chapter 5.

Finally, a word about technology. When well used, contemporary information technology provides powerful approaches to learning. Technology can bring to students whole games to which they would otherwise not have access. For instance, computer simulations, online research tools, and e-mail communication can help learners pursue collaborative investigations or thoughtful critical discussions about tricky issues. Again, some examples appear in the following pages.

However, in no way does learning by wholes require such technologies. Many social simulations do not need computers at all, simply face-to-face role-playing. Formal face-to-face debates with their whole-game character predate the Internet and discussion forums by thousands of years.

In summary, rather than offering a new theory of learning, learning by wholes sits comfortably within a number of contemporary ideas about learning and teaching as an integrative theory of action. There are of course other theories of action for organizing learning. You will have to make up your mind which you like or cherry pick what parts of each you find most helpful.

To help you think about it, bear this in mind. The trend in design frameworks for learning is to address any topic without complaining much about how atomistic the topic itself is—dividing by fractions, the dates of the presidents, Newton's third law of motion. In contrast, learning by wholes emphasizes not only how learning might proceed but what the right unit of learning is—the whole meaningful game. Learning by wholes takes a strong stance against learning by elements and against extended learning *about* things when the ultimate idea is to learn to *do* them. *Part of my mission in the rest of this book is to make the case again and again that this holistic emphasis, always with appropriate attention to "the hard parts," is what works best.*

All that said, there is a very different "Yes, but . . ." that deserves a moment of attention. Sometimes people feel uneasy with the game metaphor itself.

One concern is that "game" is too light for serious matters like the plays of Shakespeare or the founding of our nation or the biological origins of human beings. Another concern is the competitive connotations. Most sports and games involve individuals or teams vying against one another, and the competitive characteristics of grades and exams may do more mischief than good.

I *half* agree with both these concerns. I wish that the metaphor of learning the whole game was not so light sounding, although I also sometimes think that we approach the entire enterprise of education too gravely and should lighten up a bit. I also wish that the competitive connotations were softer, although I think that in carefully chosen circumstances certain kinds of mild competition can help to foster learning.

No metaphor is perfect. Whatever our nation is, when we speak of "the father of our nation" (or mother) in some ways this is apt and in some ways it is not. When we say with seventeenth-century British poet and preacher John Donne, "No man is an island, entire of itself; every man is a piece of the continent, a part of the main," we acknowledge a vivid and important truth while pushing into the background some complexities of human autonomy. Metaphors are like oriental rugs: They reveal a compelling pattern, while the complicating lint gets swept underneath them.

In the balance, let me suggest that the concerns with the metaphor itself do not weigh very heavily against the integrative power, and we can learn to watch out for the downside. If you prefer, you can take the seven principles literally and never mind the game metaphor. They might sound something like this:

1. Engage some version of the holistic activity, not just bits and pieces.
2. Make the activity worth pursuing.
3. Work on the hard parts (at least this one sounds the same).
4. Explore different versions of and settings for the activity.

And so on. Doesn't have the zip, does it? But the points are essentially the same and fundamentally important.

So I'm hoping that you will read on to discover the rest of the story. And as you read, if you are in an educative role—teacher, mentor, coach, parent, or even a student managing your own learning—I hope you will try a few things. You might want to construct your own junior version of learning by wholes rather than attempting everything at once! Just focus on the basic principles without worrying too much about the details. Just take two or three of the principles and tease them into motion in simple ways.

In fact, you can probably do a lot with a principle without even looking that far into its details. I've discovered that as soon as I name the seven, they stimulate elaboration from people's own experience without a lot of prompting on my part. Also, at the end of each chapter you will find "Wonders of Learning," a boxed summary of the key ideas. It's written in the first person, as though you were thinking things over, with a series of "I wonder . . ." questions leading into brief answers drawn from the chapter. You are invited to take these questions and others like them to heart and ask and answer them in real contexts of teaching and learning.

After some road testing, if you then turn back to the book, you are likely to find many particulars all the more meaningful. To put everything together, the Afterword offers some reflections on the experience of learning and teaching by wholes, what principles to foreground early and why, how the craft of learning and teaching by wholes builds over time, and the challenges of educating for a complex globalized and changing world. Remember, we are learners too, and the power of a well-chosen junior version applies to our own learning to teach just as much as to others' learning what we would like to teach them.

On Fruitful Mediocrity

Meanwhile, there is one more doubt worth taking up right here. If learning by wholes is so powerful, why wasn't I better at baseball? In fact, since people usually learn sports and games and arts and crafts in whole-game kinds of ways, how come most people are not better at them?

Of course, there is the talent factor. Remember, I was not particularly good at sports in general. However, this is not the heart of the matter. Besides playing the whole game, there are six more principles of learning by wholes. These were not always operating in my favor. Here is a scorecard with a little explanation.

DAVE'S SCORECARD

- ☑ Play the whole game.
- ☑ Make the game worth playing.
- ☒ Work on the hard parts.
- ☒ Play out of town.
- ☒ Uncover the hidden game.
- ☒ Learn from the team . . . and the other teams.
- ☒ Learn the game of learning.

I played the whole game of baseball and found the whole game worth playing. I didn't just play junior versions either. The one summer in Little League and many games during recess and physical education in school were nearly full-scale versions. However, except for my Little League summer and some early tips from my father, no one got me to work on the hard parts much, and I didn't take playing baseball seriously enough to work on the hard parts by myself. As to playing out of town, there was no out of town for us, just the usual gang of kids at school and in the neighborhood. No one ever told me anything about the hidden game until I was much older. Learning from the team? Only very incidentally. We certainly were not studying one another or trying to mentor one another. Learning the game of learning simply didn't come up.

If more of the magic seven principles had been in place, I would have learned to play baseball with more magic than I did. The moral: Good learning by wholes reaches well beyond playing the whole game a lot. Just as *elementitis* and *aboutitis* offer an overly reductive approach, so only playing a surface version of the whole game makes for an overly holistic approach. People remain mediocre at many sports and games, arts and crafts, and professional endeavors because they spend too much time playing the whole game without putting the other six principles to work.

But perhaps we should recognize a certain value even in this sort of mediocrity. At least it achieves a general sense of and participation in the whole game. Sure, I would like to have been great at baseball, but at least I had learned to *do* something meaningful and had become somewhat better at doing it. I was reasonably happy with my limited skills and well equipped to play now and then, understand baseball talk, follow games on TV, and, decades later, play backyard baseball with my own children. That's worth a lot!

Much of the rhetoric around education emphasizes excellence, and indeed excellence is a fine grail to seek. However, imagine a world where almost any adult had a kind of energetic if simple sense of civic engagement or ecological responsibility or avoidance of prejudice. Starting from the baseline of today's indifference and neglect, these "games" do not have to be played in very sophisticated ways to do substantial good! The world would be a better place if in areas like these most people achieved active mediocrity rather than passive erudition.

Let's take a longer look at playing the whole game in the next chapter, going on from there to each of the other six principles in turn, for the sake of understanding better how learning works and to make learning work better.

I

Play the Whole Game

YOU KNOW HOW MOUNTAINS ON THE HORIZON CAN LOOK SMALL, BUT WHEN you actually approach them they turn out to be much higher? This was my experience as a doctoral student approaching a dissertation. From a distance, the mountain did not seem so formidable, but when I got to the base I had no idea how to climb it.

My academic degrees are from the Massachusetts Institute of Technology. I was a mathematics major. After I finished the undergraduate work, I continued into a doctoral program, developing an interest in mathematical approaches to artificial intelligence. Artificial intelligence is the study of how to get computers to undertake intelligent activities, such as playing chess or proving mathematical theorems or controlling a robot to do interesting and challenging things. My work on artificial intelligence stimulated my interest in thinking and learning in human beings. After finishing my degree, I slid over into the world of cognitive psychology and education, but the why of that is another story. Right now, you can picture me in the foothills of the dissertation range, thinking about what kind of research on artificial intelligence to attempt.

The problem was *problem finding*. There is a very useful rough distinction between problem solving and problem finding. Problem solving is the art and craft of dealing well with problems that are already reasonably clear. Sometimes we find such problems in a book.

Sometimes they emerge as blatant needs in the course of everyday life. Wherever they came from, there they are, and we burrow into them and try to dig through them. Just because they are clear in outline does not make them easy. For instance, the problem of lighting efficiently with electricity had been recognized for some time and pursued by a number of inventors, before Thomas Edison finally cracked it. Classic mathematical conjectures like Fermat's Last Theorem not uncommonly linger for centuries in very well-defined form before anyone resolves them.

Problem finding is a somewhat different matter. Problem finding concerns figuring out what the problems are in the first place. It also involves coming to good formulations of problems, formulations that make them approachable. Often it also involves redefining a problem halfway through trying to solve it, out of the suspicion that one may not be working on quite the right problem.

So my dissertation problem was problem finding. I really did not know how to go about looking for a good topic. I was very able and even creative at problem solving, with a good toolkit of technical knowledge, but problem finding was another face of the game.

I wondered, why the mountain? I thought over my undergraduate and graduate experience at MIT and realized something that surprised me at the time and has stayed with me ever since: In my technical courses, I had rarely done anything but *solve* problems. I almost always succeeded, but the problems came from the text or the instructors. I had never undertaken anything like a project or an open-ended investigation. The consequence was inevitable: I had a fierce battery of problem-solving skills and hardly any problem-finding skills.

My experience in the humanities was quite different. Contrary to what you might think for a technical school, MIT had very strong offerings in literature, philosophy, music, and other areas, as well as notable professors. I nourished a range of interests in the humanities and took a variety of courses. There, I realized, problem finding was routine. The major piece of work for a course was normally an essay or two, with great latitude about their topics. I routinely had to ask what sorts of questions were worth pursuit, whether I could assemble a good argument, where to find relevant resources, and how to bundle it all together into a compelling statement.

Let me be clear here: MIT gave me an excellent undergraduate and graduate education. The institution treated me generously with support and flexibility. It was a privilege to be there and I learned a great deal that proved both interesting and helpful ever since. I'm just pointing to this one puzzle, problem solving versus problem finding.

It's a puzzle of playing the whole game. Problem finding, after all, is part of the whole game. Look at any piece of formal instruction you want, any subject matter, any age. Apply this simple test: If there's no problem finding in sight, you can be sure that the learners are not playing the whole game.

The Quest for the Whole Game

When I think about what it looks like for learners to play the whole game, I think of teachers I know who have made whole games one of their teaching strategies. I think of how they invent and adapt whole games creatively in the service of their students' learning. One such person was Lois Hetland, now a professor and research colleague, but several years ago a seventh-grade teacher participating in a research and development project on teaching for understanding. (I'll say more about the teaching for understanding framework later in this chapter and in the chapters to come.)

Lois was teaching an integrated humanities strand that focused on colonial America. She organized the students' work around several fundamental questions that the class lived with throughout the year. Some of the questions focused on the role of land: How does land shape human culture? How do people think about the land? How do people change the land? Other questions probed the tricky issue of historical truth: How do we find out the truth about things that happened long ago or far away? How do we see through bias in sources?

Lois Hetland called all these questions *throughlines,* an allusion to a notion from the method acting school of Constantin Stanislavsky.

By throughlines he meant central themes threading through the entire course of a play. Lois Hetland made a point of bringing the class back to these throughlines no matter what the particular topic under consideration. The aim was a deeper understanding of colonial America, but more than that some insight into the character and rhythm of inquiry and students' management of their own learning.

With the same teaching for understanding project in mind, I also think of Joan Soble, a talented English teacher at Cambridge Rindge and Latin High School. Joan wondered what to do for a group of ninth graders considered at risk and as she put it, "perpetually overwhelmed" by the demands of schooling. She designed an introductory writing course for them. The course experience involved various activities, among them preparation for writing by laying out collages, maintaining and reviewing portfolios with a critical eye, and articulating and pursuing individual goals. In focusing on their individual goals, the students were aided by a form targeting various writing skills they might want to sharpen, in other words, working on the hard parts. The skills ranged from sentence structure to ways of revising to strategies for managing their own work patterns better.

Readers might recall my MIT experience at this point and speculate that whole games are much easier to put together in the humanities than in mathematics and science. Yet examples are easy enough to find in these disciplines as well. Chris Dede, a fellow professor at the Harvard Graduate School of Education, sustains a line of research and development work on the scientific method and how to get students doing it as well as learning about it. He and his colleagues have constructed a MUVE called River City. MUVE stands for multi-user virtual environment. Many popular games that adolescents and young adults play online have this characteristic; participants navigate through virtual worlds, represented by icons called avatars, encountering and interacting with other players who may be physically located in Beijing or Cape Town or Rio.

In the River City MUVE, the students face a problem. Diseases of various sorts are sweeping through the virtual population. What are the causes? Exploring River City, the students can observe at various sites, test the water, and in other ways investigate the possible sources of the epidemics. In doing so, they learn some science content, and they also engage in the process of scientific inquiry itself.

Or turning to mathematics, there is an example from Kenna Barger of Elkins, West Virginia, one of the recipients of Disney's 2001 American Teacher Awards. An excellent vignette of her teaching ninth-grade algebra can be found on a videodisc developed by my colleague Ron Ritchhart about the nature of creative teaching. She leads the students in water balloon bungee jumping, the outlines of which were developed by a program at the University of Arizona called M-PACT, learning Mathematics with Purpose, Application, Context, and Technology.

Water balloon bungee jumping is a complete exercise in mathematical modeling. The ninth-grade students have been studying linear equations. They start the activity by forming small teams and measuring the stretchiness of rubber bands with weights attached to them. The teams use their algebra to construct a model of how much weight produces how much stretch. The activity is anything but routine and formulaic. The students struggle with issues about what counts as dependent versus independent variables and how to represent the situation, while Kenna Barger circulates and coaches.

Then the entire class troops outside. The teams in turn drop water balloons attached to rubber bands from the roof of the school—this is the water balloon bungee jumping part. The students have used their equations to predict just how much elastic would bring their balloon to just above the ground. A student on a team often lies underneath the descending balloon. The challenge is to come as close as possible without breaking the balloon on the ground . . . or the student. The entire exercise involves joining experiment with mathematical modeling using linear equations to try to understand how the whole system works and make effective predictions.

Barger emphasizes that this is only one piece of a year-long effort to teach algebra, seeing it not just as an abstract system of manipulating symbols but as a process of mathematical modeling. Barger comments, "When I was a student, I was always the annoying one in the back of the classroom who kept asking 'Why?' It was not until I began teaching at a school that emphasizes real-world careers and collaboration among faculty and disciplines that I truly got this question answered."

Such examples are not hard to come by. Many others can be found on the DVD with the Barger example, or in the book *Teaching for Understanding*, or in endless other resources available to the educational community. What then are the earmarks of playing the whole game? How do we know whether we've got a whole game or not?

In settings of learning, a whole game is generally some kind of inquiry or performance in a broad sense. It involves problem solving, explanation, argument, evidence, strategy, skill, craft. Often something gets created—a solution, an image, a story, an essay, a model. Moreover . . .

It's never just about content. Learners are trying to get better at doing something. Joan Soble's students are trying to get better at writing. Lois Hetland's students are trying to get better at understanding colonial America and at historical inquiry. Kenna Barger's students are trying to get better at mathematical modeling.

It's never just routine. It requires thinking with what you know and pushing further. Rather than just standard routine problems, it involves open-ended or ill-structured problems. The writing, rethinking the throughlines again and again, modeling the fall of the water balloons, all of these endeavors asked the learners to go beyond what they already knew and extrapolate to novel and puzzling situations.

It's never just problem solving. It involves problem finding. Students in Joan Soble's writing course set their own goals. In the colonial America course, Lois Hetland expected her students to help her sharpen and interpret the throughlines in the context of new topics. Kenna Barger's water balloon project was perhaps the most defined, but even there the circumstances allowed for a number of different approaches.

It's not just about right answers. It involves explanation and justification. The learners in all the settings have had to explain and justify what they were up to and how they came to the places that they have.

It's not emotionally flat. It involves curiosity, discovery, creativity, camaraderie. Kenna Barger's students competed in a good-natured way on the water balloon task and strove to get those linear equations to do something. Joan Soble's students got into writing and aspired to do better. Lois Hetland's students found their curiosity about colonial America provoked again and again. They were not just learning but developing dispositions to learn, like curiosity and persistence. Of course, not every learner is going to be interested in everything, but the conditions favor most students getting somewhat interested (more about this in Chapter 2).

It's not in a vacuum. It involves the methods, purposes, and forms of one or more disciplines or other areas, situated in a social context. Joan Soble's students dealt with the methods, purposes, and forms of writing in collaborative ways. Lois Hetland's students dealt with the methods and purposes of historical inquiry, framing their conversations and their writing with appropriate forms of justification and explanation. Kenna Barger's students worked in teams to deal with mathematical formalisms and experimentation.

These are the earmarks of a whole game, but they can also serve as guidelines for constructing a whole game. Start anywhere you want, say, with the routines of fractions arithmetic or a couple of rules of grammar. No whole game in sight yet, but some questions lead in the right direction. Ask: What would this topic be like if it's not just about content, but learners are trying to get better at doing something? What would they be getting better at doing? Ask: What would the topic be like if it were not just routine, if it required thinking with what you know and pushing that further? Ask: If there were some problem finding involved, where would it figure? Every answer to questions like these draws a larger circle around an initially limited topic. As the circle widens it's not hard to arrive at some reasonable picture of the whole game.

Kinds of Whole Games

Of course, there is more than one good answer, more than one good version of a whole game. There are many games of thoughtful inquiry around history, for example. Learners can look carefully at original sources to form conjectures and seek evidence for them. Learners can compare and contrast alternative historical accounts, even textbooks from different countries, to discover commonalities and contrasts and consider whether the contrasts reflect biases. Learners can examine pivotal events like Caesar's ascent to power in Rome, or they can look at the characteristics of everyday Roman life in the time of Caesar. Learners can compare power grabs then and now, or everyday life then and now.

While the "games" here are not as neatly defined as baseball or chess, there is no need for them to be. Realistically, any discipline brings a diffuse cloud of practices into play. Sometimes professionals even debate which ones are right and proper—the right way to do history or economics or literary analysis—but we don't have to worry about that. The challenge of *play the whole game* is not to find the one right official canonical version, but to get some reasonable version into action. Chapter 5, "Uncover the Hidden Game," will have more to say about patterns of disciplinary thinking.

Sometimes the game is integrative. It cuts across a range of disciplines, weaving together ideas from several. A class project might involve an ecological survey of the community, in the process applying concepts from biology, using mathematics to chart problems and trends, and exercising skills of reading and writing to synthesize results and propose a community action plan. A group investigation might focus on the use of art for political purposes, studying several positive and negative cases (for example, protest art in South Africa, Nazi propaganda), considering literary and aesthetic values, identifying political manipulation, and estimating with statistics how much exposure and impact was achieved.

Community ecology surveys and group investigations of political art are examples of what might be called project-based learning, one of several ways to organize learning in a holistic way. Numerous examples of project-based learning are available. For one source, the *Edutopia* Web site, maintained by the George Lucas Educational Foundation, offers a sizable collection with brief video examples.

Project-based learning by definition involves *big* wholes that take some time to work through. But a whole game need not be a big game!

This is important to recognize, because big games do not fit very well in some educational settings with their schedules and mandates. However, there is always some room for small games, and learning by wholes can proceed quite briskly in the small. Looking at a poem or a work of art or a newspaper editorial, reflecting on it, and discussing it is an entire meaningful activity that might fit in half an hour.

Also whole games often are not played all at once anyway, but spread out over time. Lois Hetland's students visit their through-lines again and again, pursuing the same questions in greater depth. Students trying to figure out the sources of disease in the online River City environment enter multiple times.

Some other familiar practices with a whole-game spin include problem-based learning, case-based learning or the case study method, community action initiatives, role-playing scenarios, formal debate, and studio learning (see Chapter 6). These each have their own flavor, but they are hardly perfectly distinct. Often the same example can be used to illustrate two or three of these practices. Here I'll just touch on three more.

Role-playing scenarios, which also can be relatively brief, are a good way to develop perspective and open-mindedness in an area. You may think you know what your core values are and what you would do if you were running the company or running the state. However, learners are often surprised by their new attitudes when they are put in role-playing scenarios where now they occupy such positions. Mindsets are not just the products of the values we hold but the roles we play.

In problem-based learning, students in small groups tackle problems together. An episode can take a class period or much longer, depending on the scope of the problem. The problems are deliberately somewhat messy. Generally they lack perfect answers and the learners need to seek information, not just work with what is given. Teachers facilitate the process. Such previous examples as water balloon bungee jumping and River City can be seen as problem-based learning.

The Jasper Woodbury series on mathematical problem solving, developed by the Learning Technology Center of Vanderbilt University, is one version of problem-based learning. The approach uses *anchored instruction,* providing a vivid scenario, the "anchor," that can be brought into the classroom as the setting for the problem. The Jasper Woodbury series centers on a dozen videos featuring the lead character Jasper Woodbury as he deals with various situations that require mathematical reasoning.

For instance, in the first video of the series, students watch Jasper as he takes his boat upriver to inspect and ultimately purchase a new, larger boat. Then Jasper has to figure out whether he can cruise the new boat back to his home wharf before sundown, because its night running lights do not work. The students address the problem. They have to consider when sundown comes, distance, gasoline consumption, whether a single tank of gas will do it, where Jasper might get more gas if not, and other factors, including some missing information that must be guessed at. Relevant information appears at incidental moments throughout the video, in passing comments, on riverside signs, in newsprint, mixed naturalistically with irrelevant information. Students typically work in small groups and hop around in the video to hunt for needed facts. Research shows that the Jasper Woodbury adventures improve learners' flexibility as mathematical problem solvers.

Another common application of problem-based learning is medical education, where, instead of sitting through extended lectures on anatomy and physiology, doctors-to-be work in small groups on simulated cases representing maladies they do not know that much about yet. Here are the initial symptoms. What do you think might be going on? Where would you need to look to find out? What anatomy and physiology do you need to know and understand? Let's divide up our questions, find out some answers, and teach them to one another. Then let's generate a trial diagnosis and find ways to test it further. Problem-based learning is more likely than technical lectures to cultivate diagnostic reasoning based on the active use of knowledge.

Continuing for a moment at the university level, problem-based learning in this style can also be viewed as a kind of case-based learning. David Garvin, professor at the Harvard Business School, does just that in a comparison of the use of the case method at three Harvard professional schools—the medical school, the law school, and the business school. Garvin emphasizes how each setting has cultivated its own distinctive version of the case method. Medical students focus on the diagnostic process in small groups that run themselves with some help. Law students work alone for the most part and convene in large classes. Their professors call upon students randomly for the facts and issues of a case and develop whole-class discussions. The students do not address one another; most of the direct interaction occurs between students and the professor. The focus falls on critical features of the case and how small differences can have large legal ramifications.

At the business school, students prepare individually or often in study groups for participation in whole-class sessions. Business cases typically pose problematic situations and ask for next steps: If you were the boss what would you do? Students need to back their ideas with detailed analyses and arguments. The first student to speak— called upon out of the blue or at best warned a few minutes earlier— will often address the class for five or ten minutes.

Garvin notes the limits as well as the qualities of these three different versions of the case method and logs how deliberations at the three professional schools are striving to improve them. What the three share is their quest to involve learners in kinds of reasoning appropriate to their professions: medical diagnosis, discerning the legal implications of features of cases, responding to business problems with well-grounded decisions and plans.

I hope this quick review shows clearly that there are many variations of learning with a whole-game flavor, some with names— problem-based learning, case-based learning, and so on—and some simply patterns of activity that ingenious teachers have assembled. Most of them can appear in longer or shorter versions. Therefore, learning by wholes might seem straightforward. With no lack of approaches, just pick one and run with it.

Not so fast! As the saying goes, the devil is in the details. Any of these practices draw learners into something like a whole game. However . . .

It's not just the form, it's the content and thinking. When you decide upon, say, problem-based learning, you have only just begun. What problems? What content and skills are they meant to cultivate? What kinds of thinking are they meant to foster—sifting historical evidence, detecting causal influences, adopting different perspectives? The general idea of problem-based learning or any of the other types says nothing about such matters. The principal challenge of constructing a whole game is not one of choosing a framework like problem-based learning, but filling the framework with an insightful conception of the game.

Also, *it's not just playing the whole game, it's the other six principles.* One can have much better or much worse versions of problem-based learning, project-based learning, or any of them. What's done to *make the game worth playing*? Are the *hard parts* somehow isolated for focused attention and then reintegrated? How is *play out of town* attended to, encouraging transfer of learning? What are the moves that *uncover the hidden game*?

And finally, *it's not just—or even particularly—discovery learning.* A casual read might suggest that across these practices learners engage in relatively free-form open-ended inquiry. Not so! These patterns of participation in learning are generally quite structured. They often involve considerable up-front information, for instance, the written or multimedia business cases that business students pore over to prep. They incorporate expected rhythms of interaction, who talks to whom and when, and stages of development: What happens first, what happens next, and what happens toward the end? A body of research summarized by Paul Kirschner, John Sweller, and Richard Clark warns that free-form practices do not work very well for beginners in a domain. Some versions of problem-based learning, project-based learning, and so on can be too loose, especially as learners get started. The learners need clear, worked-out examples and strong guidance, gradually faded back.

The point of learning through whole games is not to liberate learners from textbooks and engage them in personal exploration. The point of whole games is that they involve students in what we really want them to get better at. But of course even at the university level beginners cannot start in hospitals, courtrooms, or boardrooms. At an earlier age, beginners working at making sense of the daily paper or

The Catcher in the Rye or pollution in the local river cannot begin with erudite essays and statistical analyses. So where can they began? This brings us to the challenge of the junior version.

The Quest for the Junior Game

Students exploring Chris Dede's MUVE are not looking for real germs and toxins. Kenna Barger's students are not launching rockets from Cape Canaveral. Lois Hetland's students are not sifting through historical archives for original documents from colonial America. Joan Soble's students are not writing articles for *The Atlantic* magazine. They are not playing real baseball so to speak, not the full nine innings, not with nine on the team, not the regulation rules.

The relationship between their endeavors and the real thing is something like the relationship between backyard baseball and full-scale baseball. The junior version is less technically demanding. The timelines are much shorter. The activity often substitutes simulations for the real thing, for instance, simulated case documentation or a whole simulated environment like the MUVE or looking at reprints of historical documents. However, these junior versions capture a range of basic structural features of the full-scale game. They demand inquiry, problem finding, justification, explanation, indeed, the full range of earmarks listed earlier.

Junior versions are the key to making learning by wholes practical and powerful. Remember from the previous chapter how education always faces the fundamental problem of approaching complexity. Every teacher, every textbook, every parent, every coach has to find ways to cope with this problem. The more straightforward solutions are elements-first and teaching-about, but these tend to degenerate into *elementitis* and *aboutitis*.

The better solution is junior versions, better because junior versions involve learners meaningfully in whole games from the beginning and situate bits and pieces meaningfully in a bigger picture. Ideally junior versions provide students with what the Introduction called *threshold experiences,* experiences that usher them into new worlds of baseball, historical inquiry, writing, mathematical modeling, or whatever. I adapted the idea of threshold experiences from a very interesting body of work focused on university-level learning. Initially developed by Ray Land and Jan Meyer, the work foregrounds the idea of threshold *concepts.* These are key concepts that, once understood, bring learners to a deeper and broader sense of a discipline. In the context of learning by wholes, I'd like to emphasize not just threshold concepts but also threshold experiences.

Choosing a good junior version for beginners is an art that Joan Soble, Lois Hetland, Chris Dede, Kenna Barger, and many other teachers, mentors, parents, and others involved in education formal and informal embrace with care and commitment. Part of the art is throwing out what is not so important yet, while leaving the general spirit and shape of the game intact. Part of the art is substitution, for instance, swapping in simulations like the MUVE and replicas of historical documents. Part of the art is simply maintaining a reasonable level of challenge, not tossing beginners in with the experts. The game may be roughly the same in its rules—people don't normally learn to play checkers on a shrunk-down 4 × 4 board—but the level of play is approachable. Game makers themselves have embraced this principle, as evidenced by junior versions of popular board games such as Monopoly Junior, Junior Scrabble, and Clue Junior.

In the quest for a good junior game, the mix of throwing out and swapping in and maintaining a reasonable level of challenge reflects not only convenience, but the teacher's sense of what the learner already knows and therefore what will prove to be an accessible next step. This requires attention not just to what individual students are supposed to have learned considering their age and history, but what they have actually learned and how agile they are as learners, leading into the many practices of differentiated instruction. Learning by wholes helps by providing latitude: There are many different ways and levels through which learners can engage in a whole game.

Prior knowledge is the platform on which learners build. It wouldn't make a lot of sense to ask youngsters to become thoughtful strategic readers when they are struggling with decoding. It wouldn't make a lot of sense to involve youngsters in mathematical modeling with linear equations when they hardly know what linear equations are. So what is one to do?

The commonplace solution is elements first. Instead, learning by wholes suggests rethinking what junior game the learners might be ready for. Children struggling with decoding may not be ready to read texts strategically, but they can begin with thoughtful strategic *listening* as they are read to. Students just beginning algebra can build simple models of situations that interest them with tables and graphs and basic formulas. How does peak daily power usage vary with peak daily temperature? According to consumer data, how much does a small raise in price reduce sales? Is this the same percentagewise for inexpensive and expensive items? What's the relation between bird size and average migration distance for migratory birds? Problem finding comes into play here when students start with questions like these and figure out how to operationalize them—or formulate their own questions altogether.

If the lack of constituent skills gets in the way of using the obvious junior game, don't give up and settle for *elementitis*. Get even more junior! This does not mean stopping work on elements of decoding or algebra or any other constituent skill. Rather, such activities become more meaningful when seen as contributing to the next stages of the evolving whole game.

Related to what learners already know is the question of developmental readiness. Here again as in the Introduction I'm going to resist any plunge into the details of particular developmental theories and practices. For one thing, it is a whole world in itself with many resources available to educators. For another, again and again teachers and investigators have found that categorical statements about what children of various ages can and cannot do are risky. Children often display more skill and insight than expected if only the task is posed in the right way, with familiar materials, avoiding language that they might misunderstand, and providing tips and hints. Much depends upon the choice of a good junior version! Developmental themes will resurface when Chapter 5 explores uncovering the hidden game. For now, it's sufficient to urge a broad experience-based awareness of what happens to knowledge, understanding, and self-awareness as children advance from kindergarten through high school and beyond.

The reality is that when you devise a junior version of the game, you make your best-informed guess as to what learners already know and their developmental level. You produce a junior version and try it out to discover where it is too difficult, too easy, or just right. The first time around involves at least as much learning for you as it does for the learners, because you are always wrong in some ways. This is certainly my experience as an educator. Only over two or three cycles of working with real learners in real situations can we expect to home in on truly well-calibrated junior versions.

But what if there just is no junior version? What if the best one can do is elements first, until the learners have a critical mass of elements? In fact, aren't many things really like that?

For instance, you might suppose that swimming is a good example. Hardly anyone jumps in the lake and swims, not even awkwardly and haltingly. The way I learned to swim, the way most anyone learns to swim, seems to be elements first, standing on your feet up to your waist in the water, bending over, face immersed, turning your head sideways to practice breathing, practicing the stroke. Or holding onto a bar and practicing various kicks. Or supported by water wings.

However, the conventional teaching of swimming is not as elements first as it appears. First and most important, children and adults learning to swim, no matter what they themselves can do, have a sense of what the whole performance looks like. They see swimmers cruising back and forth all the time. Compare this with children in the third grade studying arithmetic, who typically have no clue about what math is really for, even in junior versions.

Second, practicing kicking and breathing as you hold onto a bar *is* a junior version. It's so junior that you are not even keeping yourself afloat, but you are doing everything you can at that point in a coordinated way, except for the grip that stops you from sinking. The same holds for many other early swimming exercises. From the beginning, there is an effort to put the pieces together, just so no one drowns.

If swimming is too far away from the usual business of education, consider early reading again. The same sort of complaint about swimming might apply to reading: How can we engage youngsters in reading in any holistic sense when they can't even decode? But the whole-language approach to reading in its less abrasively ideological forms has had a good answer to this for a long time. Yes, research demonstrates clearly that the decoding side of reading benefits from a phonetics approach. However, the endeavor of understanding narratives, arguments, explanations, and other such language forms involves much more than decoding and begins with oral exchanges. Indeed, research on reading development shows that the problems young readers experience reflect a mix of decoding difficulties, limited oral language facility and vocabulary, and a lack of background knowledge. Rich oral language exchanges can help with these issues. Seen in this way, whole-game undertakings like careful listening to and discussion about a story should be considered work on the larger enterprise of reading, even when all the actual reading students are doing at that moment focuses on decoding.

Junior version hard to come by? Get a little more imaginative. See the game in larger terms. Make the adjustments needed so "no one drowns," but with that in mind put as much of the whole game together from the beginning as you can. Besides that, be sure the learners, like the children learning to swim, get to *see* the whole game and participate around the edges, developing a sense of its shape and rhythm however much of it they are playing. We do well to live by a well-known statement from the seminal cognitive and developmental psychologist Jerome Bruner, who wrote in 1973, "We begin with the hypothesis that any subject can be taught effectively in some intellectually honest form to any child at any state of development."

Finally, let's say we have found our good junior version and got learners involved. Then what? How do we get to the full version of the whole game?

The journey to the full version of the whole game amounts to a staircase of junior versions with steps that become successively more complex and demanding. Early experiences of mathematical modeling can begin with simple whole-number arithmetic representing whole-number situations, move from there to fractions and decimals, and move from there to algebra and beyond. What expands is the repertoire of mathematical concepts and tools and the complexity of the modeling challenges. What persists is the idea of representing some piece of the world mathematically to reveal patterns and calculate consequences. Early experiences of literary interpretation can begin with simple stories and questions like, "What does this mean to you?" and "What do you see in the story that makes you say that?" It can advance to consideration of mythic elements in stories or character development driven by internal conflicts, and beyond. What expands is the repertoire of literary concepts and tools and the complexity of the texts. What persists is the idea of giving some evidence-based account of the work that illuminates its significance and its craft. Each step along such a staircase of junior versions is potentially another threshold experience, an entry into a more complex and sophisticated understanding.

And where does it all end? For any rich pursuit there is no real end. The possibilities for advancing a scholarly or practical craft further are endless. Today's most sophisticated versions are likely to be junior to tomorrow's. But we hardly need worry about the top of the staircase or whether there is one. The challenge of most of education lies much earlier along the staircase, getting learners started and moving them along with meaningful versions of the whole game.

The Quest for the Right Game

Recently I ran across two intriguing approaches to teaching ideas from biology: dancing mitosis and designing a fish. Two clearly dedicated and creative teachers shared these ideas briefly at a conference. If you remember your elementary biology, you may recall that mitosis is the process of asexual cell reproduction, by which the cell splits in two, each daughter cell sharing the full genetic complement of the parent cell. The rather complex multistep process of cell division in mitosis contrasts with the even more intricate process of meiosis involved in sexual reproduction, where there is an exchange of genetic materials between two parent cells.

Learners have difficulty getting the steps of mitosis straight. Dancing mitosis is one way to help them do so. In this teacher's approach, students in small groups took on the roles of various parts of the cell, designing a dance to play out the steps of mitosis, an active energetic way of recoding and representing to oneself this fundamental biological process. While there are canned versions of dancing mitosis where students simply learn predefined steps, my understanding of this teacher's practice was that the students needed to choreograph their own versions, a much more constructive endeavor.

Designing a fish also cast students in proactive roles. There the theme was adaptation to an ecology. Each student was asked to design a fish to fit within some aquatic ecology. The student had to devise distinctive and reasonable adaptations of the fish that gave it its own ecological niche, profile the lifestyle and adaptive advantages of the creature, and also position it taxonomically. I had a chance to thumb briefly through some of the reports students had written about their fish. The reports showed impressive detail and dedication to this exercise of the biological imagination.

Both dancing mitosis and designing a fish are whole games. They involve inquiry and require creating something that gives meaning to what otherwise might seem dry information. Both provide ways to approach something complex. Yet gradually I began to realize that in one way they were quite different from one another. Designing a fish looks toward its discipline of biology much more so than dancing mitosis does.

Designing a fish asks students to think *biologically* in creating their organisms, to consider issues of available food, competition, predators, and the like. Those same patterns of thinking figure over and over again in other contexts of biological inquiry. Designing a fish could be a threshold experience in biological thinking for these learners. In contrast, dancing mitosis asks students to think *choreographically* more than biologically. The steps of mitosis are right out of the textbook. The choreography helps students to learn how the steps work, good as far as it goes. But the knowledge really doesn't go any further than that. What can you do with it then? If generative knowledge is the goal, the students are probably having more of a threshold experience with choreography than with biology.

As I look across many examples where teachers have developed learning experiences with a whole-game character, I see the puzzle of dancing mitosis versus designing a fish coming up again and again. In general terms, *just because we have a whole game of some sort does not mean it foregrounds what we want.* Most of the interesting action may focus on something else.

The moral is simple: If one wants to advance students' understanding of and engagement with a discipline or some other area of learning, it's not just enough to have any old whole game in the neighborhood of the topic. One needs a well-targeted whole game, a whole game that engages learners centrally with generative knowledge and thinking in the discipline or area. Exciting activities are so seductive for teachers and students alike that it's easy to lose track of that goal.

All this said, I'm glad that students are dancing mitosis instead of simply memorizing the stages. And I'm glad they're learning something about dance in the process. I'm inclined to think that what they come to understand about dance is probably more worthwhile than what they come to understand about so very particular a topic as mitosis.

Keeping the Game in Motion

In the 1970s and '80s, quite a body of research developed around a dry-sounding concept with practical implications: *academic learning time.* Asking, "What's all the fuss about instructional time?" educator David Berliner offers a nice synthesis of the concept and results. The tale begins with the observation that there seems to be considerable slack in many settings of learning. Some of it comes from setup and transition time, some from passive listening, some from choice of activities that do not really focus on instructional targets, some from simple boredom and inattention.

To map how much students are involved in learning, investigators have constructed a number of measures such as allocated time, engaged time, and transition time. Particularly telling is academic learning time, roughly the amount of time students are involved in activities focused on the intended goals with a medium to high degree of success step by step. A relatively high success rate seems especially important for younger learners. Low success rates are always red flags. They demoralize students and, motivation aside, suggest that the tasks posed are too difficult for efficient learning.

Academic learning time predicts rather well how much students learn, much better than time sitting in class. Such research reveals the tricky logistics of settings of learning. Just because the learners are there does not mean that they are learning much. Effective learning requires artful management of the entire situation to lift academic learning time toward something close to the total time available, making the most of it rather than letting it slip away like sand between one's fingers.

The idea of learning by wholes does not automatically address academic learning time. It is all too possible for any of us to be engaged in a whole game without doing much at the moment. Again I think of baseball, an odd sport by this measure because most players are not doing much most of the time. Baseball is 10 percent action and 90 percent waiting—waiting for your turn at bat, waiting on base for someone to hit and move you along, waiting in the outfield for a hit to come your way, waiting on third base for a ball to come down the third-base line or a runner to approach from second.

There's not much hope for baseball. Waiting is intrinsic to the rhythm of the game. But baseball is an extreme case, and the general problem of keeping the game moving is fundamental to making the most of learning by wholes.

It may be helpful in considering academic learning time to think in terms of four attributes: pace, focus, stretch, and stick. For those who like acronyms, say *pfsst.*

Pace. Is each learner actively involved most of the time? Time that is adequately paced avoids drift and slack moments.

Focus. Do learners' activities fall within the core game we would like to see them getting better at, rather than taking some other form of busyness?

Stretch. Are learners being optimally challenged? When learners are finding everything easy, they are not likely to be learning much, nor are they when they are constantly encountering deep frustrations.

Stick. Are parts of the unfolding pattern of activity designed specifically to help knowledge, understanding, and skill stick in place? Stick includes elements such as deliberate rehearsal, reflection, stock taking, and revisiting ideas and practices later and then again later.

Put all these together, and we have what might be called the momentum of the game, the seamless energetic motion of the game in the designed direction.

Good *pace* can easily fall victim to set-up times and transition times. But beyond that, problems of pace often occur between the cracks, especially in classroom contexts. When students listen to a lecture or watch a video, are they just supposed to listen, or do they have a task to do that helps to keep them processing ideas actively? When a teacher fields a question from one student, what do the others take to be their roles, and how can those roles be made active? In group work, are the groups small enough to reduce the problem of marginal participants? In whole-class interactions with the teacher, is *wait time* employed, giving students time to think after a question is posed rather than calling on someone instantly, which on the one hand allows for little reflection and on the other favors students who already think they know the answer? When students ponder a question in class, are they asked to write down a few words, because when they have to write, that means mobilizing their thoughts to the point of specificity? Good pace, in other words, is a matter of organizing the subtleties in ways that promote the active engagement of most of the learners most of the time.

Even with a good pace, problems of *focus* arise when learners find themselves playing parts of the game that are too peripheral to generate much of the desired learning. Suppose, for instance, that students set up a mock store in the classroom. The idea is to learn things about handling money and basic economics. However, it turns out that much of the time goes into the incidentals of the store, furnishing and decorating, let's say. Or suppose that university students in a course on instructional design develop computer-based lessons as a project. However, it turns out that most of the time goes to struggling with the programming language rather than refining the way the learning works.

To generalize, any learning activity has secondary dimensions that require or invite attention. A certain amount of that can be enriching, but it sometimes happens that the secondary dimensions end up gobbling much of the learning time. Sometimes one hardly notices, because the secondary dimensions are engaging in themselves. Decorating the store may be more fun than running it! But what happened to the learning agenda? Good choices about the definition and structure of the activity can ensure that most of the time goes to the core.

Perhaps the trickiest problem of *stretch* is that different learners are likely to be in different places. What one learner finds altogether too hard for fruitful learning another may find altogether too easy. Sometimes this invites informal or formal diagnostic attention from a teacher. Even better, when you can, is to get learners to figure out their own appropriate levels of challenge. If the next two problems seem easy, skip ahead ten problems. What kinds of problems are you having the most difficulty with, and where can you find more of them and tips about how to handle them? All this looks forward to the entirety of Chapter 3, "Work on the Hard Parts," and beyond that to Chapter 7, "Learn the Game of Learning."

Finally, perhaps the trickiest problem of *stick* is the tendency in formal learning to leave things behind. Once we have finished the Industrial Revolution or linear equations or Deuteronomy, we do not expect to see the topic again for awhile. There is no systematic pattern of revisiting and revivifying. There is no systematic pattern of drawing things together into a larger-scale endeavor that integrates ideas and understandings from several directions. Learning by wholes is a help here, because that is the name of the game.

Gaming for Understanding

Imagine a snowball fight in space. A dozen astronauts hang above the Earth in free fall. They have arranged themselves roughly in a circle. In pouches on their space suits are supplies of snowballs, very expensive snowballs because the cost per gram of getting something into orbit is hideous. But this is just a fantasy, so we'll pay the bill with Monopoly dollars.

A signal sounds over their communicators. Each astronaut pulls a snowball out of the pouch and fires it at an astronaut on the other side of the circle. The question: Are they likely to hit one another, assuming that they are good shots on Earth? A larger question: What will happen as they attempt to continue their snowball fight?

Perhaps this puzzle brings back vague memories of the laws of Newton, studied in high school or college. So it should. You may want to ponder some answers for a moment before we go on.

A reply that might make Sir Isaac Newton happy would go something like this: As the astronauts begin the snowball fight, they also start to move way from one another. The gesture of throwing a snowball forward also pushes the astronaut backward, the principle of action and reaction. Not only that, but throwing the snowball also puts the astronaut into a spin, because the throw occurs away from the astronaut's center of gravity. Astronauts who want to avoid this would have to push the snowball forward from roughly their midsections, so the action occurs on a vector directly outward from their centers of gravity. Beginning to move away from one another and to spin, even as the gesture of the first shot unfolds, they are not very likely to hit anything, and the crew of the nearby space shuttle is going to have to invest some serious time retrieving drifting astronauts.

Here we have an example of playing a brief version of the Newtonian game of prediction and explanation. It is also a kind of test for understanding. If you understand Newton's laws of motion, you should be able to reason with them. If you do not, simply working from everyday intuition is unlikely to yield a sound forecast.

This also gives us an opportunity to examine one of the most fundamental goals of formal and informal learning: understanding. While rote and routine learning serve some ends well enough, almost everyone agrees that the larger aspirations of education require learning with understanding. Not so easily seen, however, are the answers to two questions: *What does it mean to understand something?* And *what's the connection between understanding and playing the whole game?*

So what does it mean to understand something? Staying with Newton for a moment, consider how one might know whether a particular student understands Newton's laws of motion. Many kinds of evidence should *not* convince us. The student may recite the laws. The student may write some correct equations. The student may succeed with three or four standard end-of-the-chapter problems. Despite all of that, this same student may urge that the astronauts in the snowball fight could easily hit one another if they weren't too far away and had good aim.

Our real criterion of understanding has to be performance. People understand something when they can *think and act flexibly with what they know* about it, not just rehearse information and execute routine skills. If you can't think with Newton's laws, you don't really understand them. If you can't think and act like a citizen, you don't really understand what citizenship is all about.

Earlier, I mentioned that some colleagues and I developed a framework for teaching for understanding. The heart of that framework is a performance view of understanding, the idea that understanding needs to be viewed as a flexible performance capability. To recall a couple of earlier examples, Lois Hetland in teaching about colonial

America was helping her students to become able to think historically. Joan Soble was helping her students to become more artful writers.

Sensible though this may sound, in many ways everyday language pushes in another direction. It's commonplace to speak of understanding as a matter of "having the idea," "getting it," or "seeing" what something is driving at. Everyday mention of understanding thrives on metaphors of possession, receiving, and perception. These ways of characterizing our subjective experiences of understanding are misleading. We can easily feel that we "get it" when we in fact do not. We can be sure we understand something only when we can think and act flexibly with what we know.

That brings us around to our second question: What's the connection between understanding and playing the whole game? The performance view of understanding provides a pointed answer here. Truly playing the whole game means thinking and acting flexibly in new situations, not just repeating old patterns in a stereotyped way. Playing the whole game is always a little bit creative. If every round of a game were the same, it would not be much of a game!

There is another way of thinking about understanding that is also helpful—mental models. When you pondered the problem of the snowball fight in space, almost certainly you were manipulating a mental model. You were picturing the astronauts floating in orbit, imagining what would happen as an astronaut threw a snowball. Likewise, in preparing for a job interview, you might imagine your way through likely scenarios. When sitting down to write a letter or an essay, you might make a quick mental outline. Research even shows that mental practice of athletic performances, such as shooting free throws in basketball, can improve the real-world skill.

Mental models are an important part of the story of understanding and the story of learning by wholes. Broadly speaking, mental models are images or ideas or structures we hold in mind. They need not be visual. They can use language, or our bodily kinesthetic sense, or our emotions, or other ways we have of representing things to ourselves. Whatever form they take, they support the flexible thinking and acting that is the mark of understanding. They give us mental representations for reasoning and exploration, just as an abacus or an artist's sketch gives us external representations for reasoning and exploration. Mental models are the game board of the mind.

Learning often means changing the game board, not just learning fancier strategies on the same board with the same pieces. Sometimes the game board we begin with incorporates mistakes and blind spots and prejudices. For example, think of the game board Newton had to start with. Everyday experience gives us a limited sense of the behavior of objects in motion, a sense embraced by Aristotle where objects spontaneously slow down and stop, their motion dissipating. The Newtonian conception reassigns slowing down to friction, a fundamental shift. Newton's view therefore represents somewhat different moves in a somewhat different game. Or look at the way someone like Gandhi tried to change the game. The inclusive equitable worldview of Mohandas Gandhi or Martin Luther King does not come so naturally to humankind. The usual beginning game board of group relationships has a clear "our side" defined by nationality, ethnic group, or religion, in stark opposition to "those others." A more inclusive conception that respects the other (without necessarily embracing the other) is hard but important learning, and another change in the game.

One thing that makes more sophisticated games hard to get is simply that one never gets to see them. There is not enough Newtonian motion or Gandhian philosophy around in everyday life to develop a feel for the game. One of the jobs of creative teaching and learning is to put the intended game within reach, to provide threshold experiences with it. A very important kind of mental model is a sense of the whole game. Recall the examples of learning to swim and learning to read. Children nowhere near staying on top of the water on their own already know the rough look of the entire performance of swimming, and children who do not know how to read but who have been read to a lot by their parents also know the rough look of the performance of reading. Such top-level mental models are powerful because they provide the big picture into which learners can fit particular elements, giving them meaning and purpose. It is not so hard to do this for swimming and reading. It is rather harder to do it for Gandhi, but surely we should be trying.

WONDERS OF LEARNING

PLAY THE WHOLE GAME

I wonder how I can organize learning around a "whole game." I probably need to engage learners in some kind of inquiry or performance involving problem solving, explanation, argument, evidence, strategy, skill, or craft. Learners would often produce something—a solution, an image, a story, an essay, a model. I should take care that the inquiry or performance not only engages learners but focuses on what I really want them to learn.

I wonder how I can tell whether I have a whole game. It's likely not routine but requires thinking; it's not just problem solving but involves problem finding; it's not just about right answers but involves explanation and justification; it's not emotionally flat but stimulates curiosity, discovery, creativity, camaraderie; it's not in a vacuum but engages methods, purposes, and forms of disciplinary or other practice in a social context.

I wonder how I can get learners started with a whole game even though they're just beginners. I could try to find a good junior version, maybe a very junior one. Junior versions at their best give learners threshold experiences, inducting them into a meaningful practice.

I wonder how I can keep the game in motion, keep the learners "playing." I might pay attention to "pfsst"—pace (learners individually involved most of the time), focus (learners thoughtfully doing what they're supposed to get better at), stretch (optimal challenge), and stick (review, reflection, rehearsal, and stock taking).

If I wonder about these things and do something about them, I'll be teaching for understanding. People understand something when they can *think and act flexibly with what they know* about it in new situations, not just rehearse information and execute routine skills.

2

Make the Game Worth Playing

I REALLY ENJOY CONVERSATIONS THAT GET CLOSE TO THE LEARNING PEOPLE care about. Such chats on the one hand reveal something about the learning process and on the other hand tell us a lot about why we bother. I've enjoyed dozens of incidental conversations like that, about baseball or amateur astronomy or sailing or contemporary novels, conversations not straightforwardly about learning at all, but on the side I'm thinking to myself, "Interesting, what this says about the personal understandings people have come to and how they got there!"

But sometimes these conversations can be a little more structured, like systematic archaeological digs into people's learning histories. Here is a simple but surprisingly revealing plan for such a dig:

1. What is one thing you understand really well?
2. How did you come to understand it?
3. How do you know you understand it?

These questions have long served as part of our work on teaching for understanding mentioned earlier. The aim is to unearth people's informal sense of what it was to learn something with understanding.

When you're answering question 1 about something you understand really well, academic topics are fine. But it's also fine to pick something very nonacademic such as gardening or child rearing. You might want to spend just a minute pondering a personal answer to the three questions before we go on. They are great reflective questions to try out on others as well. They can be used with adults, with teenagers, and with younger children also. They hone in on personal experiences of learning in school and out of school that people find to be truly meaningful.

I delight in hearing how people answer these questions. For *what is one thing you understand really well,* here are some ideas that often come up: driving, gardening, running a small business, cooking, sailing, raising a child, going through a divorce, snowboarding; and sometimes academic topics—algebra, the history of the Depression Era, Spanish.

For *how did you come to understand it,* people say things like this: "I did it a lot." "I stuck with it." "I worked with someone who really knew the score." "I got lots of help and feedback." "I tried to think through what I was doing and sharpen it up." "I tackled problems as they came along and tried to solve them." "I taught others how to do it."

For *how do you know you understand it,* people's answers are not so different. They say, I know I understand it because "I can do it." "I can solve problems when they come up." "I can make the right decisions." "I get good results most of the time." "I can explain why I'm doing what I'm doing." "I've taught others how to do it."

One general result affirms the importance of learning by wholes. When people respond, they almost never mention understanding a small piece of something, like the Pythagorean Theorem or how to use crampons for climbing or Act V of Hamlet or how much cinnamon to use in deep-dish apple pie. Almost always, they put on the table whole games of one sort or another.

Another strong pattern affirms the performance view of understanding emphasized toward the end of Chapter 1 When people talk about how they came to understand and how they know they understand, always in the foreground is doing, doing, doing—practicing, problem solving, getting feedback, sticking with it, teaching others.

The third feature that shines through in example after example is people's feeling of real commitment to what they have learned. A direct sign of this is how much time people have spent and how long they have persisted. But just as important is tone of voice. People speak of their activities like going home, shoes worn to the point of perfect comfort, or familiar lovers. No matter how ordinary some of the themes might seem, to their champions they are truly worth learning, understanding, and doing.

When people bring out their favorite examples of learning for understanding, just as interesting as what they mention is what they pass by. It's only now and again that people choose academic areas. This certainly does not mean that academic areas lack the potential to fascinate. My best guess is that academic areas get less press for a couple of other reasons. First of all, many of life's most vivid and important learning paths are not particularly academic. They have to do with family, birth, death, war, vocations, and avocations. Second, the lack of learning by wholes in so much of schooling means that people do not get hooked on academic pursuits in the ways they otherwise might. What a shame!

Which brings us around to the second of the seven principles of learning by wholes, *make the game worth playing*. How interested people are in learning something isn't just or even mainly a matter of how practical they think it is. Psychologists speak of *intrinsic motivation*, the motivation one feels for a topic or activity itself, regardless of other extrinsic incentives, such as pay or grades or privileges. Intrinsic motivation is nothing to take for granted. Studies of intrinsic motivation in academic subjects at various ages reveal a somewhat discouraging picture. Children start out enthusiastic and become increasingly less so over the course of the years. In one examination of almost eight hundred third through eighth graders reported by Mark Lepper, Jennifer Corpus, and Sheena Iyengar, intrinsic motivation in academics dropped steadily from third to eighth grade.

The study measured students' intrinsic and extrinsic motivations separately, revealing that extrinsic motivation remained about the same across the grades. As expected, intrinsic motivation predicted greater achievement. Extrinsic motivation, specifically the desire for easy work and aiming to please teachers, turned out to be negatively related to achievement. One natural hypothesis about the decline in intrinsic motivation looked to social approval and the possibility that intrinsic interest in academics might carry an onus. However, the study measured the need for social approval and this turned out not to be the culprit. The authors speculated that among the likely contributing causes was that "learning becomes increasingly decon-textualized, such that students find increasingly little that is directly relevant or useful in their daily lives."

Play the whole game, the first principle of learning by wholes from Chapter 1, already offers something of an answer to that shortfall. Playing baseball is more interesting than batting practice, playing pieces of music more interesting than practicing scales, and engaging in some junior version of historical or mathematical inquiry more interesting than memorizing dates or doing sums. A brisk rhythm of learning around the whole game marked by the four attributes of pace, focus, stretch, and stick is likely to energize learners with a sense of purpose, progress, and payoff.

But a good deal more can be said. On the content side, the challenge is to choose and frame content so that it is genuinely worthwhile and its worth is transparent. On the process side, there are ways of leveraging beginnings, understanding, expectations, and choice. Each of these can contribute to making the game worth playing.

Learning What's Worth Learning

You know how people reminisce about the last time they played a game of baseball or saw an old friend or went out on a date or got really drunk. Well, a while ago I found myself musing on this question: When was the last time I solved a quadratic equation?

A nerdy question yes, but remember I was really interested in mathematics, and I actually enjoyed solving quadratic equations. So here's what I found out when I asked myself this question. Although I took a doctoral degree in mathematics, and although I pursue a technical profession of cognitive psychology and education, and although I occasionally use technical statistics, it's been decades since I solved a quadratic equation.

My high school mathematics teacher, a very good one, spent weeks working with me and the rest of the class on quadratic equations. I don't think most people particularly savored it, but I certainly did! Just about everyone I know ran the gauntlet of quadratic equations at some point. Yet hardly any of them have exercised the mysteries of the quadratic lately, and most folks probably have forgotten most of the techniques.

This illustrates a disturbing general pattern from the research on lasting learning: Most students just plain forget most of what they have been taught. What they remember they often do not understand well. And what sticks with understanding often sees little active use. Learning scientists, following Alfred North Whitehead, have characterized the problem nicely: *inert knowledge*—knowledge that students dig out for the quiz but don't connect to situations in the midst of their lives where it might contribute.

Why is forgotten, misunderstood, and inert knowledge such a plague? Surely there are many factors, but much of the blame has to fall on the basic disconnectedness of much of what students learn in schools. The typical curriculum does not connect—not to practical applications, nor to personal insights, nor to much of anything else. It's not the kind of content with high prospects for connecting. The games we play in school are not enough like the games we need to and want to play outside. To symbolize the whole by a part (a literary trope called *synecdoche* for those who like erudite words), we suffer from a massive problem of quadratic education.

We need a connected rather than a disconnected curriculum, a curriculum full of knowledge of the right kind to link richly to future insights and applications. John Dewey, the great American philosopher and educator, envisioned something like this when he wrote of instruction centered on themes abounding with possibilities and connections, what might be called *generative knowledge*. He wanted education rich with ramifications for the lives of learners. This doesn't necessarily mean handbooks full of practical applications, but it certainly calls for knowledge that relates widely and readily to the many important dimensions of life.

What does generative knowledge look like? Consider another bundle of mathematical concepts, probability and statistics. The typical precollege curriculum doesn't treat them in any depth, yet statistical information abounds in newspapers, magazines, and even newscasts. Probabilistic considerations pop up in many common areas of life, such as making informed decisions about medical treatment. Statistical and probabilistic reasoning is a "game" that connects. The National Council of Teachers of Mathematics encourages more attention to probability and statistics in its standards. If I had to choose, I would put more probability and statistics on the plate and fewer quadratic equations.

Or for instance, consider the dark theme of ethnic hatred, the psychology and sociology of why ethnic groups from Northern Ireland to Bosnia to South Africa are so often and so persistently at one another's throats. It turns out that a good deal is known about the causes and dynamics of ethnic hatred. If I were teaching social studies, I might teach about the roots of ethnic hatred instead of the French Revolution. Or I might teach the French Revolution through the lens of the roots of ethnic hatred. It's knowledge that connects!

Picking What's Worth Learning

So where might ideas for the content of this connected curriculum come from? For one fine source, teachers. The teaching for understanding model I've mentioned before encourages teachers to focus their instruction around *generative topics*. These are topics that figure centrally in the discipline or practice under study, resonate with the learners' interests and concerns and, importantly, resonate with the teacher's also. They afford recurring opportunities for insight and application.

Teachers make up generative topics based on their own experience and their sense of what they teach. There is no official list, although many examples can be found in such sources as *Teaching for Understanding* edited by Martha Stone Wiske, a synthesis of the work on the original project. With generative topics in mind, educators of all sorts at any level can ask themselves: What new topic could I teach, or what spin can I put on a topic I already teach, to make it genuinely generative?

Exploring these questions with teachers yields some wonderful ideas. Here is a small collection:

- Justice in Literature (for example, *To Kill a Mockingbird*) connects to adolescents' concerns with justice, to literature as social commentary, to matters of justice from recent times such as the Rodney King case, to the many issues of justice that constantly come up.
- What is a Living Thing? Are viruses alive? What about computer viruses (some argue that they are)? What about crystals?
- The World of Ratio and Proportion. Research shows that many students have a poor grasp of this very central concept, a concept that, like statistics and probability, comes up all the time. Dull? Not necessarily. The teacher who suggested this pointed out many surprising situations where ratio and proportion enter—musical notation, diet, sports statistics.
- Whose History? It's been said that history gets written by the victors. This theme addresses point-blank how accounts of history get shaped by those who write it—the victors, the dissidents, and those with other special interests.

It's important not to mix up generative knowledge with what's simply fun or doggedly practical. We might think of the most generative knowledge as a matter of *understandings of wide scope*, systems of concepts and examples with a whole-game character that yield insight and implications in many circumstances. Look back at the topics listed earlier. Yes, they can be read as particular pieces of subject-matter knowledge. But every one also is a powerful conceptual system. Probability and statistics offer a window on chance and trends in the world; the roots of ethnic hatred reveal the dynamics of rivalry and prejudice at any level from neighborhoods to nations; patterns of justice figure over and over again in human affairs; the nature of life becomes an ever more central issue in this era of test-tube babies and recombinant DNA engineering; ratio and proportion are fundamental modes of description; the "whose history?" theme deals with central human phenomena of group identity and point-of-view.

Added to the ingenuity of teachers are the insights of scholars toward selecting what's worth learning. For example, Neil Postman in his *The End of Education* bewails the fixation of educational psychology on means in contrast to ends. "The engineering of learning is very often puffed up, assigned an importance it does not deserve," he grumbles. In contrast, Postman characterizes the real problem as "a metaphysical one," a question of fundamental worth. He urges that to be meaningful, education needs to be organized around the right "gods" or "grand narratives" that tie everything together. Postman doesn't like very much some of today's "gods" of choice, for instance, the gods of economic utility, consumerism, or technology that often shape curricula. It's not that these gods fail to offer grand narratives, they just do not provide very rich ones. They don't tell us enough about who we are, supply strong and fruitful guidance around moral questions, and explain enough about the deep mysteries of the world— three criteria he views as fundamental.

Postman favors grand narratives that do a better job of this, for example, Spaceship Earth or the Fallen Angel. Spaceship Earth reminds us that we are all in the same ecological, political, and economic boat. The Fallen Angel concerns humankind in our greatness and weakness, striving to understand the dark sides and blind spots of the human condition. Postman offers these and other sample grand narrative themes in illustration of the sort of thematic depth and breadth that might serve education well year after year. Whatever one may think of Spaceship Earth or the Fallen Angel, what stands out here is the breadth of conception, leaving no doubt that we are dealing with understandings of wide scope and a curriculum that connects in innumerable ways.

The same can be said for a vision of education offered by my colleague Howard Gardner's *The Disciplined Mind*. Gardner suggests organizing education around three overarching themes: *the true, the good*, and *the beautiful*. Education so seen could speak deeply and honestly both to the intricacies of today's world and to academic disciplines. In illustration of the true, Gardner offers Darwin's theory of natural selection. An aria from a Mozart opera stands for the beautiful, while the good is contrasted to its dark side, the Nazi decision to attempt the Final Solution. Again, as with Postman the breadth of conception stands out. Whether Darwin, Mozart, and the Final Solution are foci you personally would choose is less to the point than reaching for understandings of wide scope out of which a connected curriculum can be woven.

Looking across Postman, Gardner, and other sources, I'm struck by how visions of meaningful education seem to speak to three basic agendas: *enlightenment, empowerment*, and *responsibility*. For example, an in-depth exploration of Postman's theme of Spaceship Earth would enlighten us about our place on this planet, empower us to take significant action, and foster our sense of responsibility. Likewise, an examination of the Final Solution and related episodes of genocide would enlighten us about powerful if unwelcome aspects of human nature (Postman's Fallen Angel theme), empower us with ideas about what to watch out for and what to do, and cultivate our responsibility to deal with the dark side.

If much of what we taught highlighted understandings of wide scope, with enlightenment, empowerment, and responsibility in the foreground, there is every reason to think that youngsters would retain more, understand more, and use more of what they learned. A maxim I suggested in my 1992 *Smart Schools* and have come to believe with even more fervor over the past few years comes down to a single sentence: *Our most important choice is what we try to teach*. Yes, how we teach is an important choice also, but no matter how we teach, many students will learn a fair amount of what we teach at least temporarily. Will they hold onto it though? Will they have a reason to want to? Understandings of wide scope can give them a reason.

What then of the fate of quadratic equations? Is it just old hat in a brave new world? Well maybe not if the agenda were enlarged. I am remembering an occasion a few months ago when I shared my worries about quadratic education with a group of educators. One responded in effect:

> Why not reframe it this way? Give the theme more scope—models of growth. Out there in the world, we see patterns of linear growth, quadratic growth, exponential growth, and others. Growth in cells, sales, bodies, populations, economies, crystals, and the universe itself is a fundamental phenomenon one runs into again and again. Quadratics might be a lot more meaningful if placed in this larger picture.

Certainly there would be other roles for quadratic equations, but models of growth is a good one, a game with legs! Certainly models of growth would shift the way quadratic equations were treated, easing off some of the techniques for solving them and bringing into the foreground their significance, but all the better for that.

Making the Most of Beginnings

"It was the best of times, it was the worst of times, it was the age of wisdom, it was the age of foolishness, it was the epoch of belief, it was the epoch of incredulity, . . ." You may recognize this as the first phrases of Charles Dickens's *A Tale of Two Cities*. It's a classic example of what writers commonly call a narrative hook. Immediately your curiosity is up. How was it the best of times and the worst of times at the same time, how wisdom and foolishness side-by-side? You want to read on.

Just as authors would like readers to read on, teachers would like learners to learn on. So we would do well to take a tip from the novelist's notebook. Beginnings are important!

This is certainly something that many teachers know in their bones. My colleague Ron Ritchhart, in *Intellectual Character*, describes how gifted teachers, the first time they find themselves facing a new group of students, try to establish a tone of enticement. He relates how one algebra teacher opened the first day of class with a disarming roll call. The teacher emphasized how hard it was to keep track of all those new faces, deliberately showing weakness. Then up on the blackboard went a puzzle problem from the daily paper. The teacher explained that a student had brought it into class. The teacher then mentioned how much he loved little problems and invited students to bring in similar puzzles throughout the year as the fancy struck them. Next the teacher wrote on the blackboard a discouragingly intricate arithmetic computation from Norton Juster's witty and popular children's book, *The Phantom Tollbooth*. The teacher asked the students to try to figure out the answer, mumbling that he had better work it through himself, again showing himself not to be on top of everything all the time. Of course, the students came up with a jumble of different answers. The teacher jotted down his own, prompting a chorus of groans, but immediately said that he doubted he got it right. His attitude for the whole range of proposed answers was clear, though. "Math is not a democracy." Never mind what's the most popular answer. We need proof.

It's not hard to see that Charles Dickens and this teacher were up to much the same thing. They were both throwing narrative hooks out into the waters of their constituencies, hoping to pull in as many as possible.

Yes, one might say to oneself, "Some people are going to like this, some are not, and that's the way it is." There is certainly a measure of truth in this—people certainly have their preferences—but the measure isn't anywhere near 100 percent. I'm reminded of the stereotypical statement people are said to make when they don't feel sophisticated enough about art: "I don't know much about art, but I know what I like." The thing is, people often *don't* know what they like, not until they've had a significant amount of experience with it.

To build that experience, people need to become a little bit involved. Remember from the previous chapters the idea of threshold experiences, where the game comes together coherently even in a junior version. The first challenge of making the game worth playing, no matter what the game, is to get people far enough into it to give the game a chance.

Of course, the process of enticement does not stop there. Whatever the intrinsic merit and allure of any topic, a great deal can be done day by day to place that topic in its best light.

Making the Most of Understanding

Let's continue with the literary theme. Say you have a class studying Irish poet William Butler Yeats's poem "Sailing to Byzantium." As the lesson proceeds, the students find it takes a surprising turn. The larger topic is not Yeats's poetry but the poetry of immortality. "Sailing to Byzantium" invokes a yearning for immortality through a journey to a mythical Byzantium where the poet imagines himself transformed into a gold statue: "such a form as Grecian goldsmiths make/Of hammered gold and gold enameling/To keep a drowsy emperor awake." Also to read and relish and ponder on the topic of immortality are Keats's "Ode to a Grecian Urn," where art achieves a timeless stasis, and the Shakespearean sonnet "Shall I compare thee to a summer's day?" which at the end promises the lady to whom it is addressed immortality through the poet's immortal words.

Revealing the theme of the poetry of immortality, the teacher also announces particular goals for understanding. The goals help to focus and energize the students' attention. The teacher also invites the students to add an understanding goal or two, which they do with zest. The goals ask everyone to understand the allure of the immortal and the different ways poets have evoked that allure. There are also activities to be done individually and in small groups, inviting lively participation and personal responsibility. One activity sends students on a hunt for a twentieth-century poem with a similar theme; in a small-group discussion, students will compare and contrast this modern poem with these more classical treatments. Another activity asks students to respond to a poem with personal connections and explain them.

As they explore the poems, students receive considerable feedback on their work, sometimes from the teacher, sometimes from others, sometimes simply from themselves. The feedback has hardly any tone of grading. It centers on deepening the students' own process. In the bigger picture, all this is part of a learning experience focused on making sense of poetry—thematic sense, aesthetic sense, technical sense, many different kinds of sense. The theme of the poetry of immortality sits within this panoramic agenda.

We have here an example of teaching for understanding, the framework I've mentioned before. All the earmarks of the teaching for understanding framework appear above:

- A *generative topic*, the poetry of immortality
- *Understanding goals* such as understanding the allure of the immortal and how poets have expressed it
- *Understanding performances*, the activities learners do to think and act flexibly with what they know
- *Ongoing assessment*, feedback early and often, directed not so much toward grades as toward expanding understanding

Readers interested in the details of teaching for understanding can find out much more in *Teaching for Understanding* edited by Martha Stone Wiske, *The Teaching for Understanding Guide* by Tina Blythe, and *Teaching for Understanding with Technology* by Martha Stone Wiske and others. WIDE World, an online program of professional development developed at the Harvard Graduate School of Education, also fosters teaching for understanding.

Teaching for understanding is a way of making the game worth playing. You see, understanding is not just an attainment but also a motivator. We are fundamentally more engaged when we understand and more enthralled when we find ourselves building understanding. This is not only common sense but also a research result. In the original research that led to the framework, students in classes featuring teaching for understanding reported valuing the various features of that style of learning.

Turning on the magnet of understanding requires more than just using a four-part framework. The kinds of thinking and doing that exercise and stretch understanding can easily slip away in favor of relatively empty fun. Suppose that the theme of the month is ecology, certainly a generative topic. We want learners to develop a broad understanding of several aspects of ecology. One tempting activity might be to ask students to assemble a giant wall chart showing the complex ecology of a pond. This certainly can be an engaging collaborative project, and it can produce a useful representation for later lessons. But is it a performance of understanding? Not quite. In itself, it doesn't involve much thinking. The students simply need to follow the instructions to piece together the pieces. Remembering the principles of pace, focus, stretch, and stick from the last chapter, it lacks focus and stretch.

Another activity might feature solving a crossword puzzle that uses vocabulary from ecology. There is plenty of thinking to be done here if the puzzle is well designed. The trouble is this kind of thinking has less to do with understanding ecologies and more to do with fitting words together. The crossword puzzle may be worthwhile for other reasons, but it is not an understanding performance about ecology. It lacks the right focus.

How about this then: The students are asked to visit a local pond, identify as many organisms of various sizes as they can, and map the ecology of the pond. This sounds more promising than the crossword puzzle. It's a little like the wall chart, only now the students have to make up their own chart.

This is certainly much better, but there is still a pothole to be avoided. A group might identify a number of organisms and produce a large diagram showing where they were found, but with nothing about how they relate to one another. The students could well call this a "map of the ecology," only it does not show food webs and similar dependency relationships, again a problem of focus and stretch.

The pothole we see here shows up in many other activities we might think of as good understanding performances: write an essay, write a story, produce a diagram, develop a discussion, create a dramatization, and so on. All these are promising because they offer ample *opportunity* for understanding performances. However, they do not typically *require* extensive on-target thinking. Students can cruise through them, filling in the essay, story, diagram, discussion, or dramatization with token information about the topic.

So how to pave over the pothole? It's not difficult to define the ecology mapping activity in a way that requires true understanding performances:

> Show with arrows the dependency relationships: X eats Y, X lives on Y, and so on; label what they are; and on the chart write down your evidence, either from observations or from the text, for the reality of each dependency relationship.

To play the game in this form, you *have* to think with what you know and what you can find out, focus and stretch in clear view.

Making the Most of Expectations

How good a learner are you? An especially provocative finding from research on learning says that the league of learner you are depends significantly on the learner you are expected to be and expect yourself to be. We tend to think of being a good learner as a matter of ability, but it is also enormously a matter of disposition, learners' confidence in and commitment to learning.

Perhaps the best-known result along these lines was reported by Robert Rosenthal and Lenore Jacobson in the 1968 *Pygmalion in the Classroom*. In the story from the Roman poet Ovid, Pygmalion was a sculptor who fashioned a statue of a woman so compelling that he fell in love with it and prayed to Venus for the statue to come to life . . . successfully. Rosenthal and Jacobson presented data suggesting that teachers' expectations had a Pygmalion-like effect. When they were told that certain students would show developmental spurts, testing months later showed those children's IQ actually went up compared to others', even though the children in fact were chosen at random in a deceptive manipulation. The authors interpreted this to mean that the teachers had behaved toward these students in ways that helped them bloom.

A warning: Although widely popularized, this particular Pygmalion effect has also been widely challenged. One of many problems was that although children K–5 were tested, only those in the lowest grades showed much of an improvement. For another problem, efforts to replicate the study generally have not confirmed it. What *has* survived, however, is the idea of expectancy effects, also called self-fulfilling prophecy—maybe not on IQ, but certainly on achievement in the content areas and other dimensions of growth.

It's not hard to imagine the kinds of teacher behaviors that might signal expectations to learners. Is the student one the teacher turns to when no one else has the answer, or the student the teacher never turns to, suggesting that he or she never has the answer? Does the teacher wait for the student's answer as though confident he or she has one in there somewhere, or quickly move on to another? When the teacher places students into pairs to help one another, is the student always paired up with one of the smart ones seemingly chosen to help? Does the student get lots of praise for solving relatively easy problems, indicating how low the bar is set for him or her? In endless ways, teachers, and peers also, can communicate intellectual expectations that create the reality they supposedly reflect.

In this spirit, Rosenthal later articulated a four-factor way of looking at how teacher expectancy effects might operate: *climate* (a warmer, more welcoming social and emotional climate for students expected to achieve more), *feedback* (more thorough, careful feedback), *input* (attempts to teach more material and more difficult material), and *output* (more opportunities to respond). Notice that the four factors do not necessarily give the advantage to students from whom teachers expect more. A "reverse-expectancy" effect is also possible. Some teachers choose to focus on the plight of students who seem weaker, creating a stronger climate, feedback, input, and output to serve their development.

Of course, self-fulfilling prophecy is not just a matter of what teachers expect of learners, but what learners expect of themselves. An intriguing perspective on this comes from Stanford University psychologist Carol Dweck and her colleagues. For a number of years, her team has investigated how youngsters think about their own intellectual abilities and how that influences their investment of effort in learning. Dweck draws a distinction between *incremental learners* and *entity learners*. Entity learners fall at one end of a continuum, buying fully into that familiar phrase, "You either get it or you don't." Incremental learners at the other end view intelligence as very stretchable. This difference of philosophy translates into a sharp contrast in learning behaviors. When entity learners run up against something hard to understand or a problem tough to solve, they become early quitters. In contrast, incremental learners chip away at a challenge like a block of stone, gradually making it manageable.

It would be natural to suppose that the entity learners are the not-so-smart ones. It's not so simple, though. The research of Dweck and her colleagues shows that there are plenty of entity learners among the best and brightest. Their own intelligence sets a kind of trap. Because they have succeeded all their lives in the various hurdles education puts down in front of them, when they come up against something not so easy to hop over they tend to think that it is too high for them.

One implication of this is quite unsettling: Initial difficulties can set entity learners up for later failure, even when the initial difficulties have little to do with what comes later. In one clever study, Barbara Licht and Carol Dweck determined the mastery or incremental mindsets of a number of fifth-grade students through a self-report questionnaire. Later the students received booklets introducing "an interesting new subject," in fact, some basic principles of psychology in five sections, the first just introductory. In some booklets, sections 2 and 3 were written in a very clear way, in others in a somewhat confusing way. The students studied the booklets and afterward took a simple multiple-choice test evaluating mastery *not* of sections 2 and 3 but rather 4 and 5, quite different topics. Those students who did not score perfectly were given encouragement, review booklets, and another simple quiz, a process repeated until time ran out.

What happened reveals the devastating influence an entity mindset can have. Students who received the booklet with clear versions of sections 2 and 3 performed reasonably well on the first quiz and improved greatly when given further study opportunities, no matter whether they had incremental or entity mindsets. This showed that students in the two groups were equally intellectually able. Turning to the students with confusing sections 2 and 3, the students with incremental mindsets were not thrown off: They still performed about the same on sections 4 and 5. However, the impact of the confusing version was dramatic for students with an entity mindset. They scored very poorly on the first quiz. Even after review opportunities, only 35 percent scored perfectly, in contrast with about 70 percent for the others, including fellow entity learners who had not encountered early confusion.

Dweck adds a Pygmalionesque twist to the story, revealing how teachers' actions create learners' entity expectations. Dweck and her colleagues looked closely at classroom interactions and exposed numerous ways in which certain teachers communicated entity attitudes to their charges. For example, a teacher might say something like, "I know everyone here finds math a tough subject, but . . ." Or, "Sandy, that's a really good try," suggesting that that's as far as it goes; there is no point in Sandy trying something else. Then there is the familiar practice of picking one of the first three or four hands to go up, suggesting implicitly that any answers worth hearing are going to come to mind at once instead of exercising wait time.

Better strategies for making the game worth playing are strikingly like what coaches try to do in baseball or football or any other sport. Good coaches accomplish what they do not only by teaching skills but by fostering dispositions. They project high expectations and build the confidence and commitment of every member of the team. This does not mean that people are all alike. Of course they are not. However, aptitude is not the same thing as attitude, and attitudes—both teachers' and students'—turn out to count for a lot!

Making the Most of Choice

My wife is a big opera fan. I am a small one. You can't blame it on general background, because both of us enjoy quite a range of classical and other music, but we don't gravitate to exactly the same genres. A great operatic experience for my wife translates into a pretty good one for me, happy to be there. A pleasant operatic experience for her translates into three very slow hours for me. This is just a reminder that even within areas of considerable basic interest learners of any age or ilk are not going to like everything put before them equally. It's obvious but important: People have their preferences, their leanings, their quirks.

Even so, people's engagement in learning something should not be considered just a matter of how much they like the something. It turns out that intrinsic motivation is not just a matter of individual preferences but the style of the overall undertaking. A good learning experience may not be able to turn me into an ardent opera fan, but it can make a considerable difference.

One fine way of stoking enthusiasm is choice. For a rule of thumb, when learners feel that they have a choice about just where they focus their attention and just how they proceed, they are more likely to show intrinsic motivation and, along with, this broader and deeper learning.

Let's begin with the dark side of the story, the negative of choice, coercion. In 1966 J. W. Brehm introduced a very interesting motivational pattern called *reactance*. This is a name for people's response when they perceive that their freedoms have been restricted. The freedoms involved can range widely, from fundamental matters of religious and political options to minor fetters such as no smoking policies or littering laws. People tend to react negatively to constraints in ways that range from passive resistance to minor sabotage to outright large-scale rebellion.

A particularly clever study was reported by J. Pennebaker and D. Sanders. University scholars taking advantage of the university setting, they posted different signs on the walls of bathroom stalls.

Some signs read *Do NOT Write on the Walls*, whereas others prefaced the sentence with the word "please." Some of the signs purported to be from the chief of the university police, with others simply from a member of the grounds committee of the university police. Which bathroom stalls do you imagine collected the most graffiti? By far those without the "please" and from the high authority figure.

The connection to formal education is hardly obscure. Classrooms involve a great deal of constraint—what you must master, when things are due, what protocols of deportment to observe. There is no question that considerable structure is necessary, but to the extent that learners experience all structure and no latitude, reactance is likely to set in and undermine intrinsic motivation. A little elbow room goes a long way.

It's not just choice but the reasons for the choice. Considerable research argues that extrinsic motivation can undermine intrinsic motivation. To the degree that strong extrinsic motivators are on learners' minds—financial rewards, grades, social status—this can obscure intrinsic values. In one illustrative investigation, some children first engaged in an art activity and then received a certificate for a reward. For others the certificate played no role. Given a chance later to work with the art materials again, fewer of the children who earned a certificate wanted to do so. In another investigation at the college level, students were asked to rank order lists of reasons for engaging in creative writing. Some students got a list biased toward extrinsic reasons like public recognition, while others received a list oriented toward intrinsic reasons like self-expression. Everyone wrote haiku immediately afterward. The haiku from the extrinsic group received lower-quality ratings from judges. So again, it's not just a matter of whether there is a choice but what factors figure in the choice—intrinsic versus extrinsic.

Even the manner in which knowledge and ideas are presented can create a greater or lesser sense of choice. Very often, the mode is decidedly imperial—this is the way things are. Believe it! In the late '90s, Harvard psychologist Ellen Langer and colleagues introduced the idea of *conditional instruction*, where the language included fewer absolutes and more phrases like "could be" and "may be." Such locutions invite learners to engage with the content and make up their own minds. Systematic studies demonstrated that retention of information was just as good, while use of the information in creativity and problem solving was better. The point is not so much that everything should be up for grabs as it is that many settings of instruction have an utterly absolutist character that deprives learners of meaningful choice and reduces their intrinsic motivation and engagement.

Choice is a good rule of thumb, but the thumb has a couple of unexpected joints. One concerns cultural variables. People of some cultural backgrounds appear to be less subject to reactance than people of other cultural backgrounds. In one line of investigation, Asian-American children, with their more interdependent conception of the self, showed fewer advantages of personal choice than did Anglo-American children. Indeed, S. Iyengar and M. Lepper reported in a 1999 study that the Asian-Americans proved most intrinsically motivated when trusted authority figures or trusted peers made their choices for them.

In a complementary 2000 study, Iyengar and Lepper found that too much choice may undermine intrinsic motivation. A number of studies have demonstrated that a few choices yield more engagement and deeper learning than none. However, when the number of choices balloons to twenty or thirty, intrinsic motivation drops. In different experiments, participants with a multitude of choices in contrast with six displayed less interest in purchasing gourmet jams; less interest in writing extra-credit essays and, for those who opted to do so, poorer-quality essays; and less tendency in a chocolate selection task to choose chocolates over money as compensation. Across these studies, choosers with many options actually enjoyed the decision-making process itself more, but they also felt more responsible for their decisions and more confused by the process. The moral: When people select from a large prescribed set of options, there can be what Iyengar and Lepper term a *choice overload* effect. Again as with intrinsic versus extrinsic reasons, it's not just *that* there is a choice but the kind of choice it is.

Above the level of single decision points lies the entire cultural tone of a setting of learning, a tone that may be more important than the careful engineering of particular moments of choice. Do we have a culture of demand or a culture of opportunity? As a learner, does one feel put upon by the demands of the situation—the rules, the assertions, even the requirement to juggle a large number of choices—or does one experience a range of opportunities? In many classrooms today, the general tone seems to be much more a culture of demand than a culture of opportunity. Cultures of opportunity help make the game worth playing.

Challenge, Imagination, and More

There is always more to be said about making the game worth playing. To celebrate this point, let me mention a couple of further ideas briefly. In making the most of expectations and choices, we can also make the most of challenge. Level of challenge is a powerful factor in motivation.

One well-known expression of this idea is the phenomenon of *flow* from Mihaly Csikszentmihalyi. His artful choice of the word evokes that experience of engagement and momentum we have when a challenging activity goes truly well. Csikszentmihalyi shows how flow reflects an ideal balance of capability and challenge. When capability trumps challenge, we get bored, and when it's the other way around we get frustrated. Between the two is the motivational sweet spot of optimal challenge.

How to hit the sweet spot? The first step echoes the previous chapter: Find a good junior version of the game. The whole point of a junior version is to engage learners in a meaningful threshold experience that dodges *elementitis* and *aboutitis*.

So far so good, but with a group mixed in initial interest, capabilities, and ambition, how does one keep learners anywhere near their individual sweet spots? Here the trick is to structure learning situations so that within the junior version learners can hone in on their own optimal levels of challenge. This is one of the most potent characteristics of video games. Typically organized by level of difficulty, they allow players to advance from tier to tier, always facing manageable challenges based on the skills developed at the previous level. Indeed, technology-based games are one powerful resource for organizing learning, a theme richly explored by David Schaffer in *How Computer Games Help Children Learn*. The more general point is not that curriculum should be laid out like a video game, but that the task should be structured so that different learners can attempt more and less ambitious goals that gradually get tougher. How? For instance, teachers can introduce inquiry and design projects that provide latitude for some learners to choose more difficult missions, or tiered problem sets where learners can attempt problems of a particular difficulty and after doing well move on.

Let's add yet another theme, making the most of the imagination. Kieran Egan, in *An Imaginative Approach to Teaching*, dedicates a whole book to this agenda. Egan works from a framework of cognitive tools chosen to charge up the imagination. Boring topic at hand? Look for its emotional meaning. Identify binary opposites that focus the mind and excite learners, such as good/bad, earth/sky, courage/cowardice. Look for the heroic, tap jokes and humor, mobilize metaphor, involve learners in a kind of gossip, raise questions about what is real and the extremes of the real, and more.

Egan fills his book with examples. For one, he demonstrates how to resurrect that moribund topic the Industrial Revolution. Perhaps, Egan suggests, a parade for a hero rather than a parade of historical facts would help. One suggested hero: Isambard Kingdom Brunel (1806–1859), a British engineer who accomplished truly remarkable things through a mix of boldness and ingenuity, including suspension bridges and ocean liners far larger than anything that had been constructed before, filled with technical innovations that continue to inform engineering today.

Egan certainly does not intend a whitewash of the Industrial Revolution's darker side. There too he finds room for the imagination, images from poets William Blake and Robert Burns, along with Mary Shelley's *Frankenstein*. Framing the topic in such heightened terms invites learners into a range of imaginative activities: storytelling, dramatization, investigations, and more.

Making the game worth playing is a mission that, like one of those video games, invites layer upon layer of refinement. My greatest concern is not so much how far to go but making a really good start. Turning back to the first themes of this chapter, the place to start is with the content of learning itself. The first step is choosing a game *worth* learning. One more time: Our most important choice is what we try to teach.

WONDERS OF LEARNING

MAKE THE GAME WORTH PLAYING

I wonder how I can teach what's worth learning. I can take advantage of the choices I have about what topics to treat and how to frame them. I might foreground generative topics and understandings of wide scope that illuminate fundamental questions of human nature, society, ethics, the nature of knowledge, and more.

I wonder how I can make the most of beginnings. For one thing, I could watch out for piling up logistics and rules at the beginning. Let me establish an open curious spirit . . . and figure out a way to get learners into some junior version of the whole game soon.

I wonder how I can make the most of understanding, a powerful motivator. It might help to organize learning with the teaching for understanding framework: generative topics, understanding goals, understanding performances, ongoing assessment. (See the Notes section at the end of this book for teaching for understanding resources.)

I wonder how I can make the most of expectations. For a start, I could watch out for sending subtle signals of low expectations. I want to cultivate confident proactive mindsets, not by propagandizing but by configuring things so students can succeed step-by-step and come to believe they can improve their capacity.

I wonder how I can make the most of choice. I'm reminding myself here that everyone does not have to do exactly the same thing. My learners could find energy in individual choices. Sure there are requirements, but I want to create a culture of opportunity rather than a culture of demand.

I wonder how I can make the most of challenge. I could start by finding an approachable junior version of the game and configure activities with elbow room so that different students can find their own best levels of challenge.

I wonder how I can make the most of the imagination. Here I might get help from cognitive tools that excite the imagination, such as story, metaphor, binary contrasts, heroes, reality and its extremes.

3

Work on the Hard Parts

LIKE SO MANY AROUND THE WORLD, WHEN I WAS A CHILD I TOOK PIANO lessons. Unlike many, I had some enduring enthusiasm for the project. My parents did not have to nag me to practice. When after a year or so they asked whether I wanted to continue to study, I said yes. When a teacher I worked with for a few years said she had done about all she could for me, I found another one. I continued to study in a semi-serious way when I was home during summers all the way through college.

It was fun, but certainly not all fun. I was never keen about working on the hard parts. I liked Plan A: Play my pieces through several times. Not so interesting was Plan B: Concentrate on a particular piece, single out the several measures that gave the most trouble, analyze what the wrinkles were, revise my hand position and fingering, and play those measures with care a number of times to iron out the wrinkles.

The problem is, Plan A doesn't work very well. There is a common phrase for what goes wrong: practicing your mistakes. By and large, the hard parts don't get any better just by playing the whole piece a number of times. Even as the rest of the piece improves in fluency and expressiveness, the hard parts remain a series of stumbles and fumbles. I never did come to enjoy working on the hard parts, although I came to pay somewhat more attention to them. I learned that it was a necessary part of the process, but for me it was always a grudging part. My heart remained with Plan A.

The tremendous importance of singling out the hard parts is more than folk wisdom. A number of years ago, the cognitive psychologist K. Anders Ericsson and his colleagues conducted and synthesized a number of studies of expertise. They focused on the development of elite skill, concentrating particularly on performance areas like music and athletics. One of Ericsson's questions concerned the relative contribution of talent versus the right kind of practice. Contrary to common belief, Ericsson and his colleagues argued that talent played a negligible role compared to what he called *deliberate practice*.

For instance, an elite golfer's practice routine may include repetitive "bunker" drills designed to improve sand shots. Although lesser golfers may be interested in improving their sand shots, their practice repertoire most likely leaves out such focused and tedious exercises. Even if the time on task is equal between elite and lesser golfers, improved performance occurs only through conscious effort invested in understanding the task better and restructuring old performances. Notice that this isn't just a matter of practicing the hard parts in the sense of repetition. It involves deconstructing them and reconstructing them so they are executed in new and better ways.

Back to the piano, besides singling out difficult passages (but not often enough by Ericsson's standards), I also learned that working on the hard parts does not always mean waiting until they come up. There are ways of working on them in advance. A standard approach is to practice scales and arpeggios, preparing for the fragments of them that appear in many whole compositions as well as building strength and flexibility in your fingers. One way or another, to get good at something you have to work on the hard parts.

Slighting the Hard Parts

So how do the hard parts get attention? Much of the time they do not, or at least not nearly enough and not quite of the right kind. Most of my experience as a learner—and I bet your memories are not very different—seems to reflect what we'll call the hearts-and-minds theory: *Take it to heart, keep it in mind, and do better next time.*

The hearts-and-minds theory is the default practice all over the world. A student works a problem set on linear equations and hands it in. A couple of days later, the student gets it back with a grade and some problems marked correct and others carrying comments like "assumption" or "forgot to change sign." The hope is that the student takes this to heart, keeps it in mind, and rarely makes those mistakes again. A student hands in an essay on Martin Luther King and gets it back a couple of days later with a grade and a few comments like "compelling beginning" but "loses momentum here" and later "needs more evidence." The hope is that the student takes this to heart, keeps it in mind, and brings plenty of momentum and evidence to future essays.

There is so much wrong with the hearts-and-minds theory that I hardly know where to begin. For one thing, hearts-and-minds assumes that the heart is there, that learners care about improving the performance in question, care even though the class is now moving on to the next topic, care enough to pay attention not just to the grade but to the feedback, trying to remember it and put it to work when attempting similar tasks in the future. For another, hearts-and-minds assumes minds with enough understanding of the topic to make sense of relatively sparse feedback and use it effectively. For yet another, the hearts-and-minds theory proceeds as though the learners will have an opportunity to try again soon. Very often they do not. Even the most committed hearts and agile minds are not likely to hold onto feedback well enough to inform a second try weeks from now, say on the final exam or when the next essay is due.

Here is a story about how even a strong version of the hearts-and-minds approach isn't strong enough. A number of years ago, an ingenious doctoral student of mine, William Kendall, conducted an investigation of students' learning of standard high school algebra. He began with a hypothesis that made good sense to both of us: If students paid more attention to the errors they made, recorded them in an errors log, diagnosed what went wrong, and reviewed their typical shortfalls before doing assignments and quizzes, their performance would improve. You see why I say this is a strong version of the hearts-and-minds theory. It includes elements to encourage students to process their feedback actively and apply it.

Bill worked with five teachers to introduce the errors log into algebra classes during the second semester of first-year algebra. Some of the students in each classroom regularly looked over their assignments and quizzes, returned by the teacher with the errors marked. They recorded the particular mishaps in their logs and attempted to jot down what had gone wrong, making rules for themselves about how to do better next time. They reviewed their logs prior to assignments and quizzes.

Bill evaluated the impact of this intervention using a standard test of algebra mastery administered at the beginning and the end of the second semester. He compared the performance of the students keeping error logs with that of students in the same three classes not keeping error logs. Disappointingly, he discovered that the error logs helped not at all. There was no significant difference in performance.

What went wrong? Along the way, Bill had conducted clinical interviews with a number of the students keeping the logs. He discovered that, as one teacher put it, the students "Didn't seem to know enough to find their errors." Most of the students lacked sufficient understanding of algebra to interpret their errors in meaningful ways. Receiving a problem set back from the teacher with an X next to their solution to a problem, they would puzzle over it but not generally arrive at interpretations that proved useful the next time around. What explanations the teachers offered in class, when discussing the various problem sets and quizzes, apparently were not enough to lift students over this barrier.

Going back to the problems with the hearts-and-minds theory, Bill Kendall's clever and committed approach to making it work better taught me something tremendously important. It revealed two of the possible weaknesses in a fatal combination: The feedback was not very informative, mostly just a matter of right and wrong; and most of the students were not fluent enough with algebra to learn effectively from this relatively sparse feedback. Sometimes circumstances are better. Sometimes learners get richer feedback, and sometimes relatively sparse feedback is enough. But it's not an uncommon problem, and it was certainly a problem there. Whatever we do about working on the hard parts, it looks as though we have to get well beyond the naïve hearts-and-minds approach.

Embracing the Hard Parts

Good timing is everything! Well maybe not everything but a lot. We recognize the importance of good timing for punch lines, stock market investments, bank robberies, gymnastics, and when to leave for work to avoid a nasty commute. Addressing the hard parts has a great deal to do with good timing also: when and where and how much of it to do. Good work on the hard parts is one of the fundamental *structural* challenges of teaching and learning. We need to build in versions of the deliberate practice Ericsson identifies as so essential to strong learning. Far from slighting the hard parts, we need to embrace them.

This is an apt moment to recall one of the four key concepts from the last chapter's teaching for understanding, *ongoing assessment*. The basic idea of ongoing assessment was assessment early and often, not just as topics wind down. Assessment in this spirit does not concern assignment of grades or evaluation of whether instruction was effective. It's assessment designed squarely to feed into the learning process and make the learning stronger. So what can we discover from the ways that savvy teachers, coaches, mentors, and others in educative roles deal with the hard parts through ongoing assessment? Here are some of the patterns that stand out.

Actionable Assessment

As in Bill Kendall's study, right-wrong feedback typically does not provide enough information for learners. Broad comments like "needs more evidence" are also not helpful.

The *water balloon bungee jumping* example from Chapter 1 offers a telling contrast. Recall how Kenna Barger led her students in a modeling exercise with linear equations. Working in teams, the students developed predictions about the lengths of elastic that would let their water balloons bungee jump from the school roof down as far as possible without hitting the ground and breaking. Throughout, Kenna Barger alerted the students to specific difficulties they could act on. Often she did so by raising questions rather than saying exactly what to do. All the better, because this way her students had to figure out some of it for themselves. Her questions were specific enough to point in the right direction.

Or turning to the Martin Luther King essay above, rather than "needs more evidence," a comment might read, "More evidence needed that not only the black community, but other significant communities were moved by his message; can you find quotes to support this?" This is specific enough to act on.

Assessment for Understanding

Kenna Barger's ongoing assessment during the bungee activity didn't just fix mistakes, it strengthened the students' understanding. Likewise, calls for evidence expand the writers' understanding of the case they are trying to make as well as the craft of writing. In keeping with the deep connection between learning by wholes and understanding, good feedback touches not just matters of correctness—computational accuracy, spelling, grammar and such—but strengths and shortfalls of understanding.

Peer and Self-Assessment

One of the practical dilemmas of ongoing assessment is teacher time. In most settings, teachers do not have the time to provide all the feedback needed for good learning every day. Kenna Barger's bungee class kept her frantically busy. Other sources of feedback need to be found. This can mean students evaluating one another's work or even self-evaluation with the help of a rubric, a specific set of guidelines about what to look for.

It's true that students are often uncertain about what to say. It's also true that they are often reluctant to correct their peers. However, simple criteria or rubrics help hugely, enabling most students to give reasonably thoughtful feedback. Besides, the students learn as much from assessing as being assessed. Giving the feedback demands a reflective stance and specific articulation of problems, so students will develop evaluative skills they can apply to their own work too. For more ideas about this, see Chapter 6, "Learn from the Team."

Communicative Feedback

Even when feedback is specific, it is still not always what we would like to see. Schools aside, my colleagues and I have also spent some time looking at learning in organizational contexts. I'm remembering a particular interchange where an employee made a proposal and received starkly skeptical feedback from his boss. "So what do you think about the plan?" asked the employee.

"Well, thanks for raising the matter," the boss responded. "It seems fine in principle. But I'm afraid I don't see how it could really work in practice. There's likely to be legal problems around intellectual property rights. Then there's the cost factor; I'd guess another 10 percent on top of the present budget. And who else would really be on board?"

Not only was the response unappreciative of the employee's efforts, it quickly became clear that the boss did not really understand the proposal in the first place. The boss's critical points were somewhat wide off the mark, nor did the boss check whether he understood. What a shame, especially as such mishaps of communication occur all the time.

One way to think about this recognizes three different styles of feedback: *corrective, conciliatory*, and *communicative*. All of them are relevant to the classroom as well as the workplace. Often feedback is simply *corrective*. The giver of feedback announces what's wrong. There's no cross-check on whether the idea or essay or other object of evaluation is truly understood. Positive features get no or only passing attention. The basic pattern of corrective feedback is, "Yes, but . . ." or "Good, but . . . ," moving quickly on to the difficulties.

Another common pattern is *conciliatory* feedback. This appears frequently in peer evaluation and in social and organizational settings where people want to be nice. So they make a few vague positive comments that are completely uninformative. "Well, basically I liked it! I thought it made some good points. So what did you do last weekend?"

In contrast, the alert boss, peer, or teacher might offer *communicative* feedback. As the name suggests, this is feedback structured to ensure good communication. It involves three key elements in roughly this order: clarification, appreciation, and concerns and suggestions.

1. *Clarification*. To guard against misunderstandings of what's on the table, communicative feedback allows for some kind of upfront check, such as questions of clarification. Although this is easiest in one-on-one conversations, the principle applies to written work also. I can remember writing students quick notes or grabbing them in class to clarify their intentions. The age of e-mail makes this all the easier.

2. *Appreciation*. Communicative feedback includes clear identification of positive features as seen by the evaluator. This may not be as elaborate as the critical comments to follow, but it is a clear developed presence. The recipient of the feedback knows what in your view worked well, what to hold onto, and what to keep doing.

3. *Concerns and suggestions*. Then communicative feedback shares concerns and suggestions. These focus on a positive future: how to improve this or do better next time. They avoid criticisms of the person's capabilities or character and address the situation.

The point of *clarification* and *appreciation* is not just to be nice but to be informative. Clarifications and positive points are information too, and often information just as important as any concerns. Also, clarification and appreciation help to avoid the trap of conciliatory feedback by establishing a positive platform from which to move to concerns and suggestions. For instance, when peers honor another's work by seeking clarification and identifying positives explicitly, they then feel freer to share their best judgment about concerns.

Peer feedback often works much better when the communicative feedback pattern is used systematically.

Implicit Assessment

Consider the following scenarios:

- Three students present their different solutions to an open-ended math problem on the blackboard and the class argues about the virtues of the alternative approaches.
- A discussion of the French resistance during World War II kindles a debate about what counts as terrorism.
- Working in small groups, class members need to arrive at consensus recommendations at a community-based ecological improvement plan.
- The teacher may hardly offer a word of feedback in such situations, only facilitate. But assessment figures abundantly in these exchanges, implicit in the dialogue among the students themselves. Some physical activities automatically generate feedback. When you hit a sour note on the piano, you generally know it. When you swing at the pitch and miss, you certainly know it!

There are many ways in which learners can receive feedback without it being given. By setting things up in such a way that there is dialogue, contrast, and juxtaposition, teachers, mentors, coaches, and others in educative positions can generate rich implicit feedback. Assessment embedded seamlessly in the flow of events often feels more authentic and arouses less defensiveness.

Ready Opportunities to Act on the Assessment

One principal difficulty with the hearts-and-minds theory is assessment too general to act upon effectively, but another principal difficulty is no ready opportunity to act on it. In contrast, Kenna Barger circulated among her student groups, providing feedback on the fly in real time that they could fold into their developing models and predictions, and then the students tried out their water balloon bungee jumps.

For a conventional algebra assignment, a teacher might assign the odd-numbered problems first, provide feedback, and then ask the students to work through the even-numbered problems applying what they had learned, followed of course by more feedback. For the Martin Luther King essay, students might produce revisions based on the feedback, with final evaluation and grading deferred to the second or third version.

Isolate and Reintegrate

Yes, sometimes quick sketchy feedback is all a learner needs, the hearts-and-minds theory triumphant, the counsel taken to heart and kept in mind for next time. But how much can we count on that?

What if a student receives the following feedback on *who's* versus *whose?*

Who's means "who is." It's a contraction; for example "Who's giving the party tonight?" *Whose* is a possessive pronoun; for example, "Whose party is it?" See the difference?

Is the student really going to remember this the next time he or she writes something? Similarly, tips about hitting curveballs probably will not prepare the player for a curveball in the next real game. Even practice with the batting machine is likely to leave a curveball gap. And likewise, in studying musical instruments, it's commonplace to isolate hard parts for concentrated attention, improve them, and find that you still stumble over them as you perform the entire piece.

In general, trouble spots improved through advice and isolated exercise often relapse in the setting of the whole game. Incorporating the improved skill or understanding into the whole game needs to be a deliberate part of the process of deliberate practice. When we take learning the hard parts seriously, the rhythm of isolation and reintegration is fundamental.

Returning once again to Kenna Barger, she might discover that her students hold a persistent misconception as they pursue the bungee jumping project. She might decide she needs a separate lesson to work through the confusion. But after the separate lesson, there should again be some kind of whole game into which the students can integrate their new understanding. Water balloon catapulting?

Turning to the Martin Luther King essay, we might find that many students in the class have difficulties with compelling argument structure that invite a separate exercise. What they learn is much more likely to stick when they have an immediate opportunity to rework their essays or write new ones with amplified attention to argument structure.

In summary, the hearts-and-minds theory generally leads to thin learning because it slights rather than embraces deliberate practice. Organizing the rhythm of learning for actionable assessment focused on understanding, peer- and self-assessment, communicative feedback, implicit assessment, ready opportunities to act on the assessment, and a pattern of isolation and reintegration can help to ensure that working on the hard parts happens in a potent way.

Anticipating the Hard Parts

Sometimes good advice is so good that the same general idea gets packaged in several different ways, say, "A stitch in time saves nine." Or "Those who cannot remember the past are condemned to repeat it," a notable quote from the philosopher George Santayana. Or the simple *Think Ahead!* Maybe we do not have to wait for learners to stumble over the same hard parts yet again. Maybe we can anticipate the hard parts and try to deal with them in advance.

My favorite way of looking at this focuses on *troublesome knowledge*. Any area of learning has its own peculiar difficulties, but certain general kinds of troubles keep surfacing over and over again. They may be worth bearing in mind, because they provide a preview of challenges on the horizon that one can to some extent guard against. In the Santayana spirit, here are several likely "hard parts" to watch out for that apply to learning any subject: *ritual knowledge, inert knowledge, foreign knowledge, tacit knowledge, skilled knowledge,* and *conceptually difficult knowledge.*

Ritual Knowledge

Knowing what to do with numbers is certainly the heart and soul of basic arithmetic. However, knowing what to do can mean rather different things. I have always been charmed by this example from an elementary school child reported a number of years ago:

> I know what to do by looking at the examples. If there are only two numbers I subtract. If there are lots of numbers I add. If there are just two numbers and one is smaller than the other it is a hard problem. I divide to see if it comes out even and if it doesn't I multiply.

This is a coping strategy at its best . . . clear, articulate, and remarkably effective in dealing with those pesky pages of arithmetic problems. It is plainly intelligent, just not intelligent in the direction we want. This is knowledge that has a rather meaningless surface character. Ritual knowledge feels like a ritual: the crank routinely turned to get a certain solution, the way we're supposed to answer when someone asks a certain kind of question. One of the basic coping strategies of all learners facing the complexities of curricula and assignments is to find rituals they can perform that satisfy immediate demands (see Chapter 7, "Learn the Game of Learning").

All educators hope for something deeper than this, but a great deal of instructional practice panders to ritual knowledge, calling it good enough. Any problem set that yields to the above strategy, any test on which students can do well enough by knowing the names and dates, any essay assignment that simply requires assembling information and writing it down plays into ritual knowledge. Sometimes ritual knowledge becomes the implicit social contract between teachers and learners. Both accept the deal to keep everything simple and straightforward.

Ritual knowledge is not always bad. There is some information it's just plain good to know, telephone numbers for instance. From the learner standpoint, sometimes ritualization may be the optimal strategy because the learning situation does not provide sufficient support and guidance for understanding. There are also areas where both a quick ritual and the understanding behind it are handy. Multiplication tables are a good example, with the number facts at your fingertips but also a behind-the-scenes understanding.

So how can teaching and learning work against ritualization? Any teaching-learning process that embraces the idea of learning by wholes helps to make ritual knowledge a weak coping strategy. The learning activities are too open-ended for effective ritualization. Such a teaching-learning process avoids elements that pander to ritualization, as with only fact-based tests or problem sets that can be gamed by arithmetic tricks like the opening example. Instead the learning involves understanding performances, for instance, project-like activities or arguments about the meaning or validity of something or explorations of alternative interpretations.

Inert Knowledge

There is an interesting family of puzzles called insight problems. Many of them are deliciously frustrating examples of the problem of inert knowledge. Here is an example:

> A man comes to a curator of rare coins in a museum and offers
> for sale a battered authentic-looking coin from early Roman times
> dated 153 B.C. Immediately, the curator has the man arrested for
> fraud. Why?

Let me put off giving the answer for a moment, so that you can ponder the puzzle if you would like to do so. Instead, let's define *inert knowledge*. This is knowledge stored away in the mind's attic, available only upon deliberate efforts to fetch it and dust it off. If you are asked for the information or ask yourself for it, you will find it. However, inert knowledge sees little active use without a direct cue. Many cases of inert knowledge are quite benign. One of the most familiar is passive vocabulary. We all have thousands of words in our vocabularies that we recognize and understand, but rarely use in our own speech and writing.

Back to the coin puzzle: The curator knew the coin was a fake because of the date. The system of dating, counting backward and forward from 0 B.C., had not even been invented in 153 B.C. You may well have figured out this problem easily, but many people do not. It's not because the problem is difficult in the sense of being complicated. Rather, solving the problem requires making just the right connection to something one already knows perfectly well. Often that connection does not get made. The knowledge is inert; it's there, but it doesn't get used.

If the coin example of inert knowledge seems like too much of a trick, an unsettling amount of research evidence exists for the hard reality of inert knowledge in much of what we learn. For example, students will study basic statistics and apply the principles to realistic problems in class, but not make the connection to problems encountered outside of class. Students who have studied computer programming when confronted with new situations may not apply commands that they know how to use until given the suggestion to do so.

In another well-known study, researchers interviewed graduating students of Harvard University, who were making a film about their ideas called *A Private Universe*. Students were asked a very basic question about how the world works: Why is it hot in the summer and cold in the winter? Many answered, "Because the Earth is closer to the sun in the summer." This is not at all the right explanation. Moreover, virtually all students at some point study why winter and summer happen. Apparently what they learned was inert, or perhaps they forgot it altogether. Even if they did so, they certainly had at least one piece of relevant knowledge: When it's summer in the northern hemisphere it's winter in the southern hemisphere, and vice versa. So summer could not possibly be explained by the Earth being closer to the sun, because then it would be summer in both hemispheres at the same time.

Inert knowledge can be seen as a problem of transfer of learning, a theme pursued further in Chapter 4, "Play Out of Town." People fail to activate knowledge that they have acquired in some other context. But, in many cases at least, it is not so much a problem of *far* transfer in the sense of making remote and imaginative connections. The applications of statistics or computer commands just alluded to are quite straightforward.

An experiment reported by John Bransford and colleagues reveals some of the factors involved that make knowledge inert or active. The experiment asked two groups of students to study the same content in somewhat different ways. The content concerned ideas about nutrition, solar-powered airplanes, water as a standard of density, and other matters. For one group, the aim was remembering the content. For the other, the aim was thinking through the challenges of a journey through a South American jungle. The experimenters tested for retention with straightforward informational questions and found it to be just as good in both groups. Active use of knowledge needs to be tested with open-ended tasks that do not cue students about exactly what is wanted. Here, the experimenters asked the students in both groups to plan an expedition to desert terrain. Students in the second group made much more active use of what they had learned than students in the first group did.

Why did the students in the second group acquire more active knowledge? Two factors seem to be at work in some mix: First, the learning process itself was more active, more problem-solving oriented. Second, the specific learning task—the journey through a South American jungle—was more like the application to the desert expedition.

What the second group did sounds something like learning by wholes, and so it should. Rather than the *elementitis* of rehearsing information, there is a holistic challenge, planning an expedition. The first time, the expedition targets a desert terrain and the students get the hang of the game. Then there's another round of the game for another setting, the South American jungle. Chapter 4 pursues the important idea of a different setting under the theme *play out of town*.

With learning by wholes and playing out of town in motion, knowledge is much less likely to be inert.

Foreign Knowledge

Many schoolchildren at one time or another find themselves discussing U.S. President Harry Truman's notorious decision to drop the atomic bomb on Hiroshima and Nagasaki at the end of World War II. Students easily veer in one of two directions. Either it was a remarkably cruel and naïve decision, not only inflicting great harm on innumerable Japanese but also ushering in the Atomic Era with all its risks and angst. Or it was just the right thing to do, bringing to a quick conclusion what otherwise might have been a prolonged and costly struggle, the common textbook explanation.

Either way, these discussions along with many other explorations of complicated issues in history show front and center a problem called *presentism*. That is, people tend to look at historical events through today's attitudes and their knowledge of how things actually turned out. The dropping of the bombs did indeed debut the Atomic Era and did indeed put a stop to the war. It's hard for us to project our minds into the complex prejudices, considerations, and available knowledge in play at the time.

The problem of presentism is a good example of a larger bundle of challenges summed up by the phrase *foreign knowledge*. This is knowledge hard to take in because it does not align well with where we are today, in our own setting, among our own friends, with our own current beliefs and prejudices and routines. The mores and practices of other cultures pose this kind of conundrum. The way those people on the other side of the ocean do things just does not make sense, and indeed often seems simply wrong. Robert Kegan of the Harvard Graduate School of Education provides a neat characterization of this dilemma in terms of *centrisms*, ethnocentrism, egocentrism, or any other centrism you might think of. Kegan points out that centrisms share a common failing. They all involve viewing what is strange and uncomfortable as also mistaken or even evil.

Culturally rooted examples of foreign knowledge are easy to find. But technical knowledge also can seem foreign. A favorite example of mine comes from science education researcher Marcia Linn. She reported with amusement a particular student's view of the well-known Newtonian principle that objects in motion maintain motion in the same direction at the same velocity unless some outside force intrudes. The student said, "Objects in motion remain in motion in the classroom, but come to rest on the playground." The student's philosophy seemed to be this: Yes, I can learn the ideas and learn how to solve the problems in the textbook, but the world doesn't really work that way. Just look!

Foreign knowledge poses a problem not only of learning but *unlearning*. Sometimes this means replacing the old knowledge altogether, but it always means loosening up the old knowledge enough so that new knowledge can live alongside it.

What patterns of learning get a grip on unlearning? One approach is direct confrontation, for instance, working with history students to help them identify their likely presentism and to project themselves more into the mindset of the times. Another is indirect, deferring the confrontation. The next chapter touches on an example where Israeli students were able to get a better perspective on the Israeli-Palestinian conflict by studying the Northern Ireland conflict. Paradoxically, sometimes foreign knowledge is not foreign enough. It was easier for them to examine the Northern Ireland conflict as something far away and make the connections later than to address the attitudes of the Palestinians as something too close to home.

A common strategy in science teaching is to expose the incoherence of the favored belief through reasoning and experiments, nudging the learner toward the foreign but more sophisticated theory. Sometimes this proves successful, although it has a rather mixed history. Learners do not always follow the paths of reasoning one would like or end up with the desired conclusions.

One effective version of this strategy uses the idea of *anchoring intuitions*. The process begins with a case where students' intuitions are right and encourages them to extend it. Science education researcher John Clement and colleagues explored situations where common sense is sometimes right and sometimes wrong, urging learners to reconcile the cases. For example, students tend to believe that a fly sitting on a table pushes down, but the table does not push up on the fly. This violates Newton's third law, which specifies equal and opposite forces. However, the same students readily accept that the table pushes up on a bowling ball. This is the anchoring intuition. Now let's imagine the bowling ball dwindling down to fly size and weight. At what point does the table abruptly stop pushing as the bowling ball shrinks? Patterns of reasoning like this help students to see the universal logic of the Newtonian principle.

Another approach I've always found attractive is explicit *bracketing*. You ask the learners simply to step outside their intuitive beliefs and learn another way of thinking about the problem. Just spend a while learning this new game. Have a threshold experience with it! After that, one returns to those intuitive beliefs and looks carefully at the trade-offs between them and the new way of thinking about the problem. The bracketing approach recognizes that knowledge appears foreign partly because learners have not had a chance to see it from the inside in an open spirit. Deliberately bracketing the conflict between old and new can sometimes buy time to get used to the new.

Tacit Knowledge

Hardly anyone can tell you how they walk. Hardly anyone can tell you how they manage to speak grammatical sentences fluently and maintain conversational turn taking. Hardly anybody can tell you exactly why their first impression of a person or poem or painting is positive or negative. They may be able to point to a feature or two, but the odds are this is far from the complete story.

A great deal of our knowledge is tacit. We arrived at perceptions and judgments and take fluent actions without knowing exactly why. Tacit knowledge in many ways is highly functional, a natural intuitive response to complicated situations. But tacit knowledge can make trouble for formal learning, and in more than one way.

Let's begin with the teachers themselves. Teachers' expectations for their students are generally partly tacit. Students can find themselves bewildered about just what is expected of them. This is why the teaching for understanding framework discussed earlier encourages explicit shared understanding goals along with frequent ongoing assessment. These elements surface the hidden game so that learners can get a grip on it.

The content we would truly like students to learn also is usually partly tacit. This makes it both hard to explain as well as cumbersome when explained.

On top of all that, certain kinds of tacit beliefs and commitments—prejudices and biases, for instance—mount barriers against more expansive and open-minded learning, sometimes subtle barriers not readily recognized by learners themselves or even teachers for that matter.

The hidden character of tacit knowledge makes it a natural theme for upcoming Chapter 5, "Uncover the Hidden Game," so more about it there.

Skilled Knowledge

I'm thinking again of my battles with the pianoforte. All too often your fingers are not good soldiers. They just won't follow orders. Likewise, the tennis player trying for a good serve or the golfer striving to avoid a slice may well have heard from the coach or read in a book what moves to make, but it is often easier said than done. The pattern won't fall into place comfortably and naturally.

In other words, sometimes the trouble lies not so much in knowing what to do as in doing it. Assiduous deliberate practice is needed to find the groove.

Areas of performance such as music and athletics bristle with troublesome knowledge of this sort, but it's not hard to find in more conventional corners of academics either. Challenges of skilled knowledge pervade second-language learning. You cannot function as a fluent speaker or writer by laboriously retrieving grammatical forms moment by moment; they need to be at your mental fingertips, the tip of your pencil, and the tip of your tongue. Reading development depends fundamentally on highly automatized patterns of response. Turning to mathematics, it's hard to use arithmetic or algebra as ways of modeling the world when constituent operations are laborious.

With the challenge of skilled knowledge in the spotlight, once again it's good to remember the risk of *elementitis*—there is such a temptation to build up the skills for a long time before ever putting them together. A much better solution recalls the isolate-integrate pattern from a few pages ago. Learners play the whole game in some appropriate junior version, whether the whole game is piano, a sport, some reading-like activity, or mathematical modeling. In parallel, learners practice constituent skills and integrate them relatively soon into the whole game.

Conceptually Difficult Knowledge

What makes the theory of relativity hard? The temptation here is to answer, "Everything!" (In case you're wondering, I don't understand it either. I understand a few things about it, but so do a lot of people.)

As it turns out, "everything" is something of an overstatement. One way of keeping score comes from an analysis of conceptual difficulty by Paul Feltovich, Rand Spiro, and Richard Coulson. They discussed what they called *advanced knowledge acquisition*, the kind of learning that reaches well beyond getting the facts and routines. They were particularly interested in the high-stakes area of medical learning.

Part of their account was a list of factors that made concepts and conceptual systems more challenging for learners. Here is their scorecard (the examples are mine).

1. *Abstract rather than concrete*: the principle rather than the example, the rule rather than the application.
2. *Continuous rather than discrete*: real numbers rather than integers or the fluid moves of a dancer or athlete rather than the discrete moves on a chess board.
3. *Dynamic rather than static*: the orbit of the moon rather than the position of the moon.

4. *Simultaneous rather than sequential*: simultaneous linear equations again or the way a line of poetry does several things at the same time.

5. *Organicism rather than mechanism*: the complexity of the jungle rather than the complexity of a Swiss watch.

6. *Interactiveness rather than separability*: the way the Moon pulls on the Earth at the same time that the Earth pulls on the Moon, or William Butler Yeats's famous phrase at the end of his *Among Schoolchildren*, "How can we tell the dancer from the dance?"

7. *Conditionality rather than universality*: qualifications such as "only when," "assuming that," "unless," and such.

8. *Nonlinearity rather than linearity*: quadratic rather than linear equations, political backlashes when one tries to force an issue.

So once again, what makes the theory of relativity hard? By this scorecard, it certainly is abstract rather than concrete, deals with continuous motion in time and space, and is dynamic rather than static. The constraints apply simultaneously rather than sequentially and in interactive and nonlinear ways. But there's some good news: It's mechanistic rather than organic and universal rather than conditional. So the theory of relativity shows six of the eight difficulty factors on the list. Not "everything."

Let's use the same scorecard to look at historical causation, what leads history to veer in one direction or another. This also is certainly abstract rather than concrete, continuous rather than discrete, dynamic rather than static, simultaneous rather than sequential, *and* organic rather than mechanistic, of course interactive rather than separable, *and* highly conditional—the notorious difficulty of making valid general rules about how historical events unfold—and of course nonlinear. Eight out of eight!

In other words, historical causation is more of a conceptual challenge than the theory of relativity. On the surface this sounds implausible, but perhaps it makes sense. Historical causation seems more accessible at first than the theory of relativity, because the ramp into it is easier. Anyone can understand some of the basic factors involved.

TOURO COLLEGE LIBRARY

However, the full explosion of its complexity might easily count as more mind-blowing than the tidy mathematical science of relativistic thinking. In any case, certainly Feltovich, Spiro, and Coulson only meant their list as a rough guide. It is one helpful way of reminding ourselves how very messy concepts and conceptual systems can become and of giving us problems to anticipate and targets to address as we engage in a teaching-learning process.

So what might we do about it? The main thing I see over and over again is this: Face up to conceptual difficulties rather than slide back into the avoidance strategies of ritual knowledge. Engage learners in junior versions that gnaw away at the complexity. Make the abstract concrete through a lively range of examples. Show the continuity and dynamic character rather than two or three still frames. Bring up the simultaneous and organic way that factors interact through examples. Play the whole game.

As though all this weren't enough, there is another layer to the problem of conceptual difficulty. Besides the list of Feltovich and others, conceptually difficult knowledge also often points to the challenge of hidden games. We struggle with new ideas not just because of their very real surface complexities, but also because they presuppose concepts, frameworks, and ways of thinking that are not apparent. Please look at Chapter 5, "Uncover the Hidden Game."

Building a Theory of Difficulty

Suppose you are playing baseball. You stand at the plate, ready to swing and hit a home run or at least achieve first base. What makes this hard?

The pitcher's job is to make it hard. Good pitchers have a number of ways to do this. They throw different kinds of pitches: fastballs, curveballs, slow balls. They switch them around so the batter doesn't know what to expect. They go for the corners of the strike zone, hoping the batter will figure the pitch will count as a ball rather than a strike. They may even deliver a "waste pitch" deliberately outside the strike zone, hoping to sucker the batter into a flailing swing. Hazards all, but knowing this is also a kind of power. It gives both batters and their coaches something to focus on and work on. They have a *theory of difficulty*.

One of the most important questions we can ask as educators is, "What makes this hard?" When we have a good answer to this question, we are anticipating the hard parts that go with a particular topic or activity. Maybe with the right approach, we can prevent those hard parts from doing their worst damage.

Any experienced teacher or parent or coach or minister or mentor always has some kind of response to the what-makes-this-hard question. Also, the six kinds of troublesome knowledge from earlier provide a very broad list of candidate answers. The eight complexity factors from Feltovich, Spiro, and Coulson offer more specific answers for challenging conceptual learning. Difficulties like presentism for history or perspective taking in moral judgment or the everyday sense of physics that people have (as in "objects in motion remain in motion in the classroom, but come to rest on the playground") are responses to the what-makes-this-hard question for common topics.

All of these, general or specific, formal or informal, from researchers or teachers, are theories of difficulty. Such theories often are not very academic, nor do they need to be to do good work. They warn teachers and learners about the potholes on the learning road and thereby tell us where we need a special spring in our educational feet.

However, theories of difficulty are not always as specific or well directed as they need to be. Let me tell you about some of my experiences here. For many years, I've taught a course to students at the Harvard Graduate School of Education called "Cognition and the Art of Instruction." The course asks participants to develop individual design projects for learning agendas of their choosing. The design projects vary widely in their learning targets and settings, from such standard in-school topics as fractions arithmetic to out-of-school themes such as pig farming and understanding knee-joint replacement. I routinely ask the students to spell out simple theories of difficulty for the topics they choose. What will make this hard for learners? And therefore, what are you going to do about it in your learning design?

The answers do not have to be very elaborate to be helpful. A student designing a decision-making program for people in management positions might note difficulties like this: In the midst of time pressure, there is a chronic problem of neglecting long-term consequences. Or: In the hierarchical management climate, a respectful and genuinely helpful pattern of consultation can go by the wayside. A student designing an intervention to foster ecological responsibility might note difficulties such as: It's one thing to understand some of the problems conceptually and even write essays about them, but another thing to discern practical actions you can take in your community beyond the really simple ones such as recycling. And it's still another thing to get around to those practical actions! Through such characterizations as these, students provide themselves with better defined design targets.

All well and good, but I've discovered over the years that some students bring forward very thin theories of difficulty; a topic or concept is difficult because "it's complicated," or because "learners usually find it boring," or because "it's so unfamiliar," or because "there's so much to remember." So I write back more or less as follows:

> Please think about this some more and give us a theory of difficulty that is more specific to your topic. Give us one that doesn't sound like something that could be said for a hundred other topics. There are a lot of topics that are complicated or commonly boring or initially unfamiliar or packed with points to remember. Please get specific! You see, theories of difficulty afford much more leverage if they target the particular learning challenges for that particular thing.

Also, students often isolate difficulties without explaining them. So for example, someone might write, "It's handling the fractions that give children the trouble," or "It's more translating the word problems into equations than solving the equations." Such a theory of difficulty offers some help. It tells us where to lavish more attention, but not much about the form the attention should take. Here the trick is to push for more of an explanation. Just where does handling the fractions go wrong? What sorts of glitches come up in translating the word problems into equations?

Here is a response I usually don't hear from my students but sometimes do hear in other settings: "It's clear enough what to do, but there's just not enough resources and not enough time." This is a kind of theory of difficulty. It locates the difficulty not in the content but in the circumstances. Well, yes, I can hardly think of any setting where serious educators would not like more resources and more time. But it also can be a way of avoiding serious engagement with the challenges of content.

Perhaps the least helpful theory of difficulty, almost a perverted one, is blame-the-learners. What makes this hard? "Well, it's these kids. They just don't study. They just don't care. They really weren't very well prepared by what they studied before." What is so insidious about this pseudo-theory of difficulty is that it functions as an excuse for not doing anything different.

In all fairness, any of these less-than-ideal theories of difficulty can easily have a measure of truth. Some learners are indeed lazy or underprepared. Sometimes time and resources are seriously lacking. Sometimes it's enough to know just what subtopics are likely to cause the most trouble. All that acknowledged, the ideal is worth holding onto: a theory of difficulty specific to the content of what's been taught, explaining what makes it hard.

Perhaps it's useful to bundle all these ideas into a diagram not about student learning but teacher learning (see Figure 3.1).

As we teach and teach the same topic again, we notice persistent trouble spots. The question is, how do we respond to them? The simplest response, tagged with *blame* on the diagram, blames something or someone else—not enough time, not enough resources, learners who aren't ready or lack the wit or will. This leads to teaching in the same way, perhaps with even less energy. A more sophisticated

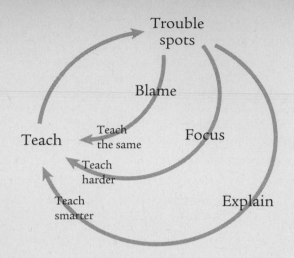

Figure 3.1. Three Responses to Trouble Spots of Teaching

response, tagged with *focus* on the diagram, is to focus on the particular parts of the topic generating the difficulty. This leads to teaching harder, pouring more time and energy into those parts.

The most sophisticated response, tagged *explain* on the diagram, doesn't just identify particular difficulties but explains their causes. Sometimes bearing in mind general theories of difficulty can help with this, remembering types like ritual knowledge, inert knowledge, foreign knowledge, tacit knowledge, skilled knowledge, and conceptually difficult knowledge; and sometimes ideas from Chapter 5 on playing the hidden game can help. Other ideas can come from anywhere: colleagues, mentors, books, and so on. The aim is always to come up with an explanatory theory of difficulty relatively specific to the content in question, all toward teaching smarter.

One more thought. The first time you try to teach anything, teaching smarter is almost never smart enough. The first theory of difficulty is like this year's new models of cars or a new operating system from Microsoft, prone to bugs. One just doesn't know enough initially about what the hard parts are going to be like. We teachers and Scout leaders and trainers and curriculum designers need to learn too. We need to work on our own hard parts. And one of the most rewarding hard parts to work on is arriving at a really good theory of difficulty for our learners.

From Exercises to Études

For a coda to these variations on the hard parts, remember that young piano player we began with trying to get his musical ducks in a row. Part of the deliberate practice needed was the playing of scales and arpeggios for fluency, velocity, and evenness of tone. This is powerful preparation, but it is not very exciting.

Around the beginning of the nineteenth century, musicians realized that there must be a way to make all that a little more interesting, and the notion of études was born. *Étude* is simply the French word for study. In music, études are pieces of music deliberately written to strengthen particular technical elements, say scales and arpeggios, without simply playing them over and over. I remember working through some of the well-known études of Carl Czerny.

Many études still veer too close to technical exercises for complete musical satisfaction. A couple of titles of Czerny's collections telegraph the problem: *The Art of Finger Dexterity, The School of Velocity*. This sounds more like drilling than thrilling. But twenty-seven pieces by nineteenth-century composer Frederic Chopin show what can really be done. Chopin's études are strikingly expressive virtuoso compositions, designed to foreground a systematic collection of technical challenges. I was never good enough to play them seriously. I could make my way through a Chopin ballade or two and even once performed a Chopin polonaise credibly at a high school concert (don't ask me today). But the études were on another planet. Still, it was satisfying to know that the planet was there. Maybe someday I would go there.

The idea of études suits just about any area of learning. Many school activities with a whole-game character are essentially études. Remember once again the water balloon bungee jumping activity. This is an étude: It's a holistic mission with a technical agenda, calculated to address learners' understanding of linear equations and mathematical modeling. In studio art, instructors commonly assign what amount to études on canvas, calling for whole works that explore this or that aspect of color or perspective or texture. When a learner is asked to look deeply into a poem, strive to understand it, develop insight into its expressive strategies, come to some insightful and defensible account of its meaning, explore its personal significance, and write about all that, this too is an étude. It is a whole enterprise, not an exercise sheet on poetic tropes, and like the études of Czerny and Chopin, it has a technical agenda, cultivating certain skills and sensitivities.

This is not to say that straight-out exercises have no place. Any discipline invites some version of scales and arpeggios. But when we can, it's worth trying to advance technical mastery of the whole game, not just with exercises but with études, all in the spirit of the third fundamental principle of learning by wholes: Work on the hard parts.

Wonders of Learning

Work on the Hard Parts

I wonder how I can help learners work on the hard parts effectively. For a start, I could arrange regular episodes of deliberate practice that feed back into the whole game.

I wonder how I can avoid the hearts-and-minds theory, assessments with the shallow form of "take it to heart, keep it in mind, and do better next time." I'll need to figure out how learners could get frequent rich feedback from me or other learners, with opportunities to use the feedback soon.

I wonder how to establish a strong rhythm of learning around the hard parts. I'm remembering that a strong rhythm embraces rather than slights deliberate practice, with ongoing action-able assessments focused on understanding, peer- and self-assessment, communicative feedback, implicit assessment, immediate occasions to apply, and a pattern of isolation and reintegration into the whole game.

I wonder how to see the hard parts coming. I could try to antici-pate my topic's most likely pattern of troublesome knowledge (ritual, inert, foreign, tacit, skilled, and conceptually difficult) and organize learning in ways that work against it.

I wonder how to develop a good theory of difficulty for what I'm teaching. Here my own experience is a key resource. I could try not only to identify but explain to myself learners' specific dif-ficulties, which would help me to teach smarter, not just harder.

I wonder how I can use not only exercises but "études." Exercises that isolate hard parts are important, but I'm thinking I might design "études," whole games chosen to provide practice with particular target difficulties.

4

Play Out of Town

A NUMBER OF YEARS AGO, I SPENT A DAY WORKING WITH A COLLEGE FACULTY (not my home institution Harvard) on how students can learn better for understanding. The event went well. The professors showed plenty of interest and made sensible connections with their own practice. However, what I most remember about that day was a side conversation during one of the breaks. A professor of physics came up to me with a furrowed brow. "My students just don't understand," he said.

"How so?" I asked.

"Let me give you an example," he continued. "I teach basic physics. It's not rocket science as the saying goes, but there is so much that the students just don't get. For instance, and this is very standard, we look at how falling objects behave. So I have problems like this: There's a one hundred meter tower. A ten kilogram object sits on top of the tower. Someone tips the object off. How long does it take the object to fall to the ground?"

I recognized this as a familiar kind of problem with a standard formula for solving it. If you know the formula, you don't even have to figure anything out, just plug the numbers into the equation. The mass of the object is a deliberate distracter. The rate of acceleration of the falling body does not depend on its mass, setting air resistance aside. "Okay," I said. "I'm with you so far."

The professor continued, "So comes the day of the final exam. I include this problem: There's a hole one hundred meters deep. A ten kilogram object sits on the edge of the hole. Someone tips the object into the hole. How long does it take the object to fall to the bottom? Believe it or not, several students failed to solve the problem. Not only that, but one student came up to me after the exam with a complaint. She said, 'Professor, I don't think that problem was fair. All semester, we never had any hole problems.'"

I tried to give the professor a little advice about how to avoid falling into such holes. I also did some private wondering about just what the teaching-learning process was like in this class, with students not making what would seem to be such an obvious connection. But the principal legacy of this experience was the story of the tower problem and the hole problem, a story I have told with relish ever since. A while ago, I included the tale as part of a larger presentation. As the audience drifted out of the session, a couple of people came up to me and said, "That story, you made it up, right, to illustrate a point?" No I didn't! It really happened!

The tale of the tower problem and the hole problem is a wonderful example of how *transfer of learning* can fail unexpectedly. The concept of transfer comes from learning theory. The idea in bare-bones form is simple: People learn something in one context, and this informs how well they learn and perform in another context. For instance, students learn about tower problems and ideally this equips them for hole problems. You learn to drive a car, and sometime later when you're moving and rent a small truck, you find that you can drive it pretty well. We all acquire skills of literacy and apply them readily to reading everything from the daily newspaper to income tax forms. You learn some ideas about the French Revolution or the Civil War, and as you read the daily paper or listen to a news broadcast, you make some comparisons and contrasts with what's happening in Iraq or Afghanistan. An elderly person hears about how colds and the flu are principally transmitted by touch and translates it into practical action: During that dangerous time of year, the person gets cautious about shaking hands and assiduous about washing hands.

In other words, transfer is a matter of "playing out of town," applying the games we learn and bits and pieces of those games not just in their original contexts but elsewhere, in some other setting where they might be helpful.

Playing out of town may sound easy, but often it is not. Remember the example from the introductory chapter about the Boston Red Sox. Baseball stadiums differ significantly, and when the Sox play out of town, they encounter stadiums that are laid out differently, with quirky advantages and pitfalls, plus a not-so-friendly crowd. The importance of the out-of-town factor varies considerably across sports and other games we play. Compare ping-pong, a highly standardized indoor sport, with mountain climbing, where every mountain is different.

In the same spirit, research on transfer of learning (more on that in a minute) warns that for some topics playing out of town is a very serious problem. Learners simply do not show the transfer of learning one would like. The educational mission has failed. As educators, we need to work to get the kinds of connection making we want. That's why "play out of town" is principle number four of learning by wholes.

The Meaning of Transfer

You might ask, "The tower problem and the hole problem—isn't that just a matter of learning, not transfer? The students didn't really learn what the tower problem was all about."

Good point. The meaning of transfer is indeed a bit slippery. Just how does it relate to learning and understanding?

In a sense, any learning at all involves some transfer. It's helpful here to invoke a rough distinction in the literature between *near transfer* and *far transfer*. Near transfer means making the connection to situations very like those of the original learning. Reading a newspaper is not that different from reading a history textbook. Driving a small truck is not that different from driving a car. As to far transfer, relating the Civil War to tensions in Iraq is much more of a stretch. Or I'm reminded of a friend of mine, out on a cheese-and-wine picnic, who found himself without a knife to cut the cheese. So he cut the cheese with a credit card instead. My friend transferred his knowledge of key features of the credit card (stiff, thin) to solve a problem in a very different context.

Back to the tower and the hole problem, it's reasonable to see the difficulty some students had with the hole problem as a failure of near transfer, missing a connection that really should not have been that hard to make. But certainly some learning was going on. The student who complained to the professor about the lack of hole problems in the curriculum apparently felt confident of her tower problem capabilities. She was prepared to apply that template to towers of different heights, objects of different weights. *Very* near transfer was doing just fine.

The contrast between near transfer and far transfer is handy but also rather crude. There is no official yardstick of how near or how far. The notion of near versus far transfer relies on our intuitions about how different situations are and how easy the bridge is to build.

Understanding is part of this story of near and far. The difficulty some students had with the hole problem meant that the professor did not get the understanding he hoped for. An expectation for at least near transfer is built into the very idea of understanding. Recalling the discussion in Chapter 1 of the performance model of understanding, understanding something involves thinking and acting flexibly with what you know about it. The thinking and acting in question needs to have some stretch beyond the formulaic. That stretch does not go very far when students find themselves baffled by hole problems.

The stumble over hole problems illustrates a common pattern in human learning, fixation on surface characteristics. This pattern figures frequently in learning science. Research shows that early on in studying a topic, students routinely code problems in terms of surface characteristics rather than underlying principles. For example, some problems about pendulums and some about inclined planes involve conservation of energy, but at first students categorize them by surface characteristics: Here there are pendulum problems and over there are inclined-plane problems, different beasts in different habitats.

To perceive tower problems and hole problems as distinctive types is an extreme case of surface coding, both a failure of transfer and a failure of understanding.

It's worth adding another twist to the meaning of transfer. When we say transfer, we usually have in mind a positive impact. However, as a technical matter, transfer can be either positive or negative. *Negative transfer* happens when something someone learns in one context undermines performance or learning in another context.

Negative transfer is commonplace. For instance, people from the United States or other settings with a righthand-side-of-the-road driving convention commonly experience negative transfer when they rent cars and drive in countries such as England, which has the opposite convention. These very out-of-town drivers need to remain constantly alert to override their old driving habits.

A certain amount of negative transfer occurs routinely in second-language learning. Some words that sound the same and even have similar origins do not mean the same thing, promoting mistakes. "Actual" in Spanish does not mean "real" but rather "current, present, present-day." Sentence organization in the second language is always somewhat different, and learners routinely export from their mother tongue sentence patterns that mangle the new idiom.

In an ever more globalized world, people constantly cross the boundaries of nations and cultures, carrying with them expectations about conversational patterns, business practices, dining rituals, and even differences about how and when to tell a white lie. What travelers do may prove confusing and even offensive, as shown by the proliferation of guidebooks about how to behave in Paris or Beijing or Tokyo.

While negative transfer is certainly a significant phenomenon, it will get no more press here. It is mostly a front-end problem, one easily overcome with some persistence and guidance. People make the transition from right-side driving to left-side driving or the other way all the time, and in language learning, the novices push past those early perversions of sentence structure soon enough. More serious is the challenge of positive near and particularly far transfer.

I have tried to characterize transfer in a straightforward way. However, controversies about how best to conceptualize it thrive today. Some learning theorists have argued that we should stop talking about transfer altogether. It's too entangled with the meaning of learning to have a separate label. Others have chafed at picturing transfer as acquiring a package of knowledge here and applying it there. They have suggested alternative, broader ways of conceptualizing transfer. I certainly agree with the problem of narrowness. From the standpoint of learning by wholes, I see transfer more as a matter of building up rich extensible action repertoires—"games" that we mix and match for other occasions. This is no place to attempt a review of the debates that rage on, so let me simply acknowledge that they are there.

But why all the fuss about transfer anyway? Beyond dictionary meanings, beyond distinctions like near and far or positive and negative, beyond even the controversies lies the central significance of transfer for teaching and learning. Without transfer understood in one or another way, under one label or another, general education would make little sense. The whole point of education is to prepare people with skills and knowledge and understanding for use elsewhere, often *very* elsewhere. As the story of towers and holes illustrates, we do not always get to the elsewhere we want. Call it a failure of transfer or call it something else, there is a serious challenge at hand.

Let us imagine for a moment what education would be like if anything beyond very near transfer was hard to get. Schools would be monasteries of learning with little to say to the outside world. Participants in these monasteries would learn to read only to continue to read more advanced texts. They would learn about long division or Newton's laws only to continue on to more advanced topics right there in those classrooms arrayed along those corridors. Their increasingly impressive mastery of facts about military coups and the Italian sonnet form would only be expressed through their own orations to one another and their debates about fine points. No more than that would be possible. They would be prisoners of the tower, learning gorgeously elaborate matters that are always delicately brittle.

The trouble is, the monastic school is not enough of a fantasy. In some ways, typical institutions of education display this monastic character. They function as closed systems, teaching and testing content much of which touches how people behave outside only in very narrow and limited ways. Transfer of learning has the potential to leap over the walls of the monastic school, but only if we can figure out how to play out of town well.

The Trouble with Transfer

From Hong Kong to Cape Town, from Melbourne to Boston, a great deal of teaching and learning shares what I like to call the Bo Peep theory of transfer. Remember how Bo Peep lost her sheep, but according to the children's rhyme did not have to worry because *Leave them alone and they'll come home/wagging their tails behind them*. In the same spirit, educators all over the world assume that the transfer we want will pretty much take care of itself. When people learn something general in principle, people will apply it in a general way. The sheep just come home. There is no problem of transfer.

This optimism is seductive because some of the time there is indeed nothing to worry about. Some knowledge and skills transfer quite readily. Reading is a good example. Text in front of one's face powerfully evokes the reading response. It's difficult *not* to read a line or two of accessible text when you are a fluent reader. Just try to look at the next paragraph without reading it!

Also, sometimes we benefit from the direct cue of being asked to do something: Write me a note, pass the salt, can you check these figures? Another kind of cue can come from what is called the *affordances* of a situation. An affordance is a feature of an object or situation that strongly lends itself to a certain use. Chairs afford sitting, but so do tree stumps or waist-high fences, and people sit on them without feeling that they are making surprising connections.

Even very far transfer is not necessarily a problem when it's strongly cued. The frequent use of metaphors and analogies in literature, science, and other domains shows how this works. When Irish poet William Butler Yeats calls an old man "a hat upon a stick," or when in discussions of hive insects like ants or bees we are invited to consider the whole colony as a single organism, we can follow along easily. But of course we have been told where to look out of town.

In summary, certain conditions facilitate transfer. Strong cues help. Once the possibility of a connection is in our mind, it helps if we can elaborate the connection readily rather than figuring it out as a complicated puzzle. Authors using metaphors and analogies naturally choose them for ready elaboration with the audience in mind.

However, such facilitating conditions also are risk factors for transfer. What about situations where the cues are not so strong or the connections not so readily elaborated? Then the sheep do not come home.

Such circumstances are commonplace. Turning to research, the previous chapter discussed *inert knowledge* as one kind of troublesome knowledge. Inert knowledge is a problem of transfer. Recall the illustrative riddle of the coin marked 153 B.C. Many people do not make the connection that this must be a fraud, because of course the B.C./A.D. dating system was formulated after the birth of Christ. Recall also the interviews showing that Harvard students thought the Earth was closer to the sun in the summer, when asked to explain why summers were warmer than winters. Whatever they preserved of their science instruction, they certainly knew that it's summer in the northern hemisphere when it's winter in the southern hemisphere and vice versa. Both of these examples illustrate the risk factor of cueing. The connection is not salient enough to trigger retrieval of the critical information, although once it's mentioned, people can readily elaborate the connection.

But sometimes elaborating the connection is a weak link. For example, people will nod when the Cambodian Khmer Rouge are called terrorists, but resist when the French Resistance of World War II are called terrorists. Quite rightly, we tend to think of the anti-Nazi French Resistance as heroes, but this can get in the way of recognizing the character of some of their tactics. As the saying goes, "One person's terrorist is another person's freedom fighter."

People encounter many ideas and practices in their formal education that would have value if widely applied—ideas about citizenship, practices of self-reflection, ways of understanding political situations, thinking skills of various kinds, practical science-related concepts like leverage, attitudes of tolerance, the basics of statistics and probability. But the risk factors are likely to rule. The payoff depends on noticing their relevance in diverse situations quite remote from classrooms and quizzes, where no one is shouting, "This would be a good time to remember the Fifth Amendment," or "This would be a good time to think about the other side of the case," or "This would be a good time to look at the odds."

The most pessimistic view of this challenge is that by and large playing out of town is a game lost before it begins. Some argue that the human mind is not equipped to achieve much transfer in the face of risk factors. There is not much to be done about the problem. We are stuck with it, not in the extreme sense of the monastic school sketched earlier, but in the still troublesome sense that most learning needs to proceed case by case, situation by situation. In contrast with the Bo Peep theory, I like to call this view the lost sheep theory. The lost sheep theory says that we just have to accept the fact that a lot of the sheep are not going to come home. We just cannot expect much transfer from most learners when the risk factors are significant.

What would lead anyone to such a pessimistic conclusion? A line of experimentation a century old documents the brittle nature of far transfer. The story begins with an early notable educational researcher by the name of E. L. Thorndike, who conducted research on transfer at the beginning of the twentieth century. At the time, it was thought that difficult subjects like Latin discipline the mind, preparing students for other kinds of learning. Thorndike decided to find out. He compared the academic success of students who had studied Latin with those who had not, and discovered no advantage whatsoever for the Latin scholars.

In earlier investigations, Thorndike and Woodworth examined a whole range of possible transfers. They concluded that transfer was hard to come by, and, when it happened, depended on concrete *identical elements* in the two performances. Consider again the example of learning to drive a car and then finding yourself able to drive a truck. This would not surprise Thorndike, because there are many identical elements. The steering wheel, the brake, the accelerator all function in more or less the same way, even though certainly there are some differences in the management of the larger vehicle. But most situations lack the critical ingredient of identical elements. Latin studies, for instance, share no obvious identical elements with mathematics, so why should the former boost the latter?

A more modern version of the idea that Latin trains the mind arose over the last couple of decades as students began to study computer programming. A number of educators suggested that the rigors and logic of programming would train the mind, enhancing thinking and learning skills generally. In the spirit of Thorndike, educational researchers began to investigate whether this was the case, and, like Thorndike, found that generally speaking it was not.

Another good candidate for training the mind was literacy itself. Surely people who learned to read and write were not *just* becoming proficient with textual communication but also picking up patterns of thought that would enhance their general cognitive performance. The great Russian psychologist Luria found results that seemed to support this idea when he investigated the impact of literacy in Siberian populations in the 1930s. Those who had a received a literacy course scored better on certain cognitive measures that appeared not to have anything directly to do with literacy.

However, later research questioned whether Luria's results meant quite what he thought they did. Sylvia Scribner and Michael Cole reported an investigation of an African tribe called the Vai. The Vai had developed their own form of writing, although they had no equivalent of schools. Using a range of instruments, Scribner and Cole found no differences in cognitive capabilities between those Vai who had mastered this script and others who had not. The authors noted that the Vai only used their script for the purpose of exchanging certain messages, nothing like the pervasive suffusion of literacy within urbanized cultures. They suggested that reading and writing per se were not the cognitive booster shot Luria supposed. David Olson has argued that it's not so much general reasoning capabilities that are at stake as a powerful stance toward language fostered by literacy. In any case, it is the whole culture of literacy and schooling taken together that has wide impact, not literacy as an isolated skill.

The many documented cases of failure of transfer have led some to suggest that we just give up on transfer beyond easy cases. Every now and then someone will make a surprising connection, but it's not anything we can educate for systematically. The skeptics argue that learning intrinsically is highly situated in particular contexts. This situated quality strongly supports learning in those contexts. Those who favor this school of thought typically critique normal classroom instruction for being far too desituated, far too lacking in the rich characteristics of disciplinary inquiry and in the social dimensions of the disciplines to provide good learning for understanding. With this one can certainly agree, but another tenet of the situated-learning perspective in its strongest form is that on the whole general understandings and skills cannot be expected.

The Hope for Transfer

Up to this point, it might seem that the lost sheep theory has won over the herd. It certainly has much more empirical support than the Bo Peep theory. However, there is a third view, one that simultaneously challenges the naïve Bo Peep theory and the pessimistic lost sheep theory. Just to keep the herd together, I like to call it the good shepherd theory.

The good shepherd theory says that transfer can be attained, but the pattern of learning has to favor it. Generally speaking, both the Bo Peep and the lost sheep theories keep educators from paying careful attention to fostering transfer, and so learners do not display the transfer one would like when the risk conditions are high. But when educators make the effort, much more transfer appears. In other words, the sheep will not come home by themselves, but they don't have to be given up for lost either. The transfer has to be "shepherded."

Evidence for the good shepherd theory comes from the same collection of studies that seem to support the lost sheep theory. Although the trend in this literature is to report no transfer, here and there clear cases appear. For instance, I mentioned that, in general, computer programming experience was not found to enhance other cognitive skills. However, in a couple of cases it did. I mentioned that the Vai tribe with their own script showed no cognitive impact of literacy. However, the researchers found that the *teachers* of the script within the Vai culture did.

If the lost sheep theory were completely right, exceptions such as those previously mentioned would not appear. Since they do, the question becomes one of understanding the exceptions. A number of years ago, my colleague Gavriel Salomon and I offered an interpretation of this literature that sought to explain when transfer occurred and when it did not.

We identified two very different mechanisms of transfer called *high road transfer* and *low road transfer*. High road transfer is a consequence of reflective abstraction. It occurs when people proceed thoughtfully and make conceptual connections. Low road transfer is a reflexive reaction to the surface characteristics of a situation. It occurs when a new situation spontaneously reminds people of a previous one.

We also noted the conditions that favored high road and low road transfer. High road transfer is more likely when the learning experiences emphasize thinking reflectively about the activity at hand, making broad generalizations, looking for possible connections, and the like. In the absence of such deliberately thoughtful activities, high road transfer is not a good prospect. Recalling the transfer risk factors of noticing the connection and elaborating the connection, reflective abstraction prepares the mind for later noticing and elaborating by coding the initial learning in more general far-reaching terms and elaborating its significance.

Low road transfer depends on extensive practice in the original context, to build up pattern recognition processes that might be triggered in other contexts. For low road transfer to reach very far, the original learning has to incorporate experience with a range of contexts, to establish a repertoire of perceptual patterns that might get activated later. Again recalling the risk factors, extensive varied practice prepares the mind for later noticing and elaborating through exercise on diverse cases in the first place.

We used the high road–low road framework to explain why the literature reported transfer only once in a while. Looking closely at the conditions of learning in a number of studies, we found that when transfer failed, either the initial learning included very little in the way of reflective abstraction (no high road), or the initial learning involved little time and variety (no low road). In those cases where significant transfer occurred, there were clear signs of the high road or the low road conditions.

For a high road example, a study of computer programming that showed transfer asked students to reflect deliberately on what they were learning. A good low road example is the impact of a culture of literacy and schooling, what Luria studied. The culture of literacy and schooling may not involve deliberate intellectualizing, but it still pervades many aspects of life, fostering low road transfer to enhance a range of cognitive performances generally. In contrast, the special-purpose literacy of the Vai touched on few aspects of Vai life and hence had no general cognitive impact. However, the teachers of the Vai script did show cognitive advantages, presumably because the teaching role led them to become much more aware of the script and its import—reflective abstraction.

Some efforts to teach thinking skills have demonstrated considerable transfer of learning. For instance, British researchers Philip Adey and Michael Shayer developed a program called CASE, Cognitive Acceleration through Science Education. They conducted an intervention in eight schools every two weeks for two years. Follow-up research looked at the students one year and two years later, and found a lasting impact on standard achievement tests in science, mathematics, and English for many although not all students.

Transfer becomes an even more promising quest when we consider *preparation for future learning*, a concept discussed by John Bransford and Daniel Schwartz. The basic idea is that what you learn today prepares you not just for direct applications but for later learning and its ripple effects. This seems to me to be very resonant with learning by wholes. Suppose today you learn about alternative political systems in a thoughtful, critical, problem-solving-oriented way cognizant of their trade-offs. Later on you find yourself better able to learn about the intricacies of the local and national politics around you, equipping you to contribute more as a citizen and perhaps even play some role in government. Or let's say that today you learn how to appreciate the works of the English novelists in an expansive thoughtful way. Later on you find yourself engaging other genres of literature and even cinema more richly and readily, learning all the more and finding yet further connections. The greatest payoff of transfer, Bransford and Schwartz suggest, may come not from direct transfer of what is learned today, but from the indirect influence of enabling future learning, through a kind of snowball effect.

Empirical studies of preparation for future learning demonstrate the power of the perspective. For example, Schwartz and Martin report a systematic exploration of the impact of preparation for future learning in developing ninth graders' statistical understanding—certainly a worthwhile whole game. All the ninth graders experienced a learning paradigm called Inventing to Prepare for Learning (IPL), where through a number of cycles they were asked to invent approaches to various statistical problems before exposure to the canonical methods. IPL asked students to work in small groups with small data sets and encouragement to arrive at methods that seemed general and that spoke to the commonsense demands of the problems. The procedures students devised included some good ideas, but fell well short of standard statistical practice. The hypothesis was that the invention phase would lead students to appreciate some of the dilemmas and prepare them for learning the canonical methods better. The canonical methods were taught in fairly straightforward ways.

In the midst of a general unit constructed this way, the experimenters included a deliberate pattern of variation to test the impact of preparation for future learning on transfer. Let's imagine Sally and some of her peers undergoing the most advantageous treatment. First Sally does some IPL, Inventing to Prepare for Learning. Then Sally reads a straightforward explanation and a worked example of an appropriate statistical technique. Then Sally takes a test where she may use some of the statistical concepts. The question is, does she transfer what she has learned to the test?

Sally does! She has learned quite a bit. However, students in the other conditions have not. Students who invent to prepare for learning without the later explanation and example do not do appreciably better than students with neither. After all, they never have a chance to learn the standard methods. More surprisingly, students without the invention phase but with the explanation and example of the standard methods do no better, even though in principle they have all the information Sally does. The powerful combination for transfer is the invention to prepare Sally for further learning, plus the explanation and example as an opportunity for further learning.

We can redescribe all this in the language of learning by wholes. By engaging in inventive explorations before getting the official story, learners acquire a much better sense of the goals of the game as well as some rough-and-ready strategies. In effect they invent their own very junior versions. This prepares them for understanding a more sophisticated standard version of the game.

The moral: The trouble with transfer is real but manageable. Transfer does not always come free as the Bo Peep theory falsely promises. But neither is it the hopeless dream the lost sheep theory suggests. We can get the learning we want with good shepherding.

Shepherding Transfer

Play out of town! Our good shepherding of transfer is as simple and as complicated as that. One of the most basic principles of learning, so basic that it is hardly ever mentioned, says that people learn to do by doing. To foster transfer, the initial learning has to include some of the connection making that we hope learners will do later on.

Consider once again the difficulties the physics professor's students had with the hole problem. If the professor had folded some out-of-town playing into the original instruction, few students would have been baffled by the hole problem on the exam. Suppose the professor had spent some discussion time around the tower problem exploring its essential features. Such reflective abstraction (the high road) would help students arrive at a more abstract representation that would help them with the hole problem too. Suppose the initial learning had touched on several examples, say, a tower problem, a cliff problem, and a twig-dropped-by-a-bird problem, while still saving the hole problem for the exam. The varied examples and more extended practice (the low road) would have prepared students for the hole problem.

For a more detailed case, let me review a personal experience. In the previous chapter, I mentioned a course I've taught for many years at the Harvard Graduate School of Education, "Cognition and the Art of Instruction." The aim of the course is to introduce students to the "whole game" of principled designs for learning, foregrounding a range of ideas from cognitive science about teaching and learning. The ideas themselves include many of those discussed in this book.

Transfer is very much a goal of "Cognition and the Art of Instruction." I want the students not just to learn about the content, but to use it actively, and not just use it actively in the sense of writing essays about it, but apply it to designing real learning, and not just designs they make up for the class, but ones important to their professional and personal lives beyond the course. So I've tried to organize the course with considerable playing out of town. Here are some of the ways.

• The classes constantly go back and forth between theory and examples. The examples have deliberate variety. They strike a balance between humanistic and scientific disciplines. They include learners of many different ages. Some of them concern adult learning and even animal learning. The class sessions feature small-group reflective discussion and evaluation of the principles and examples.

• While many nuances of theory and practice are discussed, the most important design principles are laid out in diagrams and summary charts.

• The students do design projects rather than papers. Each student needs to produce a prototype of some kind of educational intervention. Some write teachers' manuals. Some prepare workshops. Some create Web sites. Some assemble mock-ups of museum displays. Just about anything goes, so long as it constitutes a concrete expression of the educational design rather than just a high-level description. The prototype needs to demonstrate good use of several principles from the course's content, with the student explaining and justifying the connections in a report.

• Students have free choice on their design projects. They are encouraged to select something personally meaningful. Many students are maintaining jobs even as they pursue their degrees, and they are encouraged to choose projects that serve their professional settings. Sometimes students have already commenced a learning design in a previous semester, or in a professional setting, that they would like to continue. No problem, so long as their further work clearly incorporates design principles from the course.

• The students receive extensive feedback at several stages from pre-proposal to final project, look at other students' projects, identify connections with other courses they are taking, identify connections with prior and current experiences, and engage in many activities of "quick design," applying the design concepts to small problems.

Where does the "playing out of town" occur amidst all this? One way to bring it into high relief systematically is to look at the *what, to where*, and *how* of transfer—*what* is supposed to transfer, *to where* is it supposed to transfer, and *how* is the transfer accomplished.

The *what* is the content. I want students to transfer the basic design principles drawn from cognitive science. This is why the course underscores the design principles again and again and summarizes them in a series of charts. As to the *to where*, I want students to transfer the ideas to a range of practical contexts in their own lives, no matter what their particular involvement in education, whether it's as teacher, designer, corporate trainer, curriculum writer, educational administrator, or something else. Thus the course content includes a great range of practical examples, with constant looping between theory and practice; and students are encouraged to develop design projects connected with their own current professional practice and aspirations.

The *how* comes straight out of the framework mentioned earlier, the high road/low road model of transfer from Salomon and Perkins. The learning experiences in "Cognition and the Art of Instruction" are chosen to exercise both the high road of reflective abstraction and the low road of automatic triggering of well-practiced responses. Sometimes it's easier to say *bridging* and *hugging*. Bridging means playing out of town in the sense that the learners make a variety of deliberate thoughtful connections. Bridging figures in the course as students constantly reflect on principles and examples, as they practice principle-driven quick design tasks, and as they articulate the rationales for their design prototypes in terms of key concepts from the course.

Hugging means playing out of town in the sense of doing things close to the ultimate envisioned applications. Hugging figures in the course through using a wide range of examples, with the hope that every student finds some examples reflecting areas of special interest. Also, hugging enters into the choice of projects, with students encouraged to select projects close to their situations and interests, even projects that will see practical use immediately and projects that continue work they are already doing in professional settings.

Here comes the inevitable question: How well does it all work? As in any educational undertaking, the results are imperfect. On the one hand, a few students always produce projects that make thin use of the design principles the course foregrounds, despite the constant emphasis. Some students always just do not seem to invest the effort, producing shallow design prototypes. On the other hand, many projects are strikingly well developed, often far beyond the actual demands of the course, and it's commonplace for students to produce designs that they proceed to use in their various professional settings. In the balance, I'm pleased and the students seemed to be pleased. I attribute a fair measure of our satisfaction to our several ways of playing out of town.

Transfer as Importing

All the examples so far concern transfer as exporting. They ask how today's learning can prepare knowledge for wider use later. However, we can also think of transfer in the opposite direction, transfer in rather than out, transfer designed to enhance the learning of the topic at hand.

One familiar application of this principle is simply reminding learners of what they already know and don't know, or getting them to remind themselves. Just about every teacher at one time or another has used some version of the "what I already know, what I think I know, what I need to know" routine.

Here is a more surprising application. Earlier I mentioned that my colleague Gavriel Salomon and I codeveloped some of the ideas about transfer shared here. He also studies peace education. A couple of years ago, he brought to my attention an intriguing investigation conducted by I. Lustig out of the University of Haifa, Israel, a study I mentioned briefly in Chapter 3 in the section on foreign knowledge. It's not easy to teach youngsters to adopt more broad-minded, respectful, and sensitive attitudes toward rival ethnic groups in their own neighborhood. To recall the idea of threshold experiences, it's not easy to create a threshold experience of broad-mindedness in the face of so many emotional barriers.

Lustig's approach was to *transfer in* concepts and skills acquired from another context—playing out of town first in order to play in town later. Here is how it worked.

Lustig arranged for a number of Israeli twelfth-grade students to study the conflict in Northern Ireland for four months. Different perspectives on the two sides of the conflict received thorough treatment. However, not once did the program touch on the Israeli-Palestinian conflict. After the program concluded, the researchers asked the students to write two essays. One essay was to characterize an Israeli-Zionist viewpoint, the other a Palestinian viewpoint. The researchers compared the results with a control group of Israeli students who had not gone through any special program. The students who studied the Northern Ireland conflict proved much more able to write well-developed essays articulating the Palestinian viewpoint. They employed the first person more often in doing so, suggesting enhanced perspective taking. In addition, their essays included more terms relating to the possibilities of conflict resolution.

In general, patterns of thought and action likely to involve defensiveness may be hard to learn directly through cases close to home, and easier to learn through cases more superficially remote and then brought home. I'm reminded of a similar example that an Argentinian colleague, Ernesto Gore, told me. An expert on organizational development, he explained how he often helps business clients toward insight into the internal problems of their own organizations. He would tell a story about another organization, one in fact fabricated for the purpose. He would describe the miseries there, the self-defeating practices, the attempts to improve that failed. Listening to the story, his clients would begin to make their own connections, seeing how some of what they heard applied to their own self-defeating behaviors. Far more effective, Ernesto assured me, than telling his clients directly what was wrong and what to do about it.

Making the Most of Transfer

I'm imagining a school-based learning experience around the difficult process of forging the U.S. Constitution. Now I'm imagining a home-schooling experience involving kitchen and workshop chemistry. Now I'm imagining a tour of the Tower of London. These are not necessarily the best topics ever, but they are all opportunities. They all in principle afford the potential for transfer of learning. The question is: Are the opportunities taken?

There is no need to be a naïve Bo Peep expecting the sheep of transfer to find their way spontaneously. The art and craft of good shepherding—high road and low road, bridging and hugging, inventing to prepare for learning, transfer as exporting and importing—equips educators to leverage the phenomenon of transfer for much more meaningful learning, but only if we take advantage of the opportunities.

Perhaps the most important thing to mention here is pretty obvious once said: Making the most of transfer means teaching whole games in the first place. It means, for instance, looking at the development of the Constitution not just as a unique historical story, but as a complex negotiation with lessons for other settings of nation building and other negotiations in general. It means looking at kitchen and workshop chemistry as a craft one might use many times in one's life. It means looking at the Tower of London not only as a particular prison, but a pattern of architecture and a pattern of practice depressingly common throughout human history and today.

To get powerful transfer, learners need to learn something that matters widely. Almost any rich topic like the Constitution, kitchen and workshop chemistry, or the Tower of London has the potential, but that potential has to be developed. Unfortunately, a good deal of what students study in typical curricula is too narrow in its framing and detail to matter very much.

Chapter 2's exploration of *make the game worth playing* mentioned understandings of wide scope, systems of concepts and examples that map into many facets of life. Examples there included statistics and probability, the nature of justice, the nature of living things, the roots of ethnic hatred, who decides on what counts as history, and human weakness and error, to name a few. One good practice is to choose understandings of wide scope to foreground, whether the specific topic under consideration is the birth of the Constitution, kitchen and workshop chemistry, or the Tower of London. The concept and practice of democracy, the care and handling of acids, the efficacy and ethics of imprisonment and torture all can find their relevance as we navigate through a complicated world. But such large ideas only have a chance if the Constitution, kitchen and workshop chemistry, and the Tower of London are treated in ways that bring out the overarching themes.

It's not hard to list criteria for what a candidate understanding of wide scope might offer, standards for export and import if you like, standards for what makes themes especially "generative" in teaching-for-understanding terms. Here are some worth bearing in mind:

Disciplinary significance. Do the ideas have a broad significance within and beyond their own disciplinary context? Do they help us to see the world in a different way?

Societal significance. Do the ideas speak to concerns of society at large?

Personal significance. Do the ideas resonate with learners' and teachers' or mentors' or parents' hopes, desires, curiosities, and needs?

Charisma. Are the ideas magnetic, alluring, arresting? Understandings of wide scope can prove technically useful without having a lot of charisma, but charisma helps.

Import or export, high road or low road, near transfer or far, and the potentials of almost any particular topic—they all add up to a vision of how education can speak more broadly and powerfully to learners' lives. Let's make the most of what we teach and learn by playing the game out of town.

Wonders of Learning

Play Out of Town

I wonder how can I organize today's learning so it informs and empowers learners widely in their lives. For a start, I might ask myself: Where else will today's learning be useful, and how could I help learners to make the connections?

I wonder how I can recognize when transfer is likely to be a problem. Here I want to remember that transfer goes easily when the cues for use elsewhere are strong and the particulars of application elsewhere transparent, as with basic reading skills. Unfortunately, for many topics the cues are weak or the particulars subtle, and today's learning needs to anticipate that.

I wonder how to organize teaching for transfer. Ideas and skills travel to other times and places over the high road of reflective abstraction that codes knowledge with more generality and the low road of diverse applications that provides varied practice. If I could design learning activities involving bridging (reflective abstraction, the high road) and hugging (deliberate efforts to simulate diverse applications, the low road), transfer would improve.

I wonder how content can be learned in a more active way, with more bridging and hugging for better transfer. I'm recalling specific practices that could help, among them problem-based learning (Chapter 3) and Inventing to Prepare for Learning (IPL).

I wonder how to enhance content learning by transfer that imports prior knowledge. I could remind learners to remind themselves of prior knowledge in the same or related areas. For sensitive topics, students may learn better by first studying a situation well removed from their own and then bringing it home.

I wonder how to make the most of transfer. I could be ambitious here. Let me find understandings of wide scope within seemingly specific topics and skills and foreground them.

5

Uncover the Hidden Game

THE HIDDEN GAME OF BASEBALL—IF YOU TRIED TO GUESS WHAT THIS 1984 book is about, you might say "strategy" or maybe "management" or even "the commercial side of the game." Instead, the classic by John Thorn and Pete Palmer offers a statistical perspective on baseball. Perhaps most surprising of all, it's not for university mathematicians but for fans. And that's only the beginning. There is a virtual industry of books, articles, discussions, and whatnot about the statistical side of baseball.

You may remember from the opening chapter that I like baseball, but I'm not a fanatic about it. For a full confession here, I used to pay more attention to it years ago than I do now. Nonetheless, I've picked up on a couple of interesting points about this hidden game. Here's one. The batting average is a statistic you often see listed: When a particular hitter comes up to bat, how often does the batter get a hit? The batting average then is the number of hits divided by number of at-bats (times 1000 to get rid of those frightening decimal points). This certainly sounds like a good measure for planning teams or making substitutions.

However, hidden game aficionados argue that it's not as straight-forwardly informative as it appears. A superior measure involving a slightly more complicated calculation is *runs created*. This means pretty much what it sounds like. Instead of asking what percentage of time a batter gets a hit, we ask how many runs on the average does a batter generate for each time at bat. There are twists and turns to such a statistic involving walks and other factors, but that is the basic idea, and a sensible one. After all, we want batters to produce runs, not just get on base.

Runs created can rank players differently from the batting average. For instance, imagine one batter who gets short hits frequently, usually just making it to first base. Another gets long hits somewhat less often, making it to second or third or even home. The first will have a higher batting average, but the second may have higher runs created, which is what counts. Or a particular player may be a good clutch hitter, especially likely to hit in times of need or opportunity with other players on base in positions to score. The clutch hitting will increase the player's runs-created statistic even if his batting average is the same.

The statistical perspective on a sport is one kind of hidden game, a fresh window on something we usually think of as skill, spirit, and sweat. Any sport has a statistical hidden game, and so of course do many other slices of life—military matters, politics, traffic management, marriage and divorce, and health decisions. No one says we have to be interested in the statistical hidden games behind slices of life in which we're involved, but we might be, and they do afford a different kind of understanding and a different kind of leverage.

Almost everything that people learn in school and out of school has its hidden aspects, dimensions and layers and perspectives not apparent on the surface of the activity. Here are a few more examples:

- Strategy in almost any area, from sports to business to military to politics to academic publishing
- The complex influence of the world market on the prices you pay in a local hardware or grocery store
- The influence of economics and geography on history, which we tend to see as primarily political
- The impact of tipping points on trends like the spread of epidemics or spring fashions
- More generally, the role of systems phenomena like reinforcing loops, booms and busts, stocks and flows in a whole range of different settings from water supplies to industrial innovation

- The tacit messages that people send by their conduct, for instance how sitting at the head of the table implies authority and dominance
- More generally, the patterns and symbols of status in society, the subtle signals from how people dress and what they mean
- How people from different countries and ethnic groups have conversations and in general form relationships with one another
- The role of the unconscious in human thought and action

At this point, you might be thinking, "Well, those games are not all that hidden. I know a bit about most of them!" Sure you do. We all pick up something about the hidden games as we go along. A lot of us know a little about many of them and probably most of us know a lot about a couple of them. If they were completely and totally hidden, no one would know anything and we would not have to worry about it . . . blissful ignorance.

But bear in mind two things: We probably know less about these hidden games than we think we do. We know a few splinters that do not penetrate very deeply. For instance, batting average always sounded like a perfectly reasonable statistic to me until I read about runs created. Or more generally, take statistics and probability. Most of us know something there, but research also shows that what people "know" tends to be tainted by a number of serious misconceptions that can influence daily choices. The game is more hidden than we think.

Second point: Whatever people pick up incidentally about the various hidden games, here we're concerned with the place of hidden games in teaching and learning. Some rather important hidden games *stay* hidden. Learners spend most of their time playing and practicing the surface games.

However, getting really good at the overall game means learning the games underneath the surface also, layers, dimensions, and perspectives that can make big differences in understanding and performance. Earlier I emphasized how learning by wholes creates threshold experiences, strong orienting experiences of getting the hang of the game. Games hidden underneath the surface define new thresholds and invite new threshold experiences that can change fundamentally the sense of game and play. At stake here is not only technical skill but dispositional energy, the sparking of curiosity toward the discovery of new horizons. This is why the fifth principle of learning by wholes says: *Uncover the hidden game.*

The Hidden Game of Strategy

One of the odd things about hidden games is that sometimes we don't even know we are playing them. I mentioned earlier that my undergraduate and graduate degrees are in mathematics. I was pretty good at mathematical problem solving, but it was only years later that I discovered *how* I was good. When I was most involved in mathematics, I did not stand back and look at my strategic approach.

Insight came by way of a well-known classic called *How to Solve It* by the mathematician Gyorgy Polya. In this popular version and a couple of more technical books, Polya argued that the secret to mathematical problem solving was making good strategic moves, which he called *heuristics* (the word comes from a Greek verb meaning "to find"). Good heuristics included, for example, breaking a problem into parts, relating a problem to one you had solved previously, making a diagram, deliberately constructing a simpler version of a problem and trying to solve that one first, looking at specific cases to see how they illuminated the general problem, and a number of other techniques. As this sample suggests, many of the ideas on Polya's list applied not just to mathematical problem solving, but to problem solving of any kind. Even in baseball!

Years later when I ran across Polya's work, I wondered: Is Polya right? Do I use these various heuristics? I did a deliberate experiment on myself, finding three or four math problems, going to work on them, and paying close attention to my own thinking process with quick notes as I went along.

Somewhat to my surprise, I found that I was playing the Polya hidden game. During my years of studying math, I had become a

Polya-style strategic problem solver without even being aware of it. I don't mean that the heuristics were operating unconsciously. When I broke a problem into parts or made a diagram or looked at specific cases, I certainly knew I was doing so to help me move forward with the problem. However, if you asked me during those years, "What do you do to solve problems?" I would not have reeled off my list of tricks. I knew them at the level of doing in the moment but not at the level of giving an overall explanation.

This personal experience raises a serious puzzle about uncovering the hidden game: If we generally come to play hidden games automatically, why worry about them in the context of planning teaching and learning? The answer is that the strategic hidden game doesn't always develop very well. With some talent and enthusiasm and many years of experience, I had attained a good hidden game of mathematical problem solving, but most people simply don't.

So why not just teach Polya's list of heuristics? Because it's not as simple as that. There were early signs that Polya's perspective might be incomplete. Polya's work provoked considerable interest in the community of mathematics educators. Teachers and researchers tried to improve students' mathematical problem solving by teaching the practices. The results were very mixed. In general, a dose of Polya did not seem to translate reliably into a dramatic improvement.

What was going wrong? The key insight came from the research of Berkeley professor Alan Schoenfeld. Schoenfeld and his colleagues conducted careful investigations of how to teach the heuristics in a way that truly helped students. To use a concept introduced earlier (Chapters 3 and 4), Schoenfeld found that students' knowledge of the heuristics tended to be inert. Students learned about the heuristics without deploying them in the course of real problem solving.

Schoenfeld discovered that the most important missing ingredient was self-management. Students generally lacked any grand scheme by which to organize their approaches to tackling problems, a scheme that provided natural places for heuristics to come into play and guide the process. Schoenfeld introduced a five-step self-management process that began with analyzing the problem to understand it and find ways to simplify it; continued into a stage of planning an over-all approach that avoided premature calculations; and advanced to phases of exploration, implementation, and verification. Schoenfeld coupled this with direct teaching and modeling of a number of heuristics. And he hit the jackpot. The combination of instruction in heuristics and self-management doubled the number of problems students solved, compared to control groups that went over the same practice problems but without explicit attention to heuristics and self-management.

Mathematical problem solving is only one arena where strategic approaches have proved to be powerful. A further example of central significance to most of education is reading. Once students have mastered the basics of reading in their early education—in itself a considerable challenge—they need to use reading for learning in a range of other areas in school and out. Research shows that reading strategies of various sorts can make a considerable difference in learners' understanding and retention of what they read. There are many different approaches to strategic reading. One of the best-known, called *reciprocal teaching*, was developed by educational psychologists Annemarie Palincsar and Ann Brown. It emphasizes a group dialogue process with four central heuristics: questioning, clarifying, summarizing, and predicting. The "reciprocal" part means that teachers and students take turns leading the dialogue, a way of ensuring that the students accept responsibility for making the moves themselves. One could see this as a means of promoting their development of self-management processes á la Schoenfeld.

Reading strategies are not just for youngsters. For decades the Bureau of Study Counsel at Harvard University has offered strategic reading programs to Harvard students faced with the often daunting reading assignments they encounter. Michelene Chi and her colleagues have pursued a systematic program of research on *self-explanation*, much of it conducted with college students. Self-explanation means pausing to try to explain to oneself what one is reading as one goes along. In fact people often read past difficult passages and worked examples without really grappling with them. The research shows that students who understand better have strong habits of self-explanation, and students trained in self-explanation come to understand better.

Investigations have shown that a variety of reading strategies can be effective. In a 1988 synthesis, Haller, Child, and Walberg reviewed twenty studies and found a strong positive trend in the results. On the average, the programs improved students' reading on the measures used by 70 percent of a standard deviation, which is quite a lot. Two kinds of strategies proved especially effective: searching backward and forward in the text to understand puzzling points better and self-questioning strategies to gauge one's progress and redirect one's reading.

The idea of a strategic approach to anything is commonplace. It applies to mathematical problem solving, reading, sports, office management, military missions, and political campaigns. There are books full of ideas about good practices in endless areas, and, for at least some of those practices, substantiation from research. So in what sense are hidden games of strategy hidden at all? In the sense that, despite all these resources, they are hidden from most learners. Only a small percentage of teaching-learning experiences include explicit attention to the strategic dimension. The strategic game is hidden by neglect. It's hidden by the preoccupation of the teaching-learning process with the surface game, with getting the facts and routines right, with getting through the problem sets and other assignments.

This is not just the responsibility of teachers and instructional designers. Many learners themselves seem to have no time for the hidden game. Rebecca Simmons, a doctoral student of mine, conducted a study of the Harvard reading program mentioned above, a generally successful initiative. Her work looked at students four months after completing the program to examine what they got out of it. She discovered that many students gained a good deal, but some ended up avoiding the strategies for a variety of reasons. Some students felt that previewing a text or testing their understanding informally was a waste of time, even though research shows clear gains from such strategies, and the course had both taught and demonstrated this. Others displayed an aversive stance toward the reading; they just wanted to get it done in as simple a way as possible. Still others were fearful that techniques like skimming would lead them to miss something tremendously important.

With all this in mind, here are some strategies for uncovering the hidden game of strategies.

1. Find or devise a reasonable version of the hidden game, like Polya's heuristics or reciprocal teaching.
2. Include self-management, not just good moves.
3. Teach the hidden game just like teaching anything else in the spirit of learning by wholes. Find good junior versions, lay them out, involve learners in playing them, show the worth of doing it, pay attention to transfer, practice the hard parts, and so on.
4. Evoke the dispositional side of it all—curiosity, empowerment, what makes the game worth playing and worth playing better.
5. Watch out for complexity and pacing. Burdening learners with too many things to manage at once can defeat the whole purpose.

The Hidden Game of Causal Thinking

Here is a public policy question all too pertinent to the urbanized world with its spiraling populations:

Imagine a morning commute, the kind that consumes an appalling hour and a half, the kind that puts you in the middle of an implacable traffic jam with depressing reliability. So let's do something about it. Let's call upon Public Works to undertake a major reconstruction program to double the number of lanes in the artery leading into the city. If we doubled the lanes, that might cut our commuting time in half. Or would it?

I owe the gist of this question to Linda Booth Sweeney, a former doctoral student and an expert on developing systems thinking. When people ponder this question, they come up with very different responses. Some like the idea of the faster commute, although they might wonder whether the public investment and the years of disruption for reconstruction are worth it. However, some doubt whether there would be any gain. They say, "Well, those wider roads might fill up just like the narrower ones. It would be the same hour and a half all over again."

The pessimists are right. Here's why. The pool of people who want to get into the city one way or another is always going to be larger than any reasonable road can accommodate. Accordingly, people make decisions about how much time they are willing to invest in a commute by road at their ideal time of day, traded off against other options like coming in earlier or later or using some kind of public transportation like a train. The typical commuting period, say an hour and a half, represents how much time on the average people are willing to tolerate. Doubling the width of the road does not change the distribution of different people's willing investment in time, so the new road will fill up again to just about the same crowdedness, bringing in twice as many people per hour with the same frustration. You might say we have doubled the "frustration productivity" of the road.

Now here's another puzzle on a very different front. A wire from one pole of a battery leads to a switch, which leads to a light bulb, which leads to another light bulb, which leads back to the battery. You throw the switch. Does the first light bulb light up a little sooner than the second, or do they both light up at the same time? To be sure, it all happens very fast, but in principle what is the answer?

One after another is the common response. People tend to think of the battery as a kind of a reservoir, with the electricity filling up the wire from beginning to end, getting to the first bulb first and then the second one. However, this is not the way it works. The wire is already full of electrons, like marbles in a hose. When the switch is thrown, the battery, so to speak, pushes a marble into one end of the hose, forcing all the other marbles to move forward at the same time. So the simultaneous motion of the "marbles" lights up both bulbs at the same time.

Different as the worlds of highways and electrical circuits are, both these examples point to a challenging hidden game very important in understanding the world around us and indeed ourselves. My colleague Tina Grotzer calls this game *complex causality*. In many areas, learners do not understand how causal systems of various kinds work. They take in the surface story of particular cases and acquire ritual knowledge to solve standard problems without any general sense of what is going on. Confusions about causality show up in understanding topics like electrical circuits, sinking and floating, how organisms and airplanes fly, evolution, ecologies, economies, historical forces, and family relationships.

So what is complex about complex causality? Causality at its simplest is a good place to start. A great deal of our everyday reasoning depends on what might be called *domino causality*. Picture a row of dominoes each knocking over the next. The mechanism is right there on the surface: We can see the dominoes tipping. The causal relationship of the elements is very straightforward: Each domino topples the next one. It's a deterministic story: If you've set up the row correctly, the dominoes fall from beginning to end without any surprises. Finally, there is a single causal agent initiating the process, a prime mover, say your forefinger on the first domino.

Much of our causal reasoning about the everyday world is close to domino causality. Why is crime up? Not enough budget for police, so not enough police on the streets, so more opportunities for crime—a little domino chain. Why is the price of oil up? Conflict in the Middle East, so reduced oil supplies, so higher costs for oil by the law of supply and demand—another little domino chain.

Such accounts can be sound as far as they go, and they may serve well enough in everyday circumstances, but they often only tell a small part of a more complicated story. And the story can get very complicated indeed. Tina Grotzer and I, trying to map the way that causal accounts get complicated, came up with four principal dimensions: *mechanism, interaction pattern, probability*, and *agency*. These were our way of trying to map the hidden game of causal thinking.

Mechanism. This dimension involves who the players are in the causal story. The players can be dominoes, right there on the surface. However, causality often involves a story under the surface—a story about electrons or DNA or processes in the brain or germs or unconscious motives. People frequently don't know about the hidden mechanisms, or don't think about them if they do know about them (inert knowledge again), or may be skeptical of them if they do think about them. Nonspecialists can learn to reason with the mechanisms, but rarely are in a position to assess whether or not they are reasonable.

Interaction Pattern. This dimension has to do with getting beyond the simplest causal relationship where one domino knocks over another. Effects can radiate out in many directions rather than just making up a chain. Multiple causes can gang up to produce a single effect; imagine a situation where it takes five small dominoes tipping into a big one to knock it over. Many causal relationships have a mutual character, not just A to B but B to A at the same time. In a tug-of-war, the teams pull on one another, and the same holds for gravity. It's not just that the Earth pulls on the Moon, but the Moon pulls on the Earth as well. In fact, according to the laws of Newton, all forces work both ways at once.

In many systems there are causal loops. A grim example is military escalation, where one party's aggressive actions provoke the other party's even more aggressive actions. The same thing happens in family feuds. Many scientific theories take the form of constraints, such as Ohm's Law, which declares a mathematical relationship between voltage, current, and resistance and electrical circuits. Such theories don't say at all what happens first and what happens next in domino fashion. Instead, they assert that a certain relationship will always hold. This is so different from a domino story that it generates considerable confusion.

Probability. Easiest to think about are deterministic systems like the dominoes, where effects happen reliably. But uncertainty is everywhere in our world—in the spread of diseases, the fluctuations of the stock market, finding a good job or a life partner, in the flux of fundamental particles at the quantum level, and of course in the game of baseball. In fact, this is the hidden game we began with, the game of statistics and probability. Many of the large-scale patterns we see in the world, from the dominance of the New York Yankees in the World Series to the spread of AIDS and the erosion of beaches are best understood as aggregate effects of much smaller-scale events playing out according to their probabilistic trends.

Agency. This dimension has to do with what or who is the prime mover, and whether anything is. The finger starts the chain of dominoes, but who started World War II? Was Hitler the "finger?" In a sense yes, but the Treaty of Versailles, imposed by the Allies on Germany at the end of World War I, generated both great resentment and economic woes in Germany, providing the Nazis with fuel for their fire. A long history of anti-Semitism in Germany helped as well, and the looming threat of Russia under Stalin provided Hitler with a very real threat. And, of course, there were other factors at work.

In some causal systems, there is the deceptive illusion of a prime mover when in reality nothing even comes close. Many people tend to think of the queen bee as the ruler of the hive, guiding all that orderly building and foraging and rearing. However, the queen bee plays a highly circumscribed role as breeder. The large-scale orderliness of the hive's activities arises without centralized command out of instinctual rules by which the bees interact on a small scale with one another and with their environment. If bees seem too far from everyday life, healthy free-market economies work in the same way. The small-scale searches for competitive pricing and transactions generate large-scale parity of cost and value. Local needs, as for food, lead to the development through entrepreneurship of large-scale networked structures of suppliers and transporters and retailers to meet those needs.

In the previous chapter, I wrote about what made the theory of relativity complicated and also compared it with understanding historical causation. Perhaps this is a good moment to take another pass at that, with these four dimensions in mind. Far removed from a domino pattern, the theory of relativity invokes a highly nonintuitive *mechanism* where space and time are interchangeable in a complex *interaction*. It is deterministic rather than *probabilistic*, the one note of simplicity, but there is no factor that functions as a central *agency* from which everything else emanates. And, just as in the previous chapter, historical causation is even worse: *mechanisms* at many levels from individual action to economic and population trends and hideously complex *interaction patterns*, which are highly *probabilistic* and, acknowledging the important roles of figures like Hitler, greatly dependent on a panorama of other circumstances rather than a single key *agency*. Again, leading us to the conclusion that history is harder to understand than relativity.

Early on in this line of inquiry, Tina and I worked together to develop ways of describing the hidden game of causality, but Tina has gone much beyond that, investigating how to introduce learners to the hidden game. At a very general level, the answer is not so different from Alan Schoenfeld's approach to mathematical problem solving or indeed the whole spirit of this book: Get learners into the whole game in an appropriately junior version. Conventional instruction tends to settle for the surface game. The challenge is to bring the hidden game into play in a reasonable and manageable way.

Tina's approach to this is to construct a mix of experiences and conversations that uncover the hidden game. She calls these RECAST activities for activities designed to <u>re</u>veal the underlying <u>ca</u>usal <u>st</u>ructure. For instance, students are commonly confused by the distinction between weight and density in the phenomenon of sinking and floating. At first they suppose that heavy objects sink and light objects float. In one simple activity, students are offered a big piece of candle, which, when put into a beaker of clear liquid obediently sinks. A small piece of candle placed in a nearby beaker also filled with a clear liquid compliantly floats. So far so good: Heavy means sink, light means float. But then one fishes the pieces of candle out of their respective beakers and swaps them.

Uh oh, now the big piece floats and the little piece sinks. The surface rule does not hold up any more. That should generate a little curiosity! Students begin to pay attention not just to the weight of the pieces but properties of the liquids in which they are placed, liquids that of course have different densities. Together with this, students begin to construct more sophisticated accounts of what is going on with the help of various tips. Tina likes to characterize this as helping students to "trade up" for better models. Learning a complex and subtle science concept can call for several rounds of trading up.

Readers familiar with some of the ideas current in science education will notice a powerful and relatively standard move in this process: creating an anomaly. It's commonplace to devise experiences where students begin with a simplistic idea and face circumstances where it breaks down. But there is a little more to this story. The particular anomaly is calculatedly chosen to push the learners further along the dimensions of complex causality.

The candle experiment, for instance, addresses the dimension of *interaction pattern*, helping students to see that it's not just the properties of the piece of candle, but the interaction between the candle and the properties of the liquid that determine sinking or floating. Tina has accumulated a good deal of empirical evidence that experiences like this both advance learners' understanding of particular concepts in science substantially and also spill over to superior understanding of other concepts in science that they encounter later. This means that the learners are not just learning the particulars . . . they are learning something about the hidden game of causal thinking.

The Hidden Game of Inquiry

A grand experiment in unveiling the game of inquiry occurred at Harvard University in the spring of 1990, when three notable professors joined together to offer a course called "Thinking About Thinking." The course brought together Robert Nozick of the Department of Philosophy, the paleontologist Stephen Jay Gould, and Alan Dershowitz from the Law School. The lectures were hugely popular. Almost immediately, the site had to be shifted to one of Harvard's largest halls. Only a fraction of the audience members were actually enrolled. The rest were there to see what these three gurus would make of the challenge.

There was a topic of the week, the topics ranging widely across social, scientific, and philosophical themes, for instance, the nature of causality, illegal drugs, or the influence of heredity on IQ. Each of the three in turn took up the topic from his own perspective for twenty minutes, followed by a free-form conversation segueing into audience interaction.

Lecture after lecture, often arguing with one another, the three defined and categorized, clarified through analogies, offered evidence and argument, and pressed for logical coherence. They appealed to commonsense experience, considered probabilities and statistical trends, pondered underlying causal mechanisms, and asked whether systems like the law lived up to their missions. For example, a discussion about what drugs should be illegal mixed questions of evidence about the actual danger of drugs with conceptual questions about the coherence of the concept of a drug and the inconsistent relationship between the danger of particular drugs and the strength of legal sanctions against them. The right of the state to stipulate what was a dangerous drug (say, marijuana but not tobacco) was pitted against the importance of conceptual coherence and empirical evidence.

As it turned out, there was very little thinking *about* thinking despite the title of the course—the three rarely took up the topic of thinking itself—but a great deal of thinking on display. Although the three protagonists were not particularly trying to map the moves they made, I made my own chart. Here are some of the elements:

Categories and definitions. For instance, what is a drug? Are we consistent in our conceptions of a drug, and is the law consistent in what it counts as an illegal drug?

The logic of means and ends. For instance, what is the law trying to accomplish through declaring certain drugs illegal, and is the law attaining the desired results? What are the trade-offs, side effects, and competing purposes?

Logical coherence. Are we consistent in what we count as a drug? Where do inconsistencies arise? How can we resolve them? Do they matter?

Meaning and intuitive judgment. What does our intuitive sense of something, for instance what counts as a drug, have to do with legal or formal definitions? When conceptions conflict, which ought to win and why?

Probability and statistics. What are the real risks of a particular policy?
Who is at risk and how much at risk? In reaching conclusions,
are we working with an adequate sample or just proceeding
anecdotally?

Causal reasoning, as in the previous section. What are the underlying causal mechanisms? Are there multiple causes and multiple consequences? Are we at risk of being misled that one
thing causes another, just because they happen together?
Maybe they both simply have a common cause, the real story
behind it all.

Over time, I came to think of Nozick, Gould, and Dershowitz as
playing *epistemic* games: games because of the debates, the moves, the
vitality, the occasional playfulness; and *epistemic* because this word
means having to do with knowledge and how we figure out what is
sound and what is not sound. They were not just engaged in problem
solving or struggling with making a decision. They were embracing
the seething messiness of full-scale inquiry. They were trying to build
knowledge and understanding around the topic of the week.

Cultivating the sort of skill and commitment demonstrated
by Nozick, Gould, and Dershowitz is certainly an important part of
education in the disciplines and across the disciplines, and an important part of developing general intellectual competence. The problem
is, most of us don't have much of a chance to learn how to approach
inquiry at this level. The game of inquiry is another one of those
largely hidden games. There are at least three sides to the challenge:
the final score problem, the spectator problem, and the rules of the
game problem.

In a great deal of conventional learning, what learners hear is the
final score—the theory deemed correct, the court decision dismissed
or upheld by the Supreme Court, the "correct" historical account,
the "right" interpretation of the poem. Often, there is a token bow to
where the final score came from, kind of like the quick word on the
evening news that the Boston Red Sox won, with the key event a
home run in the seventh that drove in two other runs. But occasional

highlights are not nearly enough to give anyone a sense of the game. Even professional publications and technical journals do not really reveal the full game. They typically narrate the main lines of reasoning, while sharing none of the messy confusions, missteps, and backing up and trying again that stain the ragged weave of inquiry.

Then there is the *spectator problem*. This was a challenge for the thinking about thinking course. Watching Nozick, Gould, and Dershowitz go at it week after week would not necessarily make anyone in the audience a better thinker. (Those actually enrolled in the course attended section meetings, which I'm sure helped.) More generally, when education does take the trouble to get seriously beyond the final score and play out fully the game that led up to it through lectures, books, or other sources, the spectator problem still looms large. Things don't get real until the learners are actually playing the game instead of just watching.

The third challenge is the *rules of the game problem*. Different disciplines handle matters of description, explanation, and justification in different ways. The sophisticated Nozick, Gould, and Dershowitz were plainly familiar with the basic rules of the game for many disciplines and could move fluidly among them. However, conventional instruction does little to differentiate or sharpen learners' sense of the specific disciplinary game they are playing. For instance, the gold standard of evidence in mathematics is formal deductive proof. In science, empiricism rules, with theories tested against the way the world behaves. Historians look to historical documents and artifacts for evidence, but with a critical eye, because, although scientists do not expect the physical world to be out to deceive them, historians know that "history is written by the victors" and for that and other reasons words from the past may be calculatedly deceptive.

It's easy to imagine that these sorts of distinctions are obvious, but they are certainly not. For instance, I have always relished findings from an investigation by mathematics education researcher Daniel Chazen about how students of Euclidean geometry thought about proof. He asked them whether they might find exceptions to a theorem that had been formally proved. Yes, they thought! They might well find an exception if they looked hard enough. He also asked them what they might conclude about a general geometric claim supported by several diverse examples. The claim is true for sure, they said!

Their answers would send a chill down the spine of any Euclid fan. The whole point of formal proof is to establish a conclusion relative to its premises always and forever. No one should be able to find exceptions if the proof is sound. Nor should the students trust a few examples. The whole edifice of formal mathematics rests on the idea that examples are no substitute for formal proof, because it's too easy to miss the critical example that will refute the claim. Despite considerable study of a school version of Euclidean geometry, the students had missed the core of the epistemic game.

So what can be done about the final score problem, the spectator problem, and the rules of the game problem? The answer is not appreciably different from what to do about the hidden game of strategy or the hidden game of causal thinking (which in fact is part of the larger hidden game of inquiry): Surface the game and get learners involved in playing it, in appropriately junior versions.

This is the kind of mission usually thought to be suitable only for older learners, a pernicious mindset that poorly serves learners' potential. To provide a kind of counterexample, let me tell you about a charming case of kindergarten children engaged in reasoning about a painting. Of course, we would not expect them to be terribly sophisticated, but they say some things with a measure of insight that might surprise you.

For a number of years, several colleagues and myself have worked in the area of thinking skills and fashioned various approaches, the most recent called Visible Thinking. Shari Tishman has led the development of a variant to cultivate thinking skills and dispositions through using the arts with learning in the disciplines. Ron Ritchhart has led an effort to establish "cultures of thinking" around learning in the disciplines. The idea is to engage learners of all ages in deeper learning, while at the same time fostering not only thinking skills but alert proactive attitudes toward thinking and learning. We've had the opportunity to produce some videotaped examples. I'm going to tell you about one of them.

Debbie O'Hara teaches kindergarten at the International School of Amsterdam. Today she is going to work with her children on something called the *explanation game*. "Guess and say why" is the mantra encouraging the children to notice things and give reasons. Debbie explains that she tries to use the explanation game in many different ways, to foster the general mindset of alertness and reason giving. For instance, the children have played the explanation game with a box full of artifacts to introduce ideas about the postal system. Today the focus is art, in particular a large painting done by a twelfth-grade student. The painting is abstract. On a white background, hundreds of small squiggly shapes in black and gray appear. Debbie wonders what her students will make of it.

Debbie asks, "What do you notice about the painting, what do you think it is, what do you see when you look at it?"

The children begin with relatively concrete observations. The first simply says he sees black dots. Then a girl comments, "The painting looks like a Dalmatian's skin."

"What makes you say that?" Debbie asks.

"Dalmatians have dots, but those are a little bit larger; my Dalmatian in China has some."

A boy says, "It looks like they're animals going around." What makes you say that? "I can see a lion running." Debbie asks him to show everyone where he is looking. He does, and the squiggle indeed resembles a lion bounding along.

Another child identifies a crocodile. Another says the painting is like a zebra. What makes you say that? Because it's black and white. Another says it looks like Japanese words. What makes you say that? The boy points to an example, a squiggle with a remarkable resemblance to Japanese characters.

Debbie is aware that the children are picking out bits and pieces and focusing on animals. Maybe she can bump them out of this pattern. She asks, "If I were to tell you that it's nothing to do with an animal, what other explanation might you come up with for this painting?"

A boy says, "I'm going to tell a funny thing. It's about running, I think." "Can you tell me more?" Debbie asks. "These things have feet and they do like this." The child illustrates the running with his fingers.

The girl says, "It reminds me of my mommy's hair because they are gray and white and black."

A boy says that it has a lot of movement. It looks like it's going quickly.

A girl says, "It looks like skipping." What makes you say that? "The lines remind me of skipping and happiness." Why is that? "I don't know, but this just came to my mind."

Certainly the children's responses do not represent an erudite art historical stance. But the youngsters engage the work with seriousness and excitement, more seriousness and excitement than many adults manage to muster for abstract art. They make personal connections, and as the conversation moves on they respond not just to bits and pieces but to the whole work and its expressiveness. And they easily and comfortably give reasons.

Although this explanation game can be used with many objects, such as artifacts about the postal system, it actually has a pedigree in art itself. It was adapted from a procedure for examining works of art devised by Philip Yenawine and Abigail Housen for the Museum of Modern Art in New York. The procedure uses two key questions, "What's going on here?" and "What do you see that makes you say that?" These are remarkably powerful queries, just as appropriate to adults or even to experts in art history as they are to kindergarten children, because they open the opportunity for everyone to respond at his or her own level of sophistication.

In this and innumerable other ways, it's not so hard to get past the final score problem and the spectator problem, drawing learners into the game of inquiry. As to the rules of the game problem, young though these children are, there is even a nudge toward engaging the rules of the game in the way a sophisticated viewer of art would, as

Debbie leads her charges away from a piecemeal approach and toward characterizing the whole painting.

The Hidden Game of Power

Wendy Luttrell, a colleague for many years at the Harvard Graduate School of Education, likes to look at education from an anthropological perspective. One of her missions is to make visible the tacit assumptions embedded in everyday life that so powerfully shape what we believe and how we behave. A telling activity gets people to think hard about the ordinary school chair-desk.

You know what they're like. A chair and a desk are fused into the same convenient unit, the desk component a rather small platform upon which the student can rest a book or a notepad. Books usually can be stored under the seat. Wendy provokes people to realize that this very ordinary instrument of education embodies numerous tacit assumptions and expectations that deserve a second thought. Maybe you would like to guess what some of those tacit assumptions and expectations are before reading on.

For example, the conventional chair-desk favors right-handed students; the writing platform is almost always to the right. The working surface is not very large, so apparently students are not expected to coordinate multiple sources of written information or develop complex representations. Also, the chair-desk gets in the way of students forming working circles and deprives them of common desk space, as when five or six pupils sit around a table. Learners work alone! Normally chair-desks come in one size for a classroom. One-size-fits-all!

Wendy brings forward another assumption: Only those bodies that fit into the desks are appropriate for the setting. In lecture notes, she writes,

I became painfully aware of this last assumption while conducting research about teenage pregnancy as I watched the pregnant school girls try to twist their swelling bellies into desks in ways that left them feeling as if they were *misfits* in school. There were many other actions and activities that confirmed this view, that as pregnant girls they don't belong in school, but the school desk carried this message in the most subtle of ways, in a way that was hard to question because it is such a familiar and orienting cultural object in the world we call *school*.

The moral here is not that the chair-desk is an instrument of evil designed by Darth Vader to oppress innocent schoolchildren. The motive for the chair-desk is clearly efficiency and economy. The point, though, is that efficiency and economy end up trumping other factors either not thought of at all or not seen as important enough to accommodate. The chair-desk is not just an efficient design, but an expression of a mindset about what students and learning ought to be like.

So even the simple chair-desk gives us a heads up about the many ways that expressions of power, privilege, and presumption operate in the architecture of our everyday surroundings, the literature we read, the movies we attend, the television we watch, the clothing we wear and see others wearing, and endless other aspects of life. There is a game afoot here, broadly the game of hidden power, a game we live through but often do not know much about, very much in the spirit of the common saying that fish don't know anything about water.

There are, however, educational perspectives that try to awaken the sleepy citizen to the hidden games of power. One name for this agenda is *critical pedagogy*. Of many principal voices, perhaps the best known is the Brazilian educator Paulo Freire, author of *Pedagogy of the Oppressed* and other seminal works. The idea of critical pedagogy is that education should build a penetrating awareness of the ways in which literature, science, popular media, forms of governance, religions, and other aspects of society embody and express power, privilege, and presumption. In listening to rap music, reading Jane Austen, or watching the film *The Titanic*, we should, to be sure, reach for aesthetic engagement, arrive at some understanding of form and modes of expression, and so on. But we should also be asking questions like this: Who benefits here, and in what ways? Whose viewpoints and interests are represented and promoted? Whose viewpoints and interests are dismissed or marginalized?

Critical pedagogy is controversial. Sometimes it's criticized for going too far by fomenting animosity rather than thoughtful critical consideration. Sometimes it's criticized for not going far enough by substituting intellectualized discourse for social action. But whatever the challenges of striking a good balance, critical pedagogy certainly can reveal much about hidden games of power.

Let me round this out with some examples of how our favorite myths of challenging power figure in the media. Consider the movie *The Titanic*. Winner of eleven Oscars including Best Picture in 1998, the film was immensely popular. Many people I know felt it was not a very good film. I thought it was okay, but I didn't have any trouble understanding its Oscar power. Partly this was because I saw it in peculiar circumstances. I happened to be doing some educational work in Bogotá at the time, and viewing the film there made me acutely aware of how *American* a film it was.

To be sure, the Titanic was a British ocean liner, but the movie is all about how one individual of ordinary origins fights the system. Another Oscar-winning film, *Gladiator*, this time set in the Roman empire, has essentially the same theme. The American Western often celebrates the loner against the system. For a different genre, *Erin Brockovich* is the story of a single mother of three and paralegal who helped disclose a cover-up of industrial poisoning. These archetypal tales have a great appeal to the U.S. audience, indeed, to many audiences. In their better versions, I like them too.

But they are also laden with presumptions we ought to be more curious about: the individual as heroic and the system as corrupt, the individual or the small band as the agent of justice and righteousness in contrast with the sluggish futility and timidity of others, the individual or the small band as surprisingly powerful against all odds. How sound are those ideas? What kinds of justice do they promise and to whom? What paths to justice are marginalized? Who are the natural participants in such sagas and who finds it difficult to imagine himself or herself as a player?

How Games Hide

In the classic film *The Wizard of Oz*, the impressive version of the wizard is right up front: the giant head looming over Dorothy and her fellow travelers, the bursts of flame, the godlike voice. However, nosy Toto, poking around behind the curtain, shows us quite another scene, the real wizard a rather unprepossessing little fellow wielding the levers.

For hidden games of strategy, causality, inquiry, power, and other hidden games too, the story is almost the reverse. In front of the curtain, the wizardry is not so dramatic. The uninitiated who lack familiarity with the hidden games do not even see that anything special is going on. As to the initiated, often the veil of familiarity hides the wizardry from them. Remember how I was not aware of my own mathematical problem-solving practices? Likewise, a skilled baseball pitcher or poet or physicist may not be that aware of or articulate about the contributing components of the hidden game. They are just business as usual, second nature. In other words, hidden games are hidden in ways that invite neglect. That is why learning by wholes urges us to look for the hidden games and play them. And that is why it's worth asking: How do games hide?

I've counted at least five ways: *under the rug of simplicity, off the track of common sense, within the margins of "good enough," inside the cloak of the tacit*, and *beyond the horizon of readiness*. They are not completely separate, but neither are they completely the same. Here are a few words about each of them.

Under the Rug of Simplicity

The venerable TV game show *Let's Make a Deal* also is a good label for much of what goes on in conventional teaching-learning situations. Expressed from the learners' standpoint, the deal is: *You keep it straightforward, and we'll make an effort to learn it and achieve reasonable results and not complicate your life.* Such deals are not complicit private negotiations between individual teachers and their charges, but implicit in the whole system right up to the level of statewide or nationwide curriculum standards and the structure of testing. The reality is that surfacing hidden games makes things more complicated both for learners and teachers. As do other aspects of learning by wholes.

Science education is a good example. The simple layers get by far the most attention even though they involve the least real science, along these lines:

- Much of science education is given over to learning science facts.
- Of what's left, much is given over to learning and applying very specific models. For instance, students might learn the particular formula for how to calculate the time it takes for a body to fall a certain distance, as in the tower problem and hole problem from Chapter 4.
- With the time left over from that, sometimes students study entire modeling systems, for instance, the Newtonian story of velocity, acceleration, mass, and so on, which can be applied to modeling falling objects and all sorts of other things and gets closer to the hidden causal game.
- And beyond that, maybe there is a tiny bit of time left over to help learners think about scientific inquiry and their problem-solving strategies, so that they can deal with whole modeling systems by getting at the hidden strategic game.

In other words, the more scientific the story gets, the less of it you see. What a shame! The hidden games make things more provocative, creative, insightful, rich, and relevant . . . but in many settings *Arrrrgh! Too complicated!* trumps all of those.

Maybe that is because it can't be done. Maybe learners can't learn the whole games and especially not hidden games. But you see, they can, if we apply the principle of junior versions.

Off the Track of Common Sense

Another way important games hide is through departure from common sense. For example, one of our most powerful strategies for making sense of the world looks to people's intentional actions. Where did that tall building come from, or that clever bottle opener? Somebody made it that way.

This is common sense, but it is common sense uncommonly prone to overreach its boundaries. People tend to project intentions where there are not any. Remember the queen bee example from the hidden game of causal thinking, how people think the queen runs the hive, but she's really just a little DNA-programmed robot like the other bees. Or, looking to history, think about how wars happen. It's easy to suppose that they are all the plots of evil imperialists, but at least some of them come from unexpected and unwanted cycles of escalation. World War I is a common example, where a network of treaties pulled nation after nation into a quagmire of military confrontation.

The most notable and notorious example of projecting intentionality concerns Darwinian evolution. Speaking of war, today one rages between evolutionists respectful of the enormous evidence for a Darwinian account of Earth's biotic diversity and fundamentalists who advocate *intelligent design*. At one level, this is a dispute between science and religion. But, at another, it's a clash between an analytic stance overcoming the impulse toward intentional interpretations and the deeply rooted intentionality bias of the human mind. A frog, a platypus, a palm tree, or a fungus, in all their subtlety of form and survival tactics, *look* designed. The intelligent-design stance makes a powerful appeal to tendencies deep-coded in the human brain, even without the support of a particular theology.

There are endless other examples. Many elements of sophisticated causal reasoning are counterintuitive. Looking back to the hidden game of strategies, moves like thoroughly understanding the problem before trying to solve it run counter to a human impulse psychologists have called solution-mindedness. Looking back to games of inquiry, in reaching conclusions from experience we tend to take a few vivid exemplars as definitive, so attention to statistical sampling can seem convoluted.

Departure from common sense is a paradoxical signal. Sometimes departures from common sense are a red light to watch out for. But sometimes they are a green light toward better understanding. Time for another sports anecdote: My wife and I would occasionally play ping-pong, not terribly well but with good fun. Now, most novices hold the ping-pong paddle directly in their fist, as though shaking hands with it. Somewhere I read a tip about a better approach, laying your palm along one side of the paddle with your thumb gripping it from the other. The advantage lies in an easy switch between a forehand and a backhand. It felt hideously awkward for game after game, but I could soon feel the gain, and gradually the awkwardness turned into comfort and fluency.

The same kind of thing happens in a lot of learning. Sometimes what is to be learned feels wrong, generating a kind of visceral resistance. But the resistance is just transitional. The teaching-learning process needs to uncover the hidden game—not a red light here, just a bump in a road to somewhere worth going.

Within the Margins of "Good Enough"

Another place games hide is within the margins of "good enough." A longtime favorite example comes from the British poet and scholar of literature I. A. Richards. In his *Practical Criticism: A Study of Literary Judgment*, Richards wrote of the battle to get his university students to engage with poetry seriously. He logged a rogue's gallery of their difficulties. One was the tendency toward piecemeal interpretation. Asked to give an account of a poem, students would single out a few lines and tell a story about what the lines meant, sometimes quite a fanciful one. How, Richard would ask, does this fit with the rest of the poem? Often not at all, clashing with other lines and transforming the poem from a mystery into a muddle. But this did not seem to bother students very much. They would fiercely defend their piecemeal interpretations. For them, making sense of a few lines was "good enough" and the rest would fit somehow.

The syndrome of "good enough" comes up all over the place. Isn't it good enough to take the politician's speech at face value? Especially if he seems to be a regular guy you could have a beer with! Isn't it good enough if I argue my case with three points? Do I really have to review and rebut the clearly superficial view of the opposition? Isn't it good enough to say that heavy objects fall faster than light ones? Works for anvils and feathers!

New ideas generally aim to give a better account of things. However, learners may not see the need. Introducing new ideas in a compelling way is likely to involve not just elucidating the new ideas themselves, but reeducating learners' sense of what is "good enough." It's likely to involve encouraging them to get worried about what might seem to be minor discrepancies or secondary considerations. It's likely to involve making clearer what the new ideas are supposed to accomplish and why that might be worthwhile.

For instance, the experiment with big and little pieces of candle from earlier in this chapter upsets what seems to be a "good enough" explanation: Big objects sink and little objects float. When the big piece floats and the little piece sinks after switching beakers, "good enough" isn't good enough anymore, and the way toward understanding a deeper causal pattern beckons.

Inside the Cloak of the Tacit

Thank heavens for tacit knowledge! I walked down the stairway in ten seconds without a slip or a fall while figuring out what to have for lunch. The common aphorism that if we tried to think precisely about how we walked we would fall over our own feet is not entirely true, but it makes a point. We do not really know how we walk in the sense of explicit articulate knowledge. The same can be said for saying a word or sentence or holding a conversation. By and large, our knowledge about how to do that sort of thing is tacit. We speak more or less grammatically without reminding ourselves of the rules. We use tacit principles of conversational turn taking without having any reflective awareness of them.

Tacit knowledge is not always completely unconscious. In the family, in the workplace, in a supermarket we often have tacit understandings and expectations about "how things are done around here" that we could articulate if they came up. However, for the most part they operate at the level of habit without any need for deliberate attention. Recall here my story a couple of sections ago about mathematical problem-solving strategies, the ones that I did not know I had until I read the book by Polya.

Whether completely unconscious or only on the fringes of our awareness (the philosopher Michael Polanyi used the evocative term *peripheral awareness*), tacit knowledge is a powerful resource. If we had to manage explicitly all the knowledge we exercise tacitly, life would be a perpetual labyrinth of cumbersome calculations. Research shows that tacit intuitive ways of approaching problems often (not always!) prove more effective than studied deliberation. Guy Claxton summarizes the evidence in his lively *Hare Brain, Tortoise Mind*, and more recently Malcolm Gladwell has surveyed related turf in *Blink*.

That said, the virtues of the tacit sometimes turn into barriers for teachers and other mentors wanting to share their craft and understanding. As with my mathematical problem solving, people fairly skilled in an area generally do not know exactly what they do. Likewise for the hidden game of causal reasoning, people familiar with reasoning in science or economics or history are not so aware of the broad causal presumptions underlying the way they think about things.

Likewise for the hidden game of inquiry, every discipline has its own style. For instance, evidence looks different in mathematics and physics and history and literature, important in all, but its own idiosyncratic game in each. Yet almost never does instruction directly address the peculiar forms evidence takes. The smart and lucky learners pick it up from the context, but for many that is not enough. In general, the tacit character of expert knowledge is another way that hidden games hide. Surfacing the tacit becomes another part of uncovering the hidden game.

There is something of a controversy here. Some psychologists study a process called *tacit learning*, by which people pick up tacit knowledge by osmosis without explicit instruction. Some educators argue for osmosis as a better route than a tedious articulation of rules and principles. This is a complicated debate and not one to review thoroughly here, so I'll just make three points about how it looks to me. First, tacit learning is a real and well-documented phenomenon, no question about it. For instance, children learn their first languages that way, and we all absorb many aspects of "the way things are done around here" that way.

Second, it seems to me that tacit learning works best in settings saturated with the ideas and practices in question, for instance, children learning the language everyone around them is speaking. In less-saturated settings, many people miss the tacit game and remain marginal participants.

Third, surfacing the tacit certainly does not mean teaching a list of rules and saying "go thou and forever behave accordingly." To work well, it needs to involve plenty of authentic practice, putting the normally tacit game back under the surface where it does its job best, a submarine rather than a cruise ship, stealth rather than show.

The plot thickens and also darkens when we turn from the tacit knowledge of expertise to the tacit presumptions built into many aspects of society, the sorts of presumptions that people of privilege and power would generally prefer to stay at the submarine level and the sorts of presumptions that critical pedagogy and similar approaches force to the surface. No longer is the challenge of revealing the hidden game just technical. It becomes political. Added to the barriers of habit and routine are the barriers of discomfort and fear. Dare we shake the edifice, in which each of us has a place of some sort, albeit some much better places than others? Is instability the inevitable cost of insight, and, from a skeptical standpoint, can we expect anything after the revolution other than someone else's regime equally inequitable in its own way?

In any case, where one can get away with it, this is a path that the liberating course of education seems morally bound to attempt.

When done it is often overdone, but in many settings it is never done at all. Striking the generative balance is an invitation to the artist in every educator.

Beyond the Horizon of Readiness

What can kindergarten children reasonably attempt? As in the "what do you see that makes you think so" activity, kindergarten children certainly can talk about what's going on in a painting. One probably would not ask them to discuss the hidden power structures around them, not even with an example as familiar as the school desk. "Beyond the horizon of readiness" is another place where hidden games hide.

Our judgments about what learners of various ages and backgrounds are ready for is the entryway into a complex discipline, the study of human development. From an educational standpoint, perhaps the key concept in views of human development is *readiness*. Whether different models of development use the term *readiness* or not, they generally have to do with what the youngster or adult is ready to learn, which kinds of tasks and understandings are within reach, and which seem somehow beyond the horizon of the learner.

"Within reach" here has less to do with accumulating knowledge and more to do with mental stretch. One would hardly expect a student in the first semester of French to read Proust, but this is seen as essentially a matter of amassing knowledge, experience, and skill. In contrast, we would not ask the kindergarten child to think about the politics of the school desk because it's too much of a mental stretch. It represents a shift of level, attitude, dimension that we suspect the child would find difficult and disturbing.

It's challenging to map out the complexities of human development in any concise way. There are competing theories of child development and of adult development. They take conflicting stances on some important issues. For instance, some theories identify broad sweeping stages, where intellectual capability advances at more or less the same time across a wide front. During certain periods of a year or two, youngsters supposedly become broadly more capable with a range of activities from reasoning about mathematical concepts to understanding social situations from multiple perspectives. Other researchers maintain that human development is less sweeping, advancing within different areas of understanding and skill independently rather than across the whole mind at once.

Besides claims of that sort, investigators propose different kinds of causal mechanisms. A developmental advance might reflect jumps in brain function due to neurological development, or the acquisition of certain logical patterns with wide ramifications, or the accumulation of a knowledge base that passes a tipping point of richness, enabling a whole new range of understandings.

In addition, clever researchers and educators keep discovering that youngsters often prove more capable at earlier ages than they imagined before. Much depends on the use of familiar examples and ways of supporting the children's thinking so that they do not have to hold too much in memory at the same time. This is why I argued in Chapter 1 that constructing accessible versions of junior games was very much a trial-and-error process, a matter of beginning with one's best judgment, devising a first attempt, seeing how it goes, and making adjustments. It's hard to know for sure how ready any particular group is for such-and-such without constructing a version of such-and-such to try out.

So rather than step very far into the labyrinth of ideas about human development, let me just share two big ideas that seem particularly helpful across ages and stages and topics. The first is by far the most familiar, the notion of the *zone of proximal development* from the Russian psychologist Lev Vygotsky (1896–1934). Here's the very short version. Take, for example, everyday social behavior. Young children tend to be egocentric in a certain technical sense. They readily learn to follow many social rules, but they do not really see situations from the perspective of the other people involved. They do not recognize, for example, that someone might feel hurt by something they did or said. However, it's not that they are so far away from such sensitivities. A story, an explanation, a little bit of brainstorming, an invitation to think about the situation from Sally's or Alfred's perspective rather than their own may generate some real insights. What they fail to do spontaneously they can be led to do with support.

Where learners can perform well with help but not alone is their zone of proximal development. Not only is the zone where the learner is going, it's where the learner can be helped to go. The learner does not just slide forward into the next level of sophistication after a while. The learner climbs forward, by functioning occasionally in a more sophisticated way with whatever support is available. Sometimes this help is deliberate, the intervention of a mentor, a parent, a teacher. Sometimes the help is accidental, the impact of a television show or a storybook or the way older peers tend to interact. Either way, functioning in the zone of proximal development pulls the learner forward toward autonomous understanding and behavior at a new level.

The practical implication for the teaching-learning process is straightforward: Keep a little ahead of the learners but not too much. Don't let the learners just do what they can readily do without help. Raise the bar, provide the help, and then gradually fade away the help as they develop the capability to manage that level of sophistication themselves. It's like training wheels on bicycles. And it even has a name in the literature: scaffolding. In the world of builders, a scaffold is a temporary structure designed to facilitate erecting the permanent structure. The same idea applies in the world of human development and learning.

The second very general idea about human development that I'd like to sketch comes from developmentalist Robert Kegan, a colleague at the Harvard Graduate School of Education. It's called subject-object theory. Here again, social perspective-taking provides a good example. Despite their egocentricity, children deal with other children and adults all the time. But the perspectives of others are not part of their view of the world. Indeed, they don't really differentiate between their own perspective and the perspectives of others. In a sense, they don't know anything about perspectives because they only have one, their own. They are *subject to* perspectives rather than seeing their own and others' perspectives as objects that they can compare and contrast. Development into a full awareness of their own and others' perspectives involves a subject-object shift: What they were previously subject to now becomes a world of objects they can think about. Until the shift, the next game hides in the fog of *subject to*.

Almost any sort of learning can be looked at this way. It's essentially a version of surfacing the tacit. Let's take something as mundane as learning the refinements of grammar. Normally, we simply speak the way we learned as a child. We are *subject to* those habits of speech and entirely unaware of grammar as such. When we are taught some rules of officially correct speech, over time we become aware of the grammar of our speech as an object, as something that we can control and realign to new standards. To be sure, this process often advances without sufficient respect for ways of speaking natural to various ethnic groups. That acknowledged, what's involved is the sometimes awkward and painful process of a subject-object shift.

For a more sophisticated example, Einstein's theory of relativity invites us into another subject-object shift. Time à la classical physics is a very limited conception, simply a parameter that tells us how far along a process is. We are subject to this ordinary conception of time and so find it difficult to get our heads around a relativistic conception of time, which bizarrely sees time and space as interchangeable in certain ways. This is a subject-object shift that most of us have not made, indeed that most of us for ordinary purposes have no particular reason to make, but it is one essential for a sophisticated understanding of the universal clockwork.

Like Vygotsky's zone of proximal development, Kegan's notion of the subject-object shift has broad implications for the support of learning. It says: Think about what is to be learned in terms of the objects that come into view, objects to which learners were previously simply subject. Indeed, the zone of proximal development and the subject-object shift weave into a single scenario. It is the next available subject-object shift that makes up the zone of proximal development. The new objects define a horizon of curiosity and revealing threshold experiences as we uncover the hidden game.

WONDERS OF LEARNING

UNCOVER THE HIDDEN GAME

I wonder how I can uncover the hidden game for learners—really games plural. When I think about it, I begin to see hidden games of strategy, causal thinking, inquiry, power, and more. I might reveal these to learners through examples and discussion or point learners in the right direction and ask them what they see.

I wonder how I can treat hidden games accessibly, with learners feeling excited and empowered rather than burdened. I may need to keep things simple at first with very junior versions. I could awaken curiosity and appeal to growing competence. I could encourage self-management, not just good moves.

I wonder how I can get past what learners usually see to reveal the hidden games. Learners often just see outcomes—conclusions, findings, final copy—missing how the game is played to get there. I could focus them on process. Learners often play the role of spectators rather than participants. I could make them participants. The "rules of the game" often aren't explored and discussed. I could help to surface the rules.

I wonder how I can find the safety and courage to uncover sensitive hidden games, for instance, the games of power that permeate society. I could choose my battles by focusing on issues that are revealing but not so sensitive that they make trouble. I could have students study other settings that mirror our own but provide some distance and detachment.

I wonder how I can determine where the hidden games are hiding. I might bear in mind some typical hiding places: under the rug of simplicity, off the track of common sense, within the margins of "good enough," inside the cloak of the tacit, and beyond the horizon of readiness.

6

Learn from the Team

I'VE NEVER PLAYED BASEBALL ALL BY MYSELF AND NEITHER HAS ANYONE ELSE. No one but Superman could do this! From the pitcher's mound, he hurls the ball toward home plate. With the ball in the air, he super-speeds home, picks up the bat, and takes a swing at it. Let's say he connects; after all, he's Superman. The ball soars into the air, and Superman races toward the outfield, which given his superswing at the ball could be very far out indeed. He makes it to, let's say, the North Pole just ahead of the ball and catches the ball. He's flied himself out.

This image of baseball as a solo performance is certainly eso-teric, but something just about as bizarre happens all the time in many settings of group learning such as schools, professional work-shops, and religious instruction. The learner functions "solo." People are supposed to learn alone, even though several other people are sit-ting within a few feet of them. They are supposed to spend most of their time reading and listening rather than interacting. They are not encouraged to look at other learners' work, certainly not to copy it, but not even to critique it or help with it.

The game goes rather differently in most informal settings. When people learn to play baseball, they generally learn together, watch-ing one another and helping one another. When people learn various card games, they learn them from one another with lively interaction. When you acquire your first pet, maybe you get tips from a friend, an uncle, and the pet shop owner. When you learn to ride a bicycle, chances are someone is running along beside you, helping you to balance. As a broad generalization, everyday learning treats the building of knowledge, skill, and understanding as a collective enterprise. Which gives us another of the seven principles of learning by wholes: *Learn from the team . . . and the other teams.*

Just to be clear, when you "learn from the team," what's being learned does not have to be a team activity at all, nor does it have to be competitive. Learn from the team is just a loose metaphor. People can learn such generally solo activities as how to ride a bicycle or how to take care of a pet from the team, the team being whatever mix of friends and neighbors can offer some help here and there along the way.

Also, it's not just those close to one that can help. In many ways it's "the other team": strangers one can watch, sometimes competitors against whom to pit a personal-best effort, sometimes even people who are not handling the matter at hand very well. Not only might they learn from their mistakes, others can learn from their mistakes!

There is a very useful concept that puts some order to all this. It's the idea of *participation structures*. The phrase gives us a name for how activities get organized through roles and responsibilities.

Let's ponder the participation structure of a very conventional classroom. Teacher and text function as the principal sources of information, with little coming from the students. Teacher and text also are the principal sources of activities. Interaction occurs principally between each individual student and the teacher, who evaluates work and offers feedback. Interchanges among students are tenuous, a matter of hearing what others have to say during the occasional whole-class discussions. This is a participation structure, but it's a sparse one, primarily exercising the learner-teacher relationship and not making much of the other potential relationships in the room.

In contrast, much richer participation structures appear in many classrooms and beyond. In studio learning, art students daily see a great deal of what the other students are doing, and talk about it. In a strategy called pair problem solving, learners work in pairs to help each other think about their problem-solving process. In communities of practice, professionals bootstrap their own skills by learning the craft from one another, often in very informal ways. In a mentoring relationship, the mentor interacts one-on-one with the learner for a nuanced exchange of information and ideas in both directions. All of these are different participation structures for learning from the team.

So how does learning from the team help to advance knowledge, understanding, and skill? One way to look at it celebrates how rich participation structures can serve the other principles of learning by wholes:

Play the whole game. Often learners new to an activity or an area of knowledge cannot play the whole game by themselves. However, with the help of others more experienced, they can participate, initially on the edges and then moving toward the center.

Make the game worth playing. The social interactions and the assumption of responsibility for particular roles in a group generate engagement.

Work on the hard parts. Other participants can be valuable sources of information about handling the hard parts, either from the learner observing what they do or from their direct counsel and coaching.

Play out of town. Simply working with others provides a little bit of playing out of town, because people approach things differently, sometimes very differently.

Uncover the hidden game. By looking at others and hearing from others while not completely involved in the game oneself, one can sometimes more readily see hidden games at work. Discussion with others often focuses on the hidden game of strategy.

Learn the game of learning. Both the present chapter and the next, which takes up this theme directly, give examples where participation structures foster understanding and management of one's own learning process.

Of course the devil is in the details. A social setting does not help newcomers to play the whole game if the newcomers are not welcomed.

It does not help to make the game worth playing if rivalry and backbiting overwhelm camaraderie and collaboration. It does not help learners inclined to slack off unless clear roles and responsibilities draw them in and keep them active. We need some art and craft to make the most of *learn from the team . . . and the other teams.*

A Social View of Learning

A social view of learning has many offspring but certainly one father, the Russian psychologist Lev Vygotsky mentioned in Chapter 5. Vygotsky explored themes around cognition and society, language as a symbolic tool, how language supports thinking, cognitive development as fostered by social interactions, and more. One of his most familiar concepts we've already celebrated, the *zone of proximal development*, the idea that people learn by performing with social support just ahead of where they can manage by themselves. This brings into play another insight from Vygotsky, *social scaffolding*.

Thinking and learning always develop in a sociocultural context. We may think of problem solving as very much "in the head," but usually it gets considerable support from interpersonal interactions (conversation, mentoring, critiquing), group enterprises (teamwork, professional organizations, projects), and cultural artifacts (language, computers, writing, desks, books). Under the name of *activity theory*, scholars have analyzed how human enterprise unfolds within sociocultural *activity systems*. Remember, for instance, the highly social clusters of activity around parenting or plumbing or playing pool. Developmentally, internal episodes of thinking are best seen as internalizations of processes originally much more overt in conversation and physical action. Also, even when relatively internal, they still depend on socially transmitted tools such as language.

Let's pick a distinctly abstract example to underscore the point. Mathematical thinking and learning sounds like a thoroughly in-the-head solo enterprise. However, it involves induction into a highly social context of mathematical discourse. What counts as an interesting problem gets defined in considerable part by the community, where ideas thrive or die through discussion, collaboration, and critique. None of this denies that mathematicians spend a fair amount of time off in corners thinking with a pencil and a piece of paper (or these days, perhaps a computer workbench like Mathematica), but such solo episodes are situated in larger webs of social endeavor.

Situated cognition has become a key phrase signifying how effective thought and action depend on adapting to and capitalizing on particular sociocultural settings. Likewise, *situated learning* has become a key phrase signifying how meaningful learning requires an authentic context of social endeavor. The situated perspective offers a sharp critique of conventional schooling. As touched on earlier, routine patterns of interaction among teachers and learners do not really provide a very supportive structure compared with, say, good apprenticeship or mentoring relationships in collaborative home or work settings. School learning is not typically situated in authentic sociocultural practices. School math has very little to do with real mathematical inquiry. It's a pile of isolated skills, *elementitis* again. Likewise, the school version of history often has little to do with historical understanding or historical inquiry. It's a bag of information—names and dates and official stories of how things supposedly happened. Learners aren't playing the whole game.

Sometimes advocacy for situated learning seems to go too far. Sometimes ardent champions of the sociocultural perspective seem to be urging that general rather than situated knowledge is essentially useless and that there is no place for the general skills of thinking or learning or abstract notational systems. An amusing flash point for much of the debate is the famous cottage cheese story originally told by Jean Lave in her book *Cognition in Practice*.

An acute observer of situated cognition, Lave discussed how a member of a Weight Watchers group solved the problem of finding three-quarters of two-thirds of a cup of cottage cheese. The person measured out two-thirds of a cup, patted it into a circle, crisscrossed it with two lines like a pizza, and took away a quarter. This solution capitalized on the particular affordances of the circumstances—the cup at hand, the soft character of cottage cheese—with no need to remember the picky details of fractions arithmetic. It contrasts with a generic mathematical approach: $3/4 \times 2/3$, multiplying numerator and denominator yields $6/12$, which reduces to $1/2$, so take half a cup.

Champions of the situated view laud the clever contextual turn of the solution, emphasizing how it demonstrates the subtle particularity of adaptive behavior. This challenges our strong assumptions about the utility of very general and abstract notational systems. Critics in counterpoint ask what you do when you don't happen to be dealing with cottage cheese; multiplication of fractions handles any situation, however materially obdurate.

The most ardent advocates also tend to idealize enculturation as a mode of learning. No question, it can be powerful. However, it can also induct people into patterns of narrow and vicious thinking. The development of prejudice and discrimination plainly is a highly social learning process. Social learning can also reinforce mediocrity, as for instance when members of the labor force are "taught" by the group not to work too hard so that they will not end up revealing how productive people can really be.

Personally, I would like to have it all. I would like the clever adaptability of taking advantage of the particular affordances of the situation. But I would also like the general reach of arithmetic. I certainly want the power of socially and culturally situated learning. But we need to acknowledge that sometimes it can foster prejudice and mediocrity. Maybe the bottom line is a bit of irony: The advantages of situated learning in its strongest forms are . . . situated!

The point remains that considerable conventional learning is starkly impoverished from a sociocultural standpoint. It neither leverages community to forward the cause of learning nor fosters the development of skills and understandings meaningfully situated in disciplinary or other sociocultural enterprises. Of courses, this is the picture at its worst. In a number of ways in a number of settings, things can look much better. Let's examine some participation structures that put our social and cultural nature to work for the sake of learning.

Pair Problem Solving

Here is a problem to think about:

> Bill, Judy, and Sally have the occupations of teacher, plumber, and
> teamster, but not necessarily in that order. Bill is shorter than Judy
> but taller than Sally. The plumber is the tallest and the teamster is
> the shortest. What is Judy's occupation?

This problem is an exercise to foster systematic reasoning and its
management. However, the setting for the problem is not a person solo.
You can certainly figure it out by yourself, but ideally there is both a
problem solver and a listener. Here is one way the action might unfold.

> The problem solver sets out to mark down some of the relationships
> using inequality signs. The listener prompts, "Okay. So you're using
> the inequality signs here?"
>   The result is a more detailed explanation from the problem
> solver of the inequalities written down. Later on the problem solver
> falls silent, and the listener asks, "What are you thinking now?"
>   The problem solver asserts that Judy is the plumber and says that
> he is going to write "teacher" in between "teamster" and "plumber."
>   "Why?" the listener asks, even though the problem solver seems
> to have solved the problem. The listener insists on hearing the
> reasons spelled out.

This is a brief excerpt from Jack Lochhead's *Thinkback*, illustrating *think aloud pair problem solving* (pair problem solving, for short).
This widely used social learning technique was introduced in 1979
by Arthur Whimbey and Jack Lochhead in their *Problem Solving and
Comprehension*. It's a way of getting learners to help one another, but
with a curious twist. The idea is not so much for students to offer
direct assistance as it is for students to help others to become aware of
their own thinking and learning.

The pair problem solving strategy suits many kinds of learning. In
Thinkback, Lochhead offers examples from puzzle problems, dealing

with graphic organizers, writing aloud, memory work, concept maps, and knowledge as design (an approach to learning I wrote about in a book of the same name). Lochhead introduces a twist on the classic pair problem solving he and Whimbey debuted years before. He describes *thinkback* as the use of the think aloud pair problem solving strategy "with the added vision of video playback." The idea is to employ pair problem solving to create a kind of mental movie of the mind at work. The result is a *thought image*. Students are urged to hold these thought images in mind as a way of learning about thinking and learning and improving the process.

So how does pair problem solving work? Our opening story illustrated the basic pattern. Learners pair off. One learner takes the role of problem solver and the other the role of listener. There is a problem at hand, which the problem solver tackles, thinking aloud in the process. The listener listens with the goal of maintaining clarity about the problem solver's process. When the problem solver falls silent, the listener prompts for information. When the problem solver makes moves the listener does not fully understand, the listener asks for explanations. After the first problem, the two change roles, the problem solver becoming the listener and the listener becoming the problem solver.

The interactions in the Bill-Judy-Sally problem show how the listener does not give advice but instead prompts for explanations. The temptation to give advice is very strong. People get better at pair problem solving over time, and not to give advice is one of the most important things that they learn about the listener role. On the problem-solver side, many people take to thinking aloud right away, but some find it awkward at first. A key injunction is to avoid "stealth thinking," that is, don't let yourself fall silent. This skill also develops over time. In the process, the learners gain much more perspective on and management of how they think.

But why do we need the listener at all? Why not simply ask the problem solver to sit down and talk themselves through the problem aloud to get a better hold on the process?

For one thing, stealth thinking is a big trap without prompting by the listener. Problem solvers tend to get absorbed in the problems and end up paying little attention to their own thinking strategies. For another, just because you are thinking aloud does not mean that you are explaining to yourself. The listener's job is to keep the problem solver not only speaking but explaining: "Why this move?" "What do you want out of that?" "Are you getting what you wanted?" "So you changed directions, why did you do that?"

Let's examine pair problem solving from the standpoint of learning by wholes: How does it contribute to the six principles of learning by wholes besides *learn from the team?*

Pair problem solving is not so suited to *play the whole game* all the way through, because whole games typically unfold over considerable periods with many different sorts of social interactions involved. However, pair problem solving fits *work on the hard parts* very well. It's a way of concentrating on challenging aspects of an area of learning, with the cognitive mirror of the listener providing a kind of moment-to-moment feedback that would be very difficult to set up otherwise. Additionally, *make the game worth playing* gains by having a companion in the struggle as one tackles hard parts, a companion with whom you will soon switch roles to keep things even.

As to *uncover the hidden game*, the listener's questions and the problem solver's answers create a kind of cognitive mirror that reveals the problem solver's process to both. Their partnership and their switching of roles add up to some *playing out of town*, as each gets inside the head of the other.

Finally, the entire enterprise supports *learn the game of learning*: As learners become skilled at pair problem solving, they become much more self-aware and self-managing. So it is that the participation structure of pair problem solving serves the multiple agendas of learning by wholes.

Studio Learning

Recently I was having a conversation about studio learning with a friend. With considerable charm, she announced one of its most important characteristics: "No hand turkeys!"

You may remember hand turkeys. Almost everyone in U.S. schools has drawn them at one time or another. When Thanksgiving comes around, turkeys are on the agenda of the classroom as well as on the dinner table.

So how do you draw a hand turkey? One way is to put your hand down on a piece of paper at an appropriate angle and trace around it. You get most of the turkey right there and can easily fill in a head and a couple of feet. Fun enough, but not really what we want out of art. It's a good motto—"No hand turkeys!"

The very name of studio learning makes it sound like a niche enterprise, something for art and art alone; and to be sure, studio learning finds its natural home in art, but not only there. Recently my colleagues Lois Hetland, Ellen Winner, Shirley Veenema, and Kimberly M. Sheridan completed a study of high-quality studio learning at the secondary level. Their observations and findings appear in *Studio Thinking: The Real Benefits of Arts Education*. I was fascinated by the strong patterns of teaching and learning they revealed, not only for the sake of young artists but beyond.

One telling point concerned the organization of the experience. The authors identified three studio structures that promote the development of a sophisticated and refined craft: the *demonstration-lecture, students-at-work*, and *critique*. Often, they found these followed one another, beginning with the demonstration-lecture, moving into a long period of students-at-work, and rounding out with a process of critique. Sometimes more complicated interweaving occurred. In any case, what stood out for me was the highly social character of this model of teaching and learning.

In the typical demonstration-lecture, the instructor takes a few minutes to introduce some idea or technique along with a studio assignment. The demonstration-lecture foregrounds explanation and modeling, not only "these are the ideas" but "this is what it looks like to do it." The episode is usually relatively short, leaving plenty of time for students-at-work. Moreover, the practices introduced feed into application right now, not overnight or next week, a feature that helps to focus the learners' attention.

Then comes students-at-work. I suppose the cynical image of this would be the instructor heading out to the nearest Starbucks for an hour while the students labor, but that is not the plot at all. From the standpoint of *learning from the team . . . and the other teams*, there are two important features. First of all, remembering that the instructor is part of the team too, the instructor circulates all the time providing individualized guidance, a far cry from the sage on the stage model. The authors of *Studio Thinking* write about the double agenda of the instructor, who bears in mind the general ideas and techniques introduced during the demonstration-lecture, but also the development of each individual student. The students-at-work period makes room for the instructor to respond in a nuanced and individualized way to work in progress, nudging, prodding, and cajoling to help each student advance.

The second feature is a simple but tremendously important characteristic of this stage: Students can readily see one another's work and way of working. Of course, they take different approaches to the studio assignment, but each can learn something from the others' pathways.

Even more opportunities to learn from one another emerge during the third studio structure for learning: the critique. Here again as with the demonstration-lecture, the learners come together. However, this time it's not a matter of the instructor showing and explaining and the students watching and listening. Much more of a conversation ensues as students comment on one another's work, the instructor offers remarks, and a general stocktaking focuses on how matters developed, where they might go, and what the further needs are. One important effect of all this, the authors argue, is the development of "studio habits of mind," including persistence, envisioning, expression, observation, reflection, exploration, and more.

Certainly the participation structure of studio learning has some attractive features. Why don't we see it more often across the disciplines? One reason relates to the theme of this entire book: Studio learning is very whole-game oriented. Most of formal education is not. The rhythm, style, character, and energy of studio learning all take advantage of the whole-game character of producing works of art.

But there is a second more specific reason that we do not see as much studio learning as we might: Crafting works of art particularly lends itself to the "plain sight" studio experience. Visible display is, after all, the point of works of visual art. Many meaningful products that learners in other areas might craft—mathematical conjectures and proofs, poems, scientific explanations, historical interpretations—are simply not as automatically and intrinsically visible.

Perhaps the answer to this side of the dilemma is not to settle for business as usual, but to make things more visible than they normally are. Imagine a classroom where students work in small groups to do their math on big white boards, with browsing around encouraged. Imagine a setting where students studying a controversial episode in history post their arguments on the wall, written on large Post-its, so that a collective sense of the evidence begins to emerge. Key to such scenarios, and common to the studio experience, is that they do not just make work visible, they make working visible. In addition to final results, steps along the way become shared resources for further thought and action.

With all this in mind, how do studio learning and its kin score with the various elements of learning by wholes? *Learn the whole game* is the focus of the entire enterprise. That and the way the studio model puts newly introduced ideas and practices to use immediately assist with *make the game worth playing*. Troubleshooting by the circulating instructor, the opportunity to see one another's work, and well-chosen studio tasks all serve to *work on the hard parts*. The visibility of students' ongoing works as well as the discourse around them feeds *play out of town* and *uncover the hidden game*. Finally, the instructor's rich interactions with the individual students in full awareness of their diverse learning trajectories help them to *learn the game of learning*.

Of course, such settings are not always idyllic. Lois Hetland, first author of the study of studio learning, told me about a situation where the feedback a student got from a studio instructor (not one of the instructors in the study) was, "The only thing that will help this work is gesso."

Gesso is a plaster-like substance used to cover a surface in preparation for painting. In other words: Cover it up! Needless to say, such demeaning and demoralizing wit is not helpful counsel for any learner. Well, we should be warned: Any participation structure can be misused or thinly used. That said, the general shape of studio learning invites rich social exchanges that can advance skill and understanding.

Communities of Practice

Would you look for an anthropologist on the employee roster of Xerox Corporation? Probably not. But you might find some after all. Julian Orr was an anthropologist working for Xerox in the 1980s. His mission was to take a close look at how the Xerox technical representatives actually spent their time. He examined not just the hours tinkering with machines but also the minutes hanging out around coffee and snacks.

Julian Orr discovered something quite provocative. Between-the-cracks activity focused not so much on politics and sports as on how to repair Xerox machines. The technical representatives would ask one another questions about different challenges they had encountered. They would share war stories about how to handle the sometimes balky machines. The informal exchange of knowledge turned out to be tremendously important in both getting machines repaired and elevating the skills of the technical representatives.

This was just one example of a particularly provocative and suggestive participation structure, a *community of practice*. In recent years, communities of practice have received considerable attention in the world of business and beyond. In a community of practice, participants share a common mission: repairing Xerox machines, playing music, discussing old movies on the Internet, investing in the stock market. Social contact among them creates opportunities for the exchange of craft. Participants naturally talk about what's most on their mind, what they need to know today or tomorrow, or what they found out yesterday or the day before that seemed especially helpful.

Considerable learning occurs spontaneously, and it targets the here and now, not some long-term agenda that will reach realization in a year or five years.

A community of practice offers an attractive vision of collegial collaboration among people already experienced in a particular activity. What about the fate of newbies? Do they get shut out? No, and scholars of such informal learning processes have identified the way in. Jean Lave and Etienne Wenger in their book *Situated Learning* described the critical mechanism of *legitimate peripheral participation*.

This phrase is certainly a mouthful, but each word tells an important part of the story. In many communities of practice, from midwifery to technical crafts, newbies begin on the periphery. They make no attempt to tackle the hard problems, but watch and help out with simpler aspects of the enterprise—peripheral participation. But their presence is not disdained. Their contributions are welcome as assistance and respected as part of the process of induction into the full craft—*legitimate* peripheral participation. Over time, they become more sophisticated in their craft and take on more responsibility.

Communities of practice and legitimate peripheral participation are kinds of learning that bridge an important gap left by formal training toward a particular practice. Although formal training can provide an important launching pad, it typically never comes close to capturing important aspects of the day-to-day practice. Endless nuances about what goes wrong in this or that situation, how to handle this or that special case, where the resources can be found for an unusual situation, or who to consult about it are not part of that training and indeed cannot readily become part, because they arise at odd moments in highly contextual ways.

Ideas related to communities of practice and legitimate peripheral participation can be applied to students learning in formal settings. For instance, one could certainly view the studio learning process discussed in the previous section as a kind of community of practice.

In addition, communities of practice are relevant to the learning of educators. One useful pattern involves teachers looking closely at student work together with the help of simple protocols and thinking about how to improve their practice. A good general source for this is *Looking Together at Student Work* from Tina Blythe, David Allen, and Barbara Schieffelin Powell.

Here is a personal case in point. For some time, my colleagues and I have been developing a program called Visible Thinking. The program invites teachers to infuse instruction in the disciplines with a variety of thinking routines and cultural attitudes that foster deeper thinking and learning. An example appeared in Chapter 5: Debbie O'Hara leading her kindergarten class in the *explanation game* around a work of art. Besides Visible Thinking as students experience it, we also needed to figure out how teachers could learn the approach. We tackled the challenge by setting up small, intense communities of practice with some added structure—structured communities of practice, one might say.

These minicommunities are called study groups. They include about seven or eight teachers, ideally representing different grades and different disciplinary interests because this helps to break down typical boundaries and build teacher colleagueship. They meet on a regular basis, once a week initially and later perhaps once every two weeks. They collectively undertake several kinds of tasks such as studying background information and learning new techniques.

Most important, participants share their craft about how particular efforts play out in their individual classrooms, using certain conversational protocols to guide the exchange. One of the most important of these protocols is called LAST, which stands for Looking At Student Thinking.

LAST begins with the presenting teacher bringing a sample of student work to the group—say, three or four concept maps that different students made representing a particular topic, or prints of digital photographs of a whiteboard representing a class discussion. The goal of LAST is to tease out signs of student thinking in the artifacts and reflect on how the learning experience went and how it might go better. After distributing the materials, the teacher begins by describing briefly how the activity that produced them went. There is a brief period during which the other participants can ask questions for clarification.

Then something unusual happens: The presenting teacher steps back and simply listens. The rest continue to examine the students' work, describing the samples, moving on to speculating about students' thinking, generating questions that might be good to pursue, and finally discussing the implications for teaching and learning. Silent through all this, the presenting teacher steps forward again at the end, commenting on what stood out from the conversation.

Such a methodical procedure is a far cry from the Xerox technical representatives' chitchat around coffee. Why structure the process so much? First of all, there is also time for informal exchange. Second, the teachers typically do not have much contact time with one another in the natural course of events, so it's important that the time for the meetings work especially well.

Third, experience taught us that free-form conversation around student work tended to run into systematic roadblocks. For instance, what happens if the presenting teacher participates fully throughout? One consequence is a rain of further questions of clarification directed at the presenting teacher, who responds in detail. So getting clearer about the situation ends up consuming most of the group time. And in the end it's a futile quest: The other participants will never understand the fine grain of the presenting teachers' personal teaching experience. Additionally, when the presenting teacher continues as the focus of the conversation, this draws attention away from a close examination of the students' work. Fewer insights result about the character and quality of the students' thinking expressed through that work. Finally, asking the presenting teacher to step aside and listen removes any natural defensive impulses from the conversation for a while.

How does legitimate peripheral participation figure in these study groups? Not in the most straightforward way, because typically most of the members of the study group are new to Visible Thinking. Initially, a group is guided either by a person within the school who is taking special responsibility for Visible Thinking or by a veteran who participated in the study-group process previously. Even so, as the groups develop momentum, a kind of natural sifting and sorting into more proactive and less proactive participants occurs. Some particularly bold teachers step forward early, trying things and bringing in student work. Others hang back a bit, see how things go, learn from the others, and then give it a try.

In some cases, we deliberately have seeded a group with two or three veterans, who help bring along participants new to Visible Thinking. In addition, as a matter of policy, people who are not participating in any study group are always welcome to attend at their convenience, to get a sense of what is going on, and to try something in their classrooms if they are so inclined. Eventually, some of them will form study groups of their own. In this and other ways, the process fosters a looser schoolwide community of practice above the level of the intense study groups.

This work around Visible Thinking offers just one example of how the dynamics of communities of practice can be leveraged to advance learning. It also cautions that a fully spontaneous community of practice around the water cooler or coffee pot cannot always be relied upon to do the job. Meeting times, conversational protocols, and other aspects may be needed to support a rich exchange of craft.

Turning back to the general theme of learning by wholes, how do communities of practice at their best speak to its several elements? As to *play the whole game*, such collegial exchanges occur most readily around a whole-game-in-motion, whether it is repairing Xerox machines or teaching or something else. *Make the game worth playing* gains from participants' genuine interest in their craft and the social support of the group. *Work on the hard parts* is almost automatic, because the hard parts come forward in the conversation as areas of concern. The different experiences and perspectives in the group automatically generate a measure of *play out of town*. As people discuss their approaches and rationales, to some extent they *uncover the hidden game*. And finally, the community of practice itself is a setting where participants can *learn the game of learning*.

Cross-Age Tutoring

Boy 1: I have a little girl and her name is Kathy and I teach math to her. She didn't do too well at first, but now she's getting up there. When she gets her work done, I take her out and let her play what she wants to for about five minutes and then she settles down and works good.

    Boy 2: Well, I have a little girl too and I let her do what she wants for a few minutes but then she starts messing around when I'm trying to teach her and then when I turn my back, she's gone.

    Boy 3: Well, maybe you can pick up some jokes. I don't know any right off, but maybe you could make up some. There's a boy in our class who's pretty interested in math and he teaches. He gives the child jokes and this gets him interested in math.

This excerpt from Dennie Briggs's *A Class of Their Own* gives a quick picture of twelve-year-olds discussing their teaching of six-year-olds. An English despot might not be entirely pleased with their grammar, and an education expert might wonder whether jokes are just the right way to rivet young learners' attention, but even so, these twelve-year-olds are seriously involved in and concerned about the learning of their much-younger peers. This is one brief glimpse into the world of cross-age tutoring, another participation structure through which we can help one another to learn.

Adults tutoring youngsters is nothing new, but it is one of the most powerful modes of instruction we know . . . when done right. Stanford professor Mark Lepper and colleagues have conducted extensive investigations of expert adult-child tutoring. Adults with a good sense of the craft select problems to pose an approachable challenge (zone of proximal development again), guide with questions and hints rather than direct advice and feedback, encourage self-awareness and self-management, frame errors and difficulties as opportunities for good learning, and always provide enough subtle support so that the learner succeeds to some degree with the problem. The effect of this is to serve both emotional and cognitive needs. The results can be truly impressive, with learners advancing dramatically in both attitude and capability.

If society could afford and find a one-on-one expert adult tutor for every child, the impact would be quite amazing! But of course, both the affording and the finding are utopian quests. Segue then to Plan B, where with a certain amount of training and support, children take responsibility for tutoring other children. This is second-best to expert adult tutors, of course . . . well, actually, maybe not, considering the impact on the student tutors as well as the tutees.

The basic idea of cross-age tutoring comes with its name: Older students tutor younger students one-on-one. The basic logic of cross-age tutoring is just as transparent. Learning can thrive on individual attention. Given the limited resources of public schooling and the limited availability of expert adult tutors, cross-age tutoring is one way to provide younger learners with a measure of individual attention that would be hard to manage in any other way.

Moreover, the advantages suggested for cross-age tutoring go well beyond individual attention. In some cases, it seems that the tutor, just a few years older than the tutee, has a particularly good perspective on the younger peer's mindset and confusions, as well as a knack for establishing a good nonthreatening rapport. Perhaps the most natural concern is that cross-age tutoring takes inappropriate advantage of the tutors. On the contrary, it's generally good for the tutors. On the academic front, they have to polish their own understanding in order to accomplish the tutoring, playing out the familiar saying that the best way to learn is to teach. But the benefits to the tutors go beyond academic advancement. They are learning responsibility, empathy, and caring.

The teacher plays a tremendously important although less conventional role in all this, organizing and monitoring the process. Details are important. Peer tutoring seems to work best when it has a cross-age character, not the more-advanced kids helping the less-advanced kids in the same class, at least not in a formal tutoring relationship. Initial sessions go better when they are relatively short, twenty minutes or so. Tutoring does not come entirely naturally to the older children. They need a little toolbox of tricks and moves that they build over time with one another's help and the teacher's help. Preparation and debriefing are important, as in the opening example above. Furthermore, the teacher needs to exercise thoughtful consideration about pairing people up. Who needs attention? Where are the natural matches? What are the envisioned benefits to the particular tutor as well as the tutee?

What kinds of students make good tutors? The obvious answer, "the smart ones," is not particularly on the mark according to Dennie Briggs. After all, the age gap between tutor and tutee in a well-chosen match means that the tutor will be much more on top of the content anyway. A tutor who has found an area troublesome may be in a particularly good position to help a younger peer with the same woes. Finally, the tutors' efforts to get the story straight are likely to boost their own understanding and confidence.

Yet another obvious criterion for good tutors, "the well-behaved ones," also seems off center. Students who are bored and restless can find an engaging focus in their tutoring roles. Students who are rebellious can discover a settling influence in their responsibilities. Indeed, Briggs suggests that the most critical quality is wanting to give it a try. Smart or not so smart, well behaved or not so well behaved, those students that find themselves attracted to the idea for whatever reason have a considerable leg up on success.

Does it always work well? Of course not. There are many particular puzzles and problems that leave teachers with significant trouble-shooting to do. But does it basically work? This is the bottom-line question for any such pattern of practice, and the answer seems to be yes. For example, Stanford researchers conducted an elaborate study comparing four different approaches to improving instruction: cross-age tutoring, computer-assisted instruction, reduction of classroom size, and increased instructional time from adult teachers. Cross-age tutoring proved to be the most effective of the four. Moreover, cross-age tutoring was overwhelmingly more cost effective than increasing instructional time from adults or reducing class size, approaching a quarter of the cost.

What are the benefits of cross-age tutoring for learning by wholes? Here it's important to consider both the tutee and the tutor because the pictures are somewhat different. Taking the tutee first, the tutee is not necessarily encountering more *play the whole game* than in conventional instruction. This depends entirely on the focus of the tutoring, which may be routine aspects of arithmetic with *elementitis* in full bloom. However, the tutorial interaction is likely to engage young learners more than business as usual—*make the game worth playing*. As to *work on the hard parts*, the one-on-one format of cross-age tutoring makes this natural. A certain measure of *play out of town* and *uncover the hidden game* comes as a natural consequence of the cross-age relationship. After all, to a six-year-old, a twelve-year-old is very much out of town and is likely to have a better sense of the ins and outs of the game. However, this does not mean that these aspects of the learning are terribly sophisticated. Finally, skilled adult tutoring calculatedly cultivates persistence, self-monitoring, and other features toward *learn the game of learning*, but I'm not sure this can be expected for cross-age tutoring. Perhaps it's a front to be developed, though.

Turning to the tutor, certainly the tutor is playing an important whole game, the game of teaching and learning. The need of the tutors to understand the material more deeply and broadly in order to teach it pulls them somewhat toward the whole disciplinary game and perhaps toward aspects of the hidden game. Just as the twelve-year-old is out of town for the six-year-old, the reverse is also true, and the tutor is likely to gain some broader understanding of the area in question from the misunderstandings of the younger peer, as well a broader understanding of what younger people are like. Finally, certainly tutors' focus on tutoring reveals much about the game of learning.

Extreme Team Learning

Peer problem solving, studio learning, communities of practice, and cross-age tutoring—these participation structures only scratch the surface. We could add to the list project-based learning, where students join together in teams to conduct experiments, construct works of art, or investigate aspects of their local community or ecology. We could add problem-based learning, where teams address somewhat open-ended problems, drawing on different sources of knowledge as needed to advance toward potential solutions. This has become a mainstay of medical education in many settings, in contrast to the traditional intensive lecture courses, with medical students mastering content by working through a series of prepared cases in teams, studying as they need to in order to arrive at diagnoses and treatments.

We could add debate formats where students prepare arguments and counterarguments on some important historical, political, or scientific issue. Another well-known participation structure is the jigsaw method, where students form teams of four and divide up a topic to be learned. Each student takes responsibility for his or her quarter of the pie, learning it well enough to teach it to the others in the group. And the list goes on.

It's heartening that so many participation structures afford opportunities to learn from the team, because vigorous use of this principle may be fundamental to educational transformation. Instead of occasional group activities spotted here and there, instead of the rare episode of cross-age tutoring, instead of studio learning for just those subjects that particularly lend themselves, we may need *extreme team learning*—days and weeks and months with a high percentage of the learning time given over to various versions of learning from the team.

What would motivate giving *learn from the team* such a central place? Throughout this chapter, the benefits of learning from the team have been measured according to their impact on the other principles of learning by wholes. Two of these principles appear especially hard to address well in large-scale contexts without a sizable dose of learning from the team: *Make the game worth playing* and *work on the hard parts*.

Let's look first at making the game worth playing. Many factors contribute to this: having a whole game in the first place, the right balance of accessibility and challenge, transparent long-term benefits. However, amidst the mix, it's important to remember that we human beings are profoundly social creatures. Recalling the ideas outlined earlier about situated learning, our daily enterprises get not only much of their information, but much of their meaning and momentum from the social interactions woven around them. It is hard to fashion a fully motivating activity without an energizing social context of some sort, which generally means more than a detached relationship to a single teacher and grades at the end of the term.

Turning to the hard parts, learners inevitably find themselves in different places. One student of math or history or electrical engineering encounters a problem here, another there. People approach the characteristic hurdles of studies in the disciplines at different paces and find the hurdles at different heights.

However, logistical pressures push standard educational practice strongly in the direction of "one size fits all" or, when students get divided into ability levels, "three sizes fit all." More than a few slip through such coarse meshes and fall into chronic poor performance or fall out of school altogether. Similar logistical pressures tend to make the individual feedback that learners receive on assignments and tests obscurely telegraphic. Recall the story about learning algebra from Chapter 3, where students learned very little from their assignments because the feedback mostly offered corrections, and the students' understanding of algebra was not deep enough to allow them to interpret the reasons.

Enter *learn from the team . . . and the other teams*. The right participation structures escape the logistical binds that limit individual attention and rich feedback. As in the Stanford findings earlier, such practices also seem impressively cost-effective . . . and they need to be, because societies cannot afford configurations like small class sizes on a large scale.

This look at the social side of learning began with Superman playing baseball by himself. Only Superman could do it, and it wouldn't be much fun anyway! Perhaps what learning needs in order to thrive is just the opposite, patterns of endeavor and engagement where hardly anyone does anything solo for long.

Wonders of Learning

Learn from the Team . . . and the Other Teams

I wonder how to tap the promise of learning from the team . . . and the other teams. I could use various group activities to situate learning in more authentic and meaningful sociocultural contexts. It might help here to think in terms of "participation structures," different ways of organizing roles and responsibilities for learning. (See examples below and in this chapter.)

I wonder how to make the most of learning from the team. As a general strategy I could organize learning from the team to feed all the other principles of learning by wholes. Team support can help beginners play the whole game, social interactions and responsibilities can help to make the game worth playing, and so on.

I wonder how pairing up learners can serve learning. Here I have some repertoire. One participation structure is pair problem solving, where learners take turns playing the roles of listener and problem solver. Another is cross-age tutoring, where older more-experienced students tutor other less-experienced students, the teacher playing the role of mentor and organizer.

I wonder how larger groups can serve learning. The participation structure of communities of practice gives me some ideas here. Also, studio learning with its rhythm of demonstration-lecture, students-at-work, and critique allows students to watch and learn from one another as well as the instructor. Teacher study groups focusing on student work using simple protocols could make up a structured community of practice for our own development as teachers.

I wonder how I can capitalize on other strategies for learning from the team . . . and the other teams. Once I look around, I see there are many of these participation structures: debates, the jigsaw method, problem-based learning, project-based learning. I might look for what might work best with my situation and give it a try.

7

Learn the Game of Learning

RECENTLY MY WIFE AND I SPENT SEVERAL MONTHS AWAY FROM OUR USUAL home in the Boston, Massachusetts, area. When you move to a fresh setting for a while, a *what* question and a *how* question about the new neighborhood come up right away: *What* do you want to get to and *how* are you going to get there? The *what* question has a lot to do with the pragmatic and the antic sides of life, on the pragmatic side local supermarkets, drugstores, gas stations, and department stores, and on the antic side cinemas, museums, and country walks.

Then there is the *how* question. It so happens that my wife does most of our driving. A few weeks after we arrived, she needed to go back to the Boston area to take care of some things, and I found myself alone for a while. Behind the wheel at last, I discovered what many other people have stumbled over in similar situations: I wasn't really very sure about how to find some of those pragmatic and antic sites. I had been with her almost everywhere, but there is a "passenger effect." When you're a passenger, you are just along for the ride. Watching the streets go by teaches you something about navigating but leaves a lot out.

The story is not so different for *learn the game of learning. What* and *how* questions show up again: *What* might be learned about the game of learning and *how* is it going to get learned? On the *what* side, there is a great deal worth learning about the game of learning—memory strategies, problem-solving strategies, deep reading and rapid reading techniques, time management, and so on. One way or another, some students develop a collection of good moves, but some do not. In the words of the fifth principle, the game of learning is a *hidden* game. It's something that happens in considerable part in people's heads, not nearly as visible as baseball or long division.

A pretty good picture of this hidden game, not just for teachers but for learners, comes from the principles of learning by wholes themselves. For instance, suppose as a learner you have learned to look for the whole game, whether it's an academic discipline, a sport, a hobby, or managing a business. Then you've learned something important about the game of learning. Suppose you've learned to try to make the game at hand worth playing. Even if it does not seem very interesting in the first place, you've learned to look for personal connections, to reach out for a level of challenge that is neither frustrating nor boring, to persist and relish incremental progress rather than expecting everything to fall into place all at once. Then again you've learned something important about the game of learning. And so on through the rest of the principles.

All this gets more attention in the pages to come. However, still dangling is the *how* question: How is it going to get learned? Here there is hardly anything more important than the passenger effect and its positive side, the driver effect. With the game of learning, as with finding your way around the neighborhood, people are only going to learn what they need to by doing some of the driving.

The coach says it's time for batting practice. The teacher assigns these fifteen problems for next Tuesday. In many settings of formal learning, the learners themselves do hardly any of the driving. They do not have very many choices. Authors, curriculum designers, and teachers set up everything for them—define clearly and fully the game to be learned (whole game or not), motivate them through incentives and arguments for relevance, define the hard parts in advance, and ensure that the hard parts are well exercised. The general rule: Spell it out for them!

Now certainly planning is important, and indeed that is the big message of the learning-by-wholes framework. However, as with me when my wife was doing most of the driving, when we micromanage the entire process for learners, they may learn the targeted content, but they are not so likely to learn how to learn. They are not so likely to learn the skills and not so likely to learn the take-charge mindset, the disposition of managing one's own learning.

So it is that the final principle of learning by wholes, *learn the game of learning*, poses an almost paradoxical challenge. We're supposed to organize learners' experiences for learning by wholes, but not organize so much that they are never in the driver's seat. Instead, we want to put them in the driver's seat in small ways. We want to create threshold experiences for them about what it's like to drive. Then we want to make the autonomy greater, the threshold grander. We want to teach them to drive, and we can't do that without letting them drive!

The Driver's Seat

Recently I enjoyed a two-hour conversation with the principal, a teacher, and a parent from an innovative public school. Mostly I heard stories (which I will change a little for confidentiality)—what this or that activity was like, how such and such an initiative unfolded, what happened in a tricky situation. The stories revealed a lot about what it looks like to put learners in the driver's seat.

Going over the stories later, I recognized the common thread: student agency. Again and again, these relatively young students—the school only went up to grade five—found themselves in the driver's seat. This was part of the school culture, threaded through its fabric in many small ways. The "hidden curriculum" of this school (and not all that hidden!) was not so much about compliant passengers as responsible young drivers.

For instance, the principal told of a day when she agreed to keep an eye on the teacher's combined fourth- and fifth-grade class because he had to be away. The big surprise was that there was hardly anything to do. The students knew the agenda and simply set about it. Of course, a little bit of oversight was important as a sheer matter of responsibility . . . but just responsibility, not micromanagement and not even management.

Then there was the role of testing. Formal high-stakes testing was a part of this educational scene as with many others today, and the students generally did well. However, the school foregrounded diagnostic testing, ways of probing how far along each youngster had advanced in a particular area, toward deciding what needed attention next. What particularly struck me was that the students, not the teachers, took initial stock of their own progress. The tests were framed emphatically as tools to provide information, not appraisals of worth. The students judged which items they handled readily and which ones not so much. Then the question would be: Okay, what does this mean for where to focus now? Of course the faculty helped. For instance, sometimes students would not reach far enough, being too tentative in their sense of what they might achieve or too comfortable with an easy path. Teachers would explore with such students a reasonable ambition and work something out, deciding *with* the learner rather than deciding *for* the learner.

The students in various classes had certain choices to make collectively. The teacher described an occasion where his students were puzzling about how to manage a particular classroom resource. He confessed that he was tempted to intervene. There was plenty of material in the closet for what they wanted to do, but he held himself back. As the conversation developed, it turned out that having materials at hand was not the main issue. It had to do with materials that had gotten lost and whether they could be retrieved. The students sorted out the puzzle responsibly by themselves, leaving the teacher very happy that he had let them carry on.

With students more often in the driver's seat, the natural worry for any teacher is losing control, so especially impressive was a tale of a bright, mischievous, and manipulative girl. A bout of particularly offensive behavior meant that she would not be allowed to participate in a class trip. But what would happen to her instead? Suspension for a couple of days would not be productive. Schools are for learning. Instead, she would stay in school and keep learning. And what would she learn?

One exercise was writing. Rather than the teacher jotting a note to the mother, the girl was asked to compose a letter describing the situation—and a good one: neat, correct grammar, clear explanation. The letter ended up requiring three drafts. And what if the child failed to deliver the letter to her mother? Well, the principal explained, in that case, the child would speak to her mother by phone. Not me, the principal emphasized. We'll call from my office on speakerphone, I will say as little as possible, and we will see how the conversation goes.

All this is bright with democratic spirit. It's easy to acknowledge that such driver-seat school cultures are very good for building the skills and dispositions of learning to learn. Just as important, they are very good for the nitty-gritty of learning too.

The Passenger's Seat

In contrast, casting students in the perpetual role of passengers is subtly undermining, even if they get their work done today, and even if they are playing whole games in a superficial sense. For instance, many high school chemistry or physics lab experiences lead students through the "whole game" of scientific investigation, but every step of the way they are told what step to take next. Such passenger roles treat learners entirely as though they are along for a ride that someone else has planned and someone else is conducting: Please just be a good traveler, comply with the agendas of the journey, and don't make trouble.

In passenger-seat cultures of learning, students often fall into shallow patterns of learning. Considerable research exists on students' mindsets about learning, a surprising amount of it at the university level where you might expect maturity but often do not find it. In a well-known analysis, Roger Säljö of University of Gothenberg, Sweden, uncovered very different approaches to learning. Some students show a disposition toward acquiring, reproducing, and applying information of a factual character. Others put understanding at the center and eagerly explore different perspectives.

Säljö, Ference Marton, Noel Entwistle, Dai Hounsell, and many others went on to write about *shallow* versus *deep* versus *strategic* approaches to learning. The shallow approach concentrates on getting the facts and skills straight, trying to look good, and especially trying not to look bad. The deep approach reaches for comprehensive understanding and cherishes intrinsic motivation rather than looking good. A strategic approach has a little of both: It targets recognition of good performance through grades and other kudos, with an emphasis on managing the work process well. It's less superficial than the shallow approach but also less intrinsically engaged than the deep approach. In a related line of inquiry, Paul Pintrich of the University of Michigan and others characterized many students as having a performance orientation rather than a mastery orientation, striving to look good rather than genuinely to do well.

Another related line of investigation concerns students' persistence in relationship to their conceptions of ability. Chapter 2 touched on this, exploring the effect of students' expectations on performance. For a number of years, Carol Dweck and colleagues have studied how students who believe that ability has a fixed "either you get it or you don't" character turn into early quitters, figuring that when they can't grasp something relatively quickly they probably cannot master it at all. Often they also try to cover up their shortcomings.

But it's not at all a matter of individual unchanging dispositions. The culture of the setting makes a huge difference. In innumerable subtle and blatant ways, teachers send signals about the roles they expect learners to play—passive or active, compliant or adventurous, managed or self-managing. Shallow versus deep approaches, performance versus mastery orientations, early quitting versus persistence, these are not indelible characteristics like the color of students' eyes, but rather emergent qualities created by the interaction between their predispositions and the dynamics of particular settings.

Dweck illustrates this nicely by characterizing some of the very different ways in which teachers respond when students have difficulty. For instance, suppose when the teacher calls upon Johnny for his solution to math problem number seven, it turns out that Johnny is having a lot of trouble. The teacher might say, "Okay, well good try. Math is difficult! Let's see who else might have an idea." Or the teacher might say, "Okay, so you've taken the first step there. What do you think a good next step might be?" These two responses send very different messages. The first tells Johnny that the math may well be beyond him, whereas the second says take it a step at a time and see what you can figure out. The second encourages Johnny to get in the driver's seat and drive!

Sending the right message is also important for the art and craft of good tutoring, a theme of the previous chapter. According to findings from Stanford investigator Mark Lepper, expert tutors—but not those with less finesse—keep interactions centered on questions and hints rather than commands to encourage tutees to think of themselves as in control and responsible for their progress. Tutees commonly develop the impression that they are more responsible for their successes than in fact they are. This is a productive mistake! Part of their problem lies in their lack of confidence that they can direct themselves as learners.

Many students are acutely aware that they can adopt different mindsets toward learning. They recognize a tension between the way they would like learning to be and the way learning actually unfolds. I was fascinated to get acquainted with the work of Israeli scholar Linor Hadar, who spent a postdoctoral year at the Harvard Graduate School of Education. One of her research interests is students' conceptions of good learning. She had explored this in three different secondary settings in Israel.

Asked what good learning was like, a high percentage of the students quite spontaneously contrasted a typical school passenger-seat conception of learning with an ideal driver-seat conception. Here are some of the ways in which students repeatedly characterized school learning: grades (for example, "learning is when a student gets a good grade on his test; then he has most likely experienced learning"), in-class behavior (for example, "to listen to the teacher, not to disturb in class"), reception of knowledge (for example, "to know the material that the teacher had taught in class"), and being appropriately active in class (for example, "involvement in what's going on; being updated; to take an active part in the lesson").

The students' conceptions of ideal learning had a broader, more personal, and intentional character, including for instance the desire for learning (for example, "learning involves self-desire to learn . . . not in order to satisfy teachers or parents"), personal perspective (for example, "learning is helping the student to develop his own new perspective, not direct them toward something in particular"), independent learning (for example, "when you learn by yourself; you don't need a teacher to 'throw' material at you"), or implementation (for example, "being able to use things you have learned in your everyday or future life").

These contrasts do not imply that there was nothing in common. For instance, both for school learning and ideal learning, students emphasized the importance of acquiring new knowledge and achieving deep understanding. Nor is the point that the features of a passenger-seat culture are sweepingly inappropriate. The worry is more one of tone and spirit. Back to the game of learning, the students seemed to see in the classroom the school game you are supposed to play, getting along by going along, but not the larger more authentic game of learning. They were living the perpetual passenger effect and they knew it!

The Driver's View

When starting to play baseball, you naturally want to learn the basic rules early on. But what are the rules for the game of learning? The term "rules" may not really apply, but at least there should be guidelines. How does the experienced learner steer a path through the game of learning?

I have always been impressed by the following concise account from a fourth grader. Some colleagues collected this a number of years ago as part of our research:

First I would ask myself: What is it? Then, why [do] we need it?
How does it work or how does it happen? If, for example, I can't

understand a word, I read the title and think about what the title means. Then I would read the sentence before it and after it twice. Next I would read that sentence and replace the word with a word that might fit in its place.

This was one savvy learner! Her confident tone reminds us that playing the game of learning well is as much a matter of attitude as skill. Imagine an educational environment where most learners had repertoires and mindsets in this spirit!

Of course, there is a lot that learners can learn about the game of learning. Some of it we have already seen in other guises. Chapter 5 on hidden games included the hidden game of strategies and touched on reading and problem-solving strategies that serve learners well. Chapter 6 on learning from the team included a look at peer problem solving, a technique designed to cultivate metacognitive self-management, and at studio learning, which fosters a range of learning and thinking skills and attitudes.

In a broad and well-known view of fostering learning called *cognitive apprenticeship*, Allan Collins, John Seely Brown, and Susan E. Newman characterize how students can be drawn into deep and self-regulated engagement in learning. Modeling, coaching, and scaffolding are three of the key ingredients, as teachers model strategic practices, coach students in taking them on, and "scaffold," providing support and gradually withdrawing it to cultivate students' self-management, as discussed in Chapter 5. Another practice in similar spirit involves students keeping learning logs, where they reflect upon their own learning.

Proactive question asking is a further characteristic of autonomous learners. Marlene Scardamalia and Carl Bereiter reported youngsters' remarkable capacity to ask deep, far-ranging questions if only they were encouraged to do so. Indeed, their questions were better for topics they had not yet studied than for topics they had, presumably because the formal instruction had narrowed their sense of the theme. Classroom cultures that encourage broad questioning surely develop students who are broad questioners.

Alongside such ideas, we can also add memory strategies, time management approaches, creativity exercises, effective schedules of practice, argument skills, presentational skills, writing skills, and so on. Versions of these come bundled in courses and books that provide a forest of opportunities. In fact, there are so many good learning practices for one thing or another that it's easy to get lost in the trees without a good view of the forest.

Accordingly, for the rest of this chapter, I'll focus more on the general spirit and shape of self-managed learning and learning to learn. What then does it look like to manage one's own learning? Just to have a learning agenda to talk about, let us imagine learners studying *exology*, whatever that is—maybe it's the study of unknowns of all sorts, maybe the art of getting along with ex-spouses, maybe the historical study of the origins of the letter X. So here I am, studying exology. What does my management of my own learning look like with the seven principles of learning by wholes in mind?

Playing the Whole Game

The self-managed learner seeks a sense of the whole game even when it isn't provided. If I'm studying exology, I look for an early picture of the science: What are exologists trying to do and how do they go about it? How can I participate on the edges of it, what the previous chapter called "legitimate peripheral participation"? How can I take on fully a junior version of it, only the beginning but rich enough in its simplicity to provide some feel for the whole game?

Learners proactive in such ways are reaching for the whole game, not just waiting for it to be put before them nor settling for *elementitis* and *aboutitis*. Teachers who sometimes put learners in the driver's seat and encourage them to explore and define "the game" are helping learners to become proactive.

Making the Game Worth Playing

Maybe I am not that interested in exology to start with, but for some reason I need to learn it. What can I do to foster my own commitment and interest? Approaching it as a whole game already helps, but beyond that, what parts of exology connect best with what I *am* interested in? Let me try to foreground those as I work my way into exology. What is a good level of challenge for me, neither so slight as to be boring nor so overwhelming as to be discouraging? Let me find and engage junior versions that come close to this sweet spot for me.

In general, proactive learners work to make the game worth playing for themselves, not depending so much on hit-or-miss inspiration from others nor on coercion with rewards and punishments. Teachers who encourage learners to take charge to some extent of their own motivation are helping them to develop autonomy as learners.

Working on the Hard Parts

Here savvy learners say to themselves: I know it's more engaging to play the whole game of exology than to isolate the hard parts and try to master them—more engaging but less effective! Yes, I know the coach or teacher may break it down for me, but I can do some of this for myself. So what are the sticking points for me as a learner? Where am I confused and where am I poorly skilled? How can I set up the time to work on the hard parts and beyond that to integrate my improved skills and understandings back into the whole game of exology?

In general, learners proactive in such ways as these need not rely entirely on a teacher or coach or text or tip sheet to establish critical regimens of deliberate practice. Teachers who cultivate and expect such responsibility are helping learners to develop their autonomy.

Playing Out of Town

As I get going on one junior version of exology, let me keep my eye out for another. I don't always have to wait for someone to give me an assignment. To some extent, I can figure out my own best next steps. What would be a new variation, a different style, the next level of challenge? If exology has different roles, let me try them out. If exology has different approaches, let me try them out. If there are debates within exology about what the interesting questions are, let me engage in those debates and come to my own sense of the issues. If there are critics of the entire enterprise of exology, what do they have to say and how might they be answered?

In pursuing questions such as these, proactive learners dodge one of the most common pitfalls in education, where people only encounter a single canonical version of a topic and find themselves bewildered when they step outside the official curriculum into the messy real world. Learners who play out of town are more likely to transfer what they have learned far and wide later. And teachers who encourage individual connection making are helping learners to get over the mindset that everything they learn has to be served up on the platter of a text or a lecture.

Uncovering the Hidden Game

Part of the art of learning is knowing that there are always hidden games. There will be a surface version of exology, the simple moves, the straightforward plays, the correct and expected answers. But underneath all that will be not just *the* hidden game but *multiple* hidden games. Proactive learners do not always wait for revelation from teacher or text. They say: I want to be on the lookout for hidden games. There is probably a strategic layer, a matter of self-management as a problem finder and a problem solver, a matter of knowing the tricks for various situations. That's a game I want to know. If exology is an academic area, there is probably a game of evidence, what counts as good evidence and counterevidence and what the puzzles and pitfalls of evidence are. That too is a game I would like to understand better.

There are always hidden games—games of power and competition, games of deception, games of application in contrast with basic inquiry. Proactive learners search for such hidden games, and teachers concerned with developing proactive learners give them the opportunity and encouragement to do so.

Learning from the Team and the Other Teams

Chances are exology is not naturally a solitary pursuit. It depends on collaboration, perhaps on competition. Even if exology encourages solo engagement, still there is much to learn from others who have mastered the art. Even if my teacher or coach does not think this way, I can ask myself: Who can I learn from? What is my neighbor doing? What is this much more experienced learner doing? Where can I look for a mentor? Whom can I teach what I do know, thereby coming to know it all the better? With whom can I collaborate to advance a larger agenda and learn all the more along the way?

Proactive learners will have questions like these on their minds and reach out to learn from the team and the other teams where circumstances allow and encourage it. Teachers concerned with developing proactive learners will not always micromanage team learning models, but give learners the chance to mix and match and invent their own.

Learning the Game of Learning

While studying exology in a self-managed strategic way, I also have my eye out for my own learning practices more generally. I'm organizing my learning of exology, but what does that say about how I might learn atomic physics or backgammon or video editing? How can I carry over what works well here to other occasions, and get rid of what doesn't work well?

Proactive learners will ask questions like those . . . because their teachers inform, encourage, respect, and make a little time for such questions.

Of course, this picture of the proactive learner leaves open questions of when and how to put such ways of thinking on the minds of learners and help them to become attentively and enthusiastically strategic. That is a problem of "driver education."

Driver Education

Almost any setting of formal learning is a busy place, no matter whether it's summer Little League, a physics lab, a Sunday school, a Boy Scout or Girl Scout camp, a professional seminar, an apprenticeship program, or an archaeological dig. We have worked on the other six principles of learning by wholes, and now learning the game of learning gives us yet another agenda to advance. How do we fit it in?

If it's a classroom let's teach some strategic reading skills, so students will learn how to manage better that very fundamental "game" of reading to learn. Let's have students look at their own quiz results and decide where they need to focus their attention, so they will become more self-managed in working on the hard parts. Let's introduce pair problem solving (Chapter 6) as a strategy students can organize for themselves, encouraging them to self-manage learning from the team. And let's not forget memory strategies, principles of time and stress management, testmanship, active listening, note taking, methods for reviewing, strategies for checking one's work, and so on.

I'm reminded of one of the concise quips of stand-up comic Steven Wright, "You can't have everything! Where would you put it?" He might as well have had teaching and learning in mind. In the middle of pursuing such games as basketry, literacy, philosophy, biology, or exology, where can we find time to chase the game of learning too?

There are at least two different choices that might be made here. One choice concerns structure, "where would you put it," as a separate chunk of time for learning to learn—say a minicourse for half an hour every Friday morning—versus folding learning to learn into existing courses. The other choice concerns style, "where would you put it," as putting principles of learning to learn out there explicitly in speech and on posters and on the blackboard versus just creating a tacit driver-seat culture around learners that implicitly encourages learning to learn.

Let's take the first of these: separate chunks of time versus folded into existing courses. There is certainly no single answer, but some insight comes from the history of the thinking-skills movement, which has faced similar dilemmas. Just to be clear, learning to learn is not quite the same thing as thinking skills. Even so, they have a lot to do with one another, and they both have to face Stephen Wright's challenge of "where would you put it?"

In answer to this question, researchers and teachers have explored two very broad strategies, generally called the *stand-alone* approach and the *infusion* approach. The stand-alone approach advocates creating a separate course and teaching it one to several times a week according to the scope of content and available time. Such a course needs to give careful attention to transfer of learning—playing out of town—so that the ideas and practices carry over to settings outside the course.

In contrast, the infusion approach recommends working the ideas and practices into the regular pattern of teaching and learning. The study of linear equations or Chaucer or the history of Rome or exology incorporates attention to more general attitudes and strategies.

Many teachers gravitate to the infusion approach, recognizing that instruction in the disciplines could use the boost of more mindful attention, valuing the richness of learning that can result, and realizing that it might be easier to weave in another thread than to find blocks of time for a whole new course. All these are smart considerations. However, the decision is trickier than it looks. Although infusion sounds attractive in principle, it's easy for the intended attention to the general craft of thinking and learning to get lost amidst the general busyness and reduced to a kind of a tokenism, a tip here and there, a brief exercise now and again. A virtue of a well-done, stand-alone approach is that it guarantees targeted time for learning to think and learn.

So what do the track records of the two approaches say? To my knowledge, there are no systematic studies that juxtapose a stand-alone version of an intervention with an infused version of the same intervention. Indeed, it would be difficult to conduct such investigations because the characteristics of stand-alone versus infusion are so different. That acknowledged, the general sum of experience around the teaching of thinking gives a clear although not very decisive answer: Both can serve well. It depends on what's most workable in the context.

What does this mean for learning by wholes and in particular learning the game of learning? First and foremost, it's a recommendation to take stock of the context. If in a particular school at a particular time a particular educator has the vision and energy to put together and sustain a course on learning to learn, let it happen. If elsewhere the infusion approach seems more readily deployed, then let that happen. So long as something serious happens!

All this granted, when there is a choice I would lean toward infusion approaches for learning the game of learning, or a mix of a stand-alone element with strong infusion. Why? Learning by wholes focuses directly and emphatically on the learning of academic disciplines, professional practices, skills and crafts, and sports and games. Learning by wholes is not just about learning the game of learning but the first six principles as well. For learning by wholes or something in that general spirit to have momentum, those principles need to be thriving hour by hour, day by day, making the settings natural environments for encouraging students to take charge of themselves as learners.

Now let's look at the second choice, explicit versus implicit. Some educators feel that general principles and styles and patterns of practice are most effectively learned by osmosis. The best way to cultivate better thinking and learning is simply to get learners learning in thoughtful ways—questioning, debating, grappling with rich problems, attempting penetrating analyses, and often finding their own pathways to their own conclusions with appropriate help. Explicitness intrudes rather than assists. Leave the strategies in the drawer, the concepts on the shelf, and just do it!

The appeal is natural, but the research about what works goes the other way. While there have not been direct comparisons of stand-alone versus infusion, there have been studies of the teaching of thinking juxtaposing implicit and explicit approaches. Explicit wins. The problem with the implicit approach is that many students do not pick up on the message. Chapter 5, exploring the games hidden beneath the surface of any endeavor, touched briefly on the work of Berkeley's Alan Schoenfeld, emphasizing the importance of self-management strategies for problem solving. Schoenfeld also explored the influence of tacit versus explicit attention to strategies.

In a small but carefully controlled study, some college mathematics students participated in a series of five sessions where the students tried to solve problems and then saw solutions demonstrated using several powerful problem-solving strategies without naming or explaining them—osmosis at work, or so it was hoped. Other students participated in similar sessions where the strategies were labeled and the key moves explained as they were made. The sessions featured the same topics and problems.

All the students took a test with several problems before the instruction and then a test afterward with different problems. The students in the implicit condition did not do any better on the post-test than the pretest. But the students in the explicit condition did more than twice as well. Besides this research, there are other findings to the same effect.

But just because the explicit is important doesn't mean the implicit is not. Those drawn to the implicit approach are certainly right about the power of a generally mindful driver-seat culture of learning. Indeed, there is a kind of dishonesty in teaching practices of thinking and learning explicitly while the rest of the educative process allows little room for them. We don't want the explicit to take the place of the tacit but rather to punctuate it from time to time, like a porpoise occasionally leaping out of the water. If learning by wholes is generally in motion, a little bit could go a long way: a label here, a phrase there, perhaps a list of the principles on the wall, a quick explanation, a moment of encouragement, an occasional exercise, a three-minute demonstration, a five-minute debriefing, all toward learning the game of learning.

In contrast, whatever ideas about thinking and learning are made explicit, the cultures of many settings of learning work against them implicitly, not through some deliberate plot but simply because business-as-usual often ends up leaving little room for them. The learning process is organized along the lines of *elementitis* and *about-itis*, a matter of mastering bits and pieces of knowledge and skill about games that learners might be playing instead. Even if there is a whole game in play, most of the time learners may be micromanaged passengers, doing what they're told. Because they do not have to take any driver's responsibility for their learning, they do not learn much about how to drive the route themselves.

In contrast, choice points, self-assessment, different roles to try out, open-ended projects, varied styles of interaction from debates to conversations to collaborative initiatives and beyond, different levels of challenge adopted by the learners themselves—such elements as these are the mainstays of a driver-seat culture. To help learners become more thoughtful about engaging the whole game, one might even sometimes offer multiple ways in and let them choose. Some might like first to hear a seasoned practitioner of exology talk about it. Others might like to dip cautiously into the action as peripheral participants. Others might like to attempt a very junior version of exology. Or turning for a moment to working on the hard parts, make it each learner's responsibility to figure out what his or her own profile of hard and easy parts is. Or touching on the principle of playing out of town, ask the learners to explore and articulate individual connections, ways they might put exology to work or to play.

In summary, for learning the game of learning, it might make sense to lean toward an infused rather than a stand-alone approach, but if stand-alone is more viable in the context fine. Either way, explicit principles are likely to serve learners well, not as a catechism to memorize, but as objects of reflection and plans of action—specific principles about, say, strategic reading, and general overarching principles like the learning by wholes principles themselves. But none of this should turn into a substitute for a strong implicit culture of thoughtful learning by wholes. Without a driver-seat culture, the game of learning won't have a place to play.

A good mix of counsel, encouragement, and elbow room means that learners can find their own ways into the game and further along in the game. This does not call for absolute freedom, but rather a measured latitude that supports as much as it frees, guides as much as it permits, shapes as much as it allows.

Driving to Tomorrow

What strange lives we would lead if, except for very immediate needs, we stopped learning new ideas after our formal education. Yes, we learned about presidents and kings and equations and orbits and bacteria and sonnets and even baseball. So far so good, but as someone who survived all my graduations some time ago, there is a lot I would know very little about had that been the end of it.

Here are some of the gaps I have had to fill in along the way: ecology and the care of the planet, complexity and systems thinking, the histories of other cultures and particularly non-Western cultures, the complex tensions of race and ethnicity, contemporary conceptions of the universe and its makeup, the vexed role of special interest groups in politics, the rise and fall of communism, and the rise and fall of the Roman Empire. Some of these themes I didn't happen to encounter during my formal education, some were thinly represented or ignored, and some had not come into prominence yet.

The reality is that when we step down off the platform with degrees in hand, most of what we need to learn still lies ahead of us. This includes not only areas of academic knowledge but also understanding in professional realms, interpersonal dimensions of life, encounters with the ideas and arts of other cultures, and so on.

Not only that, but exactly what it is we as individuals might eventually need to know is unknown. For one thing, much of it is likely to be very different from person to person. For another, in our rapidly changing world, nobody or hardly anybody knows yet what in a decade or two many of us will need to know. Some of the games that will be worth learning have not even been invented. This is why the last principle of learning by wholes is perhaps the most important: *Learn the game of learning*.

WONDERS OF LEARNING

LEARN THE GAME OF LEARNING

I wonder how I can foster learning the game of learning. Most broadly, I had better avoid the "passenger effect" and capitalize on the "driver effect"; learners are not likely to learn the game of learning unless they often get behind the wheel and exercise some self-direction.

I wonder what to encourage toward a driver-seat culture. I could foster patterns of interaction that allow learners significant autonomy and choice, promoting reflection and self-management.

I wonder how to guard against a passenger-seat culture. I could try to dodge some typical hazards: a shallow rather than a deep approach to learning, an either-you-get-it-or-you-don't mindset, expectations that learning is a matter of acceptance, compliance, orderliness, and pursuit of nothing but conventional mastery and good grades.

I wonder just what needs to be learned to learn the game of learning. Here I might turn to the seven principles of learning by wholes, which provide a broad framework for students' self-management of learning, not just for my management of teaching. Besides that, there are many specific skills I could help students pick up: good reading practices, time management, problem-solving strategies, and so on.

I wonder how to find room for all that. With so much for me to manage, what would "driver education" be like? Either a stand-alone or infused approach might work, but infused or a mix seems better when possible. I also want to bear in mind that strategies of good learning benefit from explicit attention, not just osmosis from a generally positive driver-seat culture. However, they won't thrive without a driver-seat culture around them.

I wonder whether learning the game of learning is worth the effort. And then I think: For long lives in a world of change, the game of learning could be the most important game to learn.

AFTERWORD: THE FUTURE OF LEARNING

LEARNING IS SUCH AN ORDINARY THING, SO MUCH A PART OF OUR LIVES; one never knows when one is going to get ambushed into learning something.

Here's an example. My wife and I are museum fans. A few months ago, we were enjoying the de Young Museum in San Francisco. Browsing through the American collection, I noticed an attractive painting by Alfred Bierstadt, a well-known nineteenth-century painter of the American West, prolific in his output of large and lovely, albeit somewhat romanticized, landscapes. The painting showed a forbiddingly rugged mountain pass in the foreground overlooking a distant lake, beyond which the landscape receded toward a hazy sun hovering a few degrees above the horizon. Pretty, but I wondered why the foreground seemed so stark. I took a quick look and moved on.

A few minutes later, my wife, who was making her own circuit of the gallery, passed by and said, "Did you notice the Bierstadt? It's kind of interesting."

The painting had seemed pleasant enough to me, but I wouldn't have used the word *interesting*. I looped back for a more careful look. This time I did what I had not bothered to do before, I read the title: *View of Donner Lake*. All of a sudden, this 1871 work began to change before my eyes. The name Donner Lake triggered vague recollections of the Donner Party and cannibalism.

To fill in the story, in 1846 over eighty settlers led by George Donner made a journey westward, encountering endless troubles and delays along the way. They arrived dangerously late, at the end of October, at what is today known as Donner Pass of the Sierra Nevada, with a snowstorm blocking their path. They camped at Donner Lake and a nearby site to try to wait it out, but the winter set in hard and their supplies dwindled. A small group ventured westward through the snow to try to get help while the rest hunkered down. Some of the group seeking help died. Their companions ate them and kept going. Some eventually made it through, and rescue parties were sent back. By the time all was said and done, many in the larger group also died of cold and starvation, and the survivors resorted to cannibalism to survive. In the end, forty-eight made it, but the episode became notorious.

Back to Bierstadt's *View of Donner Lake*, painted just twenty-five years later: Now the desolate foreground leading back to the lake made more sense. This was not meant to be an idyllic scene. Gnarled trees clung to the rocky slopes. A closer look revealed a simple wooden cross erected on a ledge in the middle distance. A rough road snaked down toward the lake, surely nothing the Donner Party would have encountered, but some later construction that made the pass more passable. Surveying the wall text revealed more. On the right of the scene in the middle distance, a railway was under construction.

In fact, the painting was both a reminder of the enormous difficulties of the westward journey and a celebration of progress, the deadly pass tamed first by the rough road and now by the railway, the painting commissioned by the builder of the railroad. You may like the message or not, you may like the painting or not, but unquestionably far more was going on than I originally saw or imagined.

Learning Today for Tomorrow

Let me say it again: One never knows when one is going to get ambushed into learning something. Maybe you're in a museum and something surprises you on the first look, the second look, or the third look. Maybe it's my dad with a baseball bat and glove for me, saying, "Let's learn how to play baseball." Maybe you are visiting a new shopping mall and you have to get oriented—where's the RadioShack, the Sears, the food court? You might even get a lesson from the map kiosks that malls provide. Maybe you are tracking a political candidate, and the constant maneuvering of the candidate to say the right thing becomes increasingly off-putting, dulling the shine. Maybe you have a problem with the switch of a table lamp and need to figure out how to fix it. Maybe a first-time business trip to Barcelona or Boston is on your calendar, so you prepare for your meetings and do some side research to plan a pleasant extra day.

Such episodes do not always work out so well, of course. I would have missed the layers of the Bierstadt without a cue from my wife. However, what stands out in these very ordinary cases of learning at their best is their natural engaged purposefulness. We don't generally view these episodes as matters of studying. We see them as matters of getting surprised or getting oriented or solving a problem or making a decision or making a plan or making sense. We are learning from today, from right now, from the situation at hand in its immediate meaningfulness.

So what does this have to do with learning by wholes? Simply that the natural engaged purposefulness of such occasions is what learning by wholes aims to capture. Let me spell out some of its qualities.

The endeavor is experienced as immediately meaningful and worthwhile in itself . . . as well as representative of something larger. For instance, looking at the Bierstadt was revealing in itself as well as informative about the social symbolism that works of art can carry. In general, learning by wholes aims to engage learners in a whole game now as a step toward larger more sophisticated games later.

Knowledge is woven in here and there from the past as needed . . . as well as revealed by the unfolding experience. For instance, I used what I already knew about the Donner Party as well as observing how Bierstadt treated the theme. In general, learning by wholes invites learners to bring to the game what they already know from general experience or immediately previous instruction, but to discover new skills, knowledge, and insights through the game itself.

Conflicting knowledge from past experiences converges . . . and resolutions are negotiated through thought and experiment. For instance, I didn't look carefully originally because I categorized the painting too quickly as a conventional pretty landscape. However, my wife's comment conflicted with this so I took a second look. In general, a whole game generates dilemmas about what to do next, dilemmas that learners can pursue and strive to resolve, expanding their repertoire.

Considerable learning occurs automatically . . . extended by knowledge teased out through underscoring, reflection, and targeted rehearsal. For instance, besides taking it all in, I found myself reflecting about the Bierstadt and how blindly I had originally approached it. In general, the principles of learning by wholes invite strategic reflection before, during, and after to harvest the significance for the future.

Schoolish learning often feels very different from this. It's less like natural engaged purposefulness in the now and more like learning solely for a vaguely envisioned later. Learning by elements and learning about dominate. Students find themselves laboring over something not because it is meaningful in the moment but because it's supposed to be important next year or the year after that. Many are willing to trudge along with this, and sometimes for some content it may be the best we can do, but the learning-for-later style raises severe problems of both engagement and retention of knowledge.

Let's take a familiar example, doing the math problems at the end of the chapter. Full disclosure: I often *liked* the math problems at the end of the chapter. We all have our favorite areas. But that does not mean they served my learning as well as they might have. Consider the standard problem set through the same four points as above.

Is the endeavor experienced as immediately meaningful and worthwhile in itself . . . as well as representative of something larger? The math problems are probably not experienced as immediately meaningful and worthwhile. The problems are plainly exercises without any larger significance. They may be engaging as puzzles (worked for me!) but that's about it. Students are told they are representative of something larger, a body of skill and insight eventually to be mastered, but what that is lies beyond the horizon.

Is knowledge woven in here and there from the past as needed . . . as well as revealed by the unfolding experience? Learners are expected to weave knowledge in from the chapter they have just read as well as from earlier learning, but the exercises themselves are designed almost entirely to practice the knowledge already presented, with very little new knowledge revealed as part of the process. End-of-the-chapter problems are usually designed so that they specifically do not mention anything unfamiliar and do not require gathering information beyond the brief problem statement. This contrasts sharply with, for instance, problem-based learning and project-based learning.

Does conflicting knowledge from past experiences converge . . . with resolutions negotiated through thought and experiment? The chapter of the day tends to be isolated from previous chapters, without posing dilemmas of conflicting knowledge. This works for the moment, with the unfortunate consequence that students do not learn to integrate what they know and make choices about different methods. Later in more open-ended situations, they often do not know which approach to pick.

Does considerable learning occur automatically . . . extended by knowledge teased out through underscoring, reflection, and targeted rehearsal? Through working the exercises, some learning certainly occurs automatically. However, there is very little to cue deliberate reflective strategizing or drawing conclusions toward the future.

The lazy moral would be: Don't use the problems at the end of the chapter. However, that is much too categorical. For one thing, sometimes the problems at the end of the chapter are much richer. For another, within learning by wholes we might well use the conventional problems at the end of the chapter to good effect. Remember, *work on the hard parts* is one of the fundamental principles. A page of exercises is fine if they are seen and experienced as part of a larger enterprise clearly in view.

So this is what learning by wholes is all about. Learning by wholes aims squarely at learning from the lively now. Its goal is to build learning out of endeavors experienced as immediately meaningful and worthwhile—junior versions of the whole game that build toward more sophisticated versions. Its commitment is to leverage features of good naturalistic learning, whether we are talking about Bierstadt, baseball, or Barcelona. Its method is to systematize important features of such learning through the seven principles. Its credo says that good learning is learning from a richly experienced today with tomorrow in view.

Teaching Today for Tomorrow

I certainly do not think that this mission is easy. Thoughtful compelling education is never easy. It requires care, thought, energy, and commitment. At the same time, there is no need to harass ourselves with principle upon principle, concept upon concept.

I'm remembering the early years of my own development as a teacher at the Harvard Graduate School of Education. Of course I'm still learning, but one of the frustrations then was too many principles. I had made friends with this and that learning theory, this and that perspective on the acquisition of difficult concepts, this and that view of motivation, this and that model of thinking and understanding. I remember one time crafting a long list of the biggest ideas I knew about how to foster learning. I was planning my teaching, and I asked myself, "How can I make all of these part of what I do?"

It took me a couple of days to realize that this was a very foolish question. There was no way I could take serious account of even a tenth of the list. Juggling all the principles to keep them in action week by week would have been rather like juggling a banquet's worth of steak knives, with a few of my fingers lost to the process.

What made things harder at the time was that I had not done enough bundling and prioritizing. But even seven principles are not so few, and inside each of the seven hide multiple concepts and tactics. So here's my counsel for people who would like to give learning by wholes a serious try: There is absolutely no need to start with a full-scale effort to deploy all seven. Instead, start with a junior version (where have we heard that before?).

The essential ingredient is the first principle, *play the whole game.* One isn't working with learning by wholes at all unless one has figured out a suitably junior version of a whole game for the topics and learners concerned. Maybe it's a simple version of mathematical modeling using ordinary arithmetic. Maybe it's a simple version of literary analysis or applying the lessons of history to current times or testing a scientific hypothesis. Maybe it's a simple version of baseball. Whatever it is, without a whole game in motion there's no learning by wholes.

Another wise choice at the beginning is to *make the game worth playing*. Without a strong engaging aura around the learning, it will be uphill all the way. To make the game worth playing for the learners is to make it worth playing for oneself as well. We can never stoke everyone's enthusiasm; it's naïve to think that we can, but there is nothing more disenchanting for teachers than learners who don't care and would much rather be doing something else.

Establish some momentum on these two fronts—*play the whole game* and *make the game worth playing*—and you buy time to incorporate other principles as they seem to be important. Soon you will want learners to *work on the hard parts*. You might not be in such a rush to get them to *play out of town* or *uncover the hidden game*, but in a while yes.

One more principle will make life easier from the first: *Learn from the team*. Here I don't mean the students' learning (*learn from the team* might be good for them early on or not) but our own learning from others in the setting—other teachers, mentors, consultants, whomever. If you can establish a reading group, by all means do so. If you can establish a regular meeting of a few colleagues to look thoughtfully at student work and discuss it, by all means do so (recall the example of teachers using the LAST protocol for looking at students' thinking from Chapter 6). If you can set up a simple pattern of observing in one another's classes, by all means do so. Learning by wholes, like any other approach to educating, is much easier to tackle together than alone.

A final point, perhaps the oddest one: Do not read this book too carefully. By all means look through it, but if you discover ideas that seem provocative, try something soon. As urged in the Introduction, you'll find these pages much more useful if you make your first pass the basis for attempting a few simple things, your own personalized junior version. Then look back, and you'll find some further ideas that speak to needs you did not even know you had.

And well, yes, I'm sure you will also encounter some challenges of practice with nary a helpful word in the whole book. When do we ever get it all right? My aspiration is not to have gotten it all right but to have gotten it mostly helpful, and I hope you find it that way.

Tomorrow's Knowledge

In a way, the problem of content is simple: Teach today what learners will need to understand and act on tomorrow. Unfortunately, both as individuals living our personal lives and in a larger social sense we only know roughly from trends and guesses what tomorrow will be like. Tomorrow is a moving target.

Even so, we can explore what might help us hit the target. In *Five Minds for the Future*, Howard Gardner identifies five fundamental ways to engage emerging challenges, five "minds" metaphorically speaking, and urges that education pay more attention to their development. The disciplined mind refers to disciplinary knowledge and thinking, the synthesizing mind to assembling diverse knowledge into insightful and useful syntheses, the creative mind to truly novel insights and products, the respectful mind to respecting others near and far, and the ethical mind to a fundamentally ethical stance on challenging issues and relationships. With these five in full play, Gardner argues, people would be much better prepared to face the intricacies of the next decades. For instance, recognizing the risks of hyperspecialization and the hurdles of complex inquiry, Gardner draws a useful distinction between "laser intelligence" and "searchlight intelligence." Laser intelligence looks deep, as in fine-grained work within a discipline. Searchlight intelligence ranges broadly across multiple disciplines and perspectives to try to put things together. We need them both!

A number of authors offer views of how the target shifts as people advance through their lives and through sometimes precarious and certainly complicated times. For instance, Michael Eraut of the

University of Sussex emphasizes in his *Developing Professional Knowledge and Competence* how much professional education leaves out in preparing people for the world of work. Huge amounts of fundamental learning occur later, on the job, where people acquire personal knowledge of an informal and tacit character that empowers them to deal with a range of sometimes remarkably subtle practical challenges. Very much oriented toward playing the game, such knowledge is *process knowledge* rather than *propositional knowledge*. Eraut maintains that truly effective professional education should have a process basis rather than a propositional basis for a good part of initial qualifications. Action in the world, not just answers on the test, is the right mark of readiness.

Of course, none of this says that the school of experience provides anything like ideal learning when finally we walk through its doors. Yes, when we learn on the job, most likely we are playing the whole game, at least from one of its positions—maybe first base, maybe outfield, maybe pinch-hitter. However, in the absence of mentoring or other mechanisms, there may be little time for, say, isolating the hard parts to develop targeted skills or playing out of town to expand capacities or uncovering the hidden game. Leveraging workplace experience effectively requires all seven principles, not just the first one.

Some approaches to professional education move decidedly closer to immediately meaningful active engagement. Even so they will inevitably leave much to be learned. The reality is that some tomorrows rise over the horizon in ways complex and hard to anticipate. Eraut's insights into the demands of professional education are one reason out of many that education needs to produce nimble learners who have *learned the game of learning* and also acquired a repertoire of understandings of wide scope (Chapters 2 and 4)—powerful conceptual systems and exemplars that inform our understanding of human nature, systemic change, the roots of conflict, patterns of scientific and humanistic inquiry, clear expressive communication, creativity and critical thinking, and more.

This has always been true, but it is especially true these days. The easy argument would be to say that the pace of change is increasing.

Actually I'm not so confident about that. What is the speedometer that tells us how fast change is happening? For sure, previous centuries have included many wrenching transformations of lifestyle, fortunes, and prospects. Is the pace of change today any more drastic than let's say around Manchester and Liverpool in the midst of the Industrial Revolution or for the merchant class during the heyday of Renaissance Florence?

So never mind the general pace of change, but instead consider some specific features of current times. One of the simplest is an increase in the human lifespan, a slowly rising index that could truly take off. Contemporary work in the medical sciences seems likely to extend our lives considerably. In the course of the next fifty years, the expected lifetime for a reasonably healthy adult may well leap forward by fifty years. Even today, many people play out two careers, so imagine what a difference living to 130 or 140 would make, and imagine the multiple rounds of learning entailed. Formal education would become not just a tide that rises at the beginning of one's life and then recedes but instead a recurrent cycle.

Besides life expectancy, let's add physical, social, and economic mobility to the list. One simple index of this is accents. Recall how in the musical *My Fair Lady* and the classic play on which it is based, George Bernard Shaw's *Pygmalion*, Professor Henry Higgins, expert on phonetics, could read people's birthplaces from their accents with startling accuracy. How could this be? Because people did not move around very much either geographically or socially, so highly specific accents could develop. The constant geographical and social churn of contemporary society makes Higginsesque feats of detection much more difficult today. People are constantly up to something new: a new place, a new job, a new social circle, a new country.

Today on top of physical, social, and economic mobility there is information mobility. Sophisticated communications have made the one-way and two-way travel of information dramatically more rapid and less costly. Background data that would require a tedious trip to a large library now can often be pulled from the Internet in a matter of minutes. Rather than write to a hotel in Paris or Beijing to explore a booking, you can take an online video tour to size up whether you like the looks of the place and then sign up online too. In many cases, the principal challenge of finding information has shifted from one of gaining access to filtering down. Chris Dede, technology education expert at the Harvard Graduate School of Education, writes about the neomillennial learning styles this calls for, including the knack of "collectively seeking, sieving, and synthesizing experiences rather than individually locating and absorbing information from some single best source."

Unsurprisingly, massive social and technological shifts such as these are pushing useful knowledge in the world in the direction of understandings of wide scope. Richard Murnane and Frank Levy in their *Teaching the New Basic Skills* document the trend for the contemporary world of work to demand higher levels of cognitive functioning than was previously the case, skills such as "problem solving . . . the ability to work in groups, and to make effective oral and written presentations." During the final twenty years of the twentieth century, workers with only high school degrees and less equipped with such skills faced a flat income in constant dollars for similar jobs despite an expanding economy. In contrast, college graduates enjoyed an income that nearly doubled in terms of constant dollars.

Levy and Murnane pursued the theme further a few years later in *The New Division of Labor*, charting how information processing technologies are changing the character of work. They found a "hollowing out" of the job market in industrialized nations due to the use of computers to handle relatively routine activities and to offshoring made possible by communications and transportation technologies. The market for secretarial, clerical, and assembly-line work suffers relative to the market for creative work and work demanding interpersonal skills.

At the other end of the spectrum, many jobs characterized as relatively unskilled—janitorial, street repair, waste collection—resist replacement and off-shoring because they require physical presence and physical and pattern recognition skills that cannot readily be programmed. However, these roles are both low prestige and relatively low wage, especially with competition for them increasing as some of the people who might have occupied the disappearing blue-collar, secretarial, and clerical positions slip down the ladder. The big message: Learning to learn and understandings of wide scope are at a premium.

Recognition of the continuous challenge of learning in our lively globalized culture is widespread, but it is rarely so frank as to look ignorance squarely in the face. This is what gives the program on medical ignorance at the University of Arizona's College of Medicine a particularly refreshing feel. With variations for medical students, teachers, and high school students, the program emphatically puts questions in front of answers. Founded by medical doctor Marlys Witte in the mid-1980s, it makes one of its basic tools an "ignorance map" designed to acknowledge and articulate not what we know but what we don't know. *Known unknowns* are all the things you know you don't know. *Unknown unknowns* are all the things you don't know that you don't know. *Errors* are all the things you think you know but don't. *Unknown knowns* are all the things you don't know you know. *Taboos* are dangerous, polluting, or forbidden knowledge. And finally, *denials* are all the things too painful to know, so you don't.

Medical ignorance is certainly frightening to contemplate when we walk in the door of a clinic. However, medical ignorance and its kin in any area are tremendously empowering ideas—understandings of wide scope again—because ignorance acknowledged and identified has taken its first step toward resolution. This, as with so many aspects of contemporary education, reinforces my sense that we should think of the multiple fronts of learning that invite or may soon invite attention in terms not just of educating for the known but educating for the unknown.

Overwhelmingly, our conventional efforts to educate focus on educating for the known, for the tried and true, for the signed and sealed. To be sure, a certain measure of this makes good sense. One of our most remarkable and powerful qualities as a species is the capacity to pass along facts, ideas, practices, and indeed wisdom to the next generation. At the same time, as examples from the theme of medical ignorance to contemporary labor trends to the growth of the human lifespan testify, alongside education for the known we need education for the unknown, for how to map it and how to cope with it and how to master large understandings that can help us make sense of it. Which is the most we can hope for, because one thing for sure about the unknown is that there is always more of it.

So to the fact that one never knows when one is going to be ambushed into learning something, let's add that we do know it is likely to happen a lot. Let's not be like the Donner Party, arriving late in the season and getting ambushed by a blizzard. Let's build our conceptual roads and our conceptual railroads through the pass. The more schools attend to learning by wholes or something like it, the more summer camps and workplaces respect learning by wholes or something like it, the more technology-based learning environments attempt learning by wholes or something like it, and the more those wholes represent proactively exercised understandings of wide scope that allow for flexible sense making and wise action, the better off we will be. The more we as individuals, our society, and its institutions take this challenge seriously and respond to it energetically and strategically, the more people will be ready to catch the changing rhythms of tomorrow.

NOTES

Introduction: A Whole New Ball Game

Approaching Complexity (pp. 3–7)

Narrow curriculum standards . . .: Darling-Hammond, L. (1997). *The right to learn: a blueprint for creating schools that work*. San Francisco: Jossey-Bass.

Narrowing effects of NCLB: Au, W. (2007). Hi-stakes testing and curricular control: A qualitative meta-synthesis. *Educational Researcher, 36*(5), 258–267.

Mindlessness, mindfulness, and mindful learning: Langer, E. J. (1989). *Mindfulness*. Menlo Park, CA: Addison-Wesley. Langer, E. J. (1997). *The power of mindful learning*. Reading, MA: Addison-Wesley.

"Other people's facts": Holt, T. (1990). *Thinking historically: Narrative, imagination, and understanding*. New York: College Entrance Examination Board.

Learners' science misunderstandings—the literature is vast. Here are some summary sources foregrounding the physical sciences: Driver, R., Guesne, E., & Tiberghien, A. (Eds.). (1985). *Children's ideas in science*. Philadelphia: Open University Press. Gentner, D., & Stevens, A. L. (Eds.). (1983). *Mental models*. Mahwah, NJ: Lawrence Erlbaum. Grotzer, T. A. (2003). Learning to understand the forms of causality implicit in scientific explanations. *Studies in Science Education, 39*, 1–74. Novak, J. D. (Ed.). (1987). The proceedings of the 2nd misconceptions in science and mathematics conference. Ithaca, NY: Cornell University.

Seven Principles of Learning (pp. 7–15)

Study of adventure racing: Wilson, D. (2007). *Team learning in action: An analysis of the sense making behaviors in adventure racing teams as they perform in fatiguing and uncertain contexts*. Unpublished doctoral dissertation, Harvard Graduate School of Education, Cambridge, Massachusetts.

Hidden game: Thorn, J., & Palmer, P. (1984). *The hidden game of baseball: A revolutionary approach to baseball and its statistics*. New York: Doubleday Books.

Yes, But . . . (pp. 15–21)

Good source on learning theory and education: Bransford, J. D., Brown, A. L., & Cocking, R. R. (Eds.). (1999). *How people learn: Brain, mind, experience, and school*. Washington, DC: National Academy Press.

Behaviorism, constructivism, and so on: It's assumed that most readers will have some sense of these, and I won't take space to give characterizations of them. Wikipedia has decent brief accounts, or consult the Bransford, Brown, & Cocking source above or any basic text on learning.

Alternative frameworks for organizing learning: A good compendium here spans these two volumes: Reigeluth, C. (Ed.). (1999). *Instructional design theories and models: Volume II*. Mahwah, NJ: Lawrence Erlbaum. Reigeluth, C. M. (Ed.). (1987). *Instruction theories in action: Lessons illustrating selected theories and models*. Mahwah, NJ: Lawrence Erlbaum.

"No man is an island . . .": John Donne, Meditation XVII from *Devotions upon Emergent Occasions*, 1623.

1. Play the Whole Game

The Quest for the Whole Game (pp. 27–31)

On teaching for understanding: Blythe, T., & Associates. (1998). *The teaching for understanding guide*. San Francisco, CA: Jossey-Bass. Wiske, M. S. (Ed.). (1998). *Teaching for understanding: Linking research with practice*. San Francisco: Jossey-Bass. Examples from Lois Hetland and Joan Soble: See Wiske, op. cit.

The River City MUVE: Clarke, J., Dede, C., Ketelhut, D. J., & Nelson, B. (2006). A Design-based Research Strategy to Promote Scalability for Educational Innovations. *Educational Technology* 46(3), 27–36. Ketelhut, D., Dede, C., Clarke, J., Nelson, B., & Bowman, C. (2007). Studying situated learning in a multi-user virtual environment. In E. Baker, J. Dickieson, W. Wulfeck, & H. O'Neil (Eds.), *Assessment of problem solving psing simulations* (pp. 37–58). Mahweh, NJ: Lawrence Erlbaum.

Kenna Barger *water balloon bungee jumping* example: Inside the Creative Classroom—Five Case Studies. (2004). Volume 4 of the Creative Classroom Series, VHS Videos. DisneyHand, Disney, developed in collaboration with Project Zero, Harvard Graduate School of Education.

Kinds of Whole Games (pp. 31–37)

The *Edutopia* Web site for examples of project-based learning: http://www.edutopia.org/projectbasedlearning.

The Jasper series and findings: for example, Bransford, J. D., Zech, L., Schwartz, D., Barron, B., Vye, N., & The Cognition and Technology Group at Vanderbilt. (1996). Fostering mathematical thinking in middle school students. In R. J. Sternberg & T. Ben-Zeev (Eds.), *The nature of mathematical thinking* (pp. 203–250). Mahwah, NJ: Lawrence Erlbaum. Cognition and Technology Group at Vanderbilt. (1997). *The Jasper project: Lessons in curriculum, instruction, assessment, and professional development*. Mahwah, NJ: Lawrence Erlbaum.

On three versions of the case method: Garvin, D. A. (2003). Making the case: Professional education for the world of practice. *Harvard Magazine, 106*(1), 56–65, 107.

The problem with discovery learning: Kirschner, P. A., Sweller, J., & Clark, R. E. (2006). Why minimal guidance during instruction does not work: An analysis of the failure of constructivist, discovery, problem-based, experiential, and inquiry-based teaching. *Educational Psychologist, 41*(2), 75–86.

The Quest for the Junior Game (pp. 37–42)

Threshold concepts: Meyer, J.H.F., & Land, R. (Eds.) (2006). *Overcoming barriers to student understanding: Threshold concepts and troublesome knowledge*. London: Routledge.

The importance of knowledge and oral facility in reading development: for example, RAND Reading Study Group, C. Snow, Chair. (2002). *Reading for understanding: Toward an R&D program in reading comprehension*. Prepared for the Office of Educational Research and Improvement (OERI). Santa Monica, CA: RAND Education. Snow, C., & Juel, C. (2005). Teaching children to read: What do we know about how to do it? In M. J. Snowling & C. Hulme (Eds.), *The science of reading: A handbook* (pp. 501–520). Oxford: Blackwell.

"We begin with the hypothesis . . .": Bruner, J. S. (1973). Readiness for learning. In J. Anglin (Ed.), *Beyond the information given* (pp. 413–425). New York: Norton.

Keeping the Game in Motion (pp. 44–48)

On academic learning time: Berliner, D. (1991). What's all the fuss about instructional time? In M. Ben-Peretz & R. Bromme (Eds.), *The nature of time in schools: Theoretical concepts, practitioner perceptions* (pp. 3–35). New York: Teachers College Press. Available online at http://courses.ed.asu.edu/berliner/readings/fuss/fuss.htm.

Gaming for Understanding (pp. 48–51)

Performance view of understanding: Perkins, D. N. (1998). What is understanding? In M. S. Wiske (Ed.), *Teaching for understanding: Linking research with practice* (pp. 39–57). San Francisco, CA: Jossey-Bass. Perkins, D. N., & Unger, C. (1999). Teaching and learning for understanding. In C. Reigeluth (Ed.), *Instructional design theories and models: Volume II* (pp. 91–114). Mahwah, NJ: Lawrence Erlbaum.

Mental models and understanding: Chapter 4, Perkins, D. N. (1992). *Smart schools: From training memories to educating minds.* New York: The Free Press. See also Perkins, D. N., & Unger, C. (1994). A new look in representations for mathematics and science learning. *Instructional Science, 22,* 1–37.

Mental practice effects: for example, Murphy, S. M. (1990). Models of imagery in sport psychology: A review. *Journal of Mental Imagery, 14,* 153–172. Murphy, S. M. (1994). Imagery interventions in sport. *Medicine and Science in Sports and Exercise,* 26(4), 486–494. Peynircioglu, Z. F., Thompson, J. L., & Tanielian, T. B. (2000). Improvement strategies in free-throw shooting and grip-strength tasks. *Journal of General Psychology, 127*(2), 145–156.

2. Make the Game Worth Playing

On intrinsic motivation: Lepper, M. R., & Greene, D. (Eds.). (1978). *The hidden costs of reward: New perspectives on the psychology of human motivation.* Mahwah, NJ: Lawrence Erlbaum.

Decline of intrinsic motivation: Lepper, M., Corpus, J., & Iyengar, S. (2005). Intrinsic and extrinsic motivational orientations in the classroom: Age differences and academic correlates. *Journal of Educational Psychology, 97*(2), 184–196.

"Learning becomes increasingly decontextualized . . .": Lepper, Corpus, & Lyengar, op. cit., p. 192.

Learning What's Worth Learning (pp. 56–58)

On forgotten knowledge: see, for instance, Ravitch, D., & Finn, C. (1987). *What do our 17-year-olds know? A report on the first national assessment of history and literature.* New York: Harper & Row. On problems of understanding a good summary source: Gardner, H. (1991). *The unschooled mind: How children think and how schools should teach.* New York: Basic Books. On the problem of active use of knowledge: see, for instance, Bransford, J. D., Franks, J. J., Vye, N. J., & Sherwood, R. D. (1989). New approaches to instruction: Because wisdom can't be told. In S. Vosniadou & A. Ortony (Eds.), *Similarity and analogical reasoning* (pp. 470–497). New York: Cambridge University Press. An extended summary of these problems appears in Chapter 2 of Perkins, D. N. (1992). *Smart schools: From training memories to educating minds.* New York: The Free Press.

On inert knowledge: see, for instance, Whitehead, A. N. (1929). *The aims of education and other essays.* New York: Simon & Schuster. Bereiter, C., & Scardamalia, M. (1985). Cognitive coping strategies and the problem of inert knowledge. In S. S. Chipman, J. W. Segal, & R. Glaser (Eds.), *Thinking and learning skills, Vol. 2: Current research and open questions* (pp. 65–80). Mahwah, NJ: Lawrence Erlbaum. Bransford, J. D., Franks, J. J., Vye, N. J., & Sherwood, R. D. (1989). New approaches to instruction: Because wisdom can't be told. In S. Vosniadou & A. Ortony (Eds.), *Similarity and analogical reasoning* (pp. 470–497). New York: Cambridge University Press.

Dewey on curriculum and rich themes: Dewey, J. (1969). *The child and the curriculum;* and *The school and society* (joint ed.). Chicago: University of Chicago Press. Mayhew, K. C., and Edwards, A. C. (1966). *The Dewey School; The laboratory school of the University of Chicago, 1896–1903.* New York: Atherton Press.

National Council of Teachers of Mathematics recommendations on statistics and probability: http://www.nctm.org/uploadedFiles/Math_Standards/12752_exec_pssm.pdf; http://standards.nctm.org/document/chapter3/data.htm.

Picking What's Worth Learning (pp. 58–62)

On generative topics: Wiske, M. S. (Ed.). (1998). *Teaching for understanding: Linking research with practice.* San Francisco: Jossey-Bass.

Postman's "grand narrative": Postman, N. (1995). *The end of education: redefining the value of school* (1st ed.). New York: Knopf. "The engineering of learning . . ." from Postman, p. 3.

The good, the true, and the beautiful: Gardner, H. (2000). *The disciplined mind: Beyond facts and standardized tests, the K–12 education that every child deserves.* New York: Penguin Books.

Our most important choice . . . : Perkins, D. N. (1992). *Smart schools: From training memories to educating minds.* New York: The Free Press, pp. 69–72.

Making the Most of Beginnings (pp. 62–64)

The first day of class: Ritchhart, R. (2002). *Intellectual character: What it is, why it matters, and how to get it.* San Francisco: Jossey-Bass.

Making the Most of Understanding (pp. 64–67)

On "making the most of understanding": The ideas here are adapted from an earlier article, Perkins, D. N. (2001). Thinking for understanding. In A. Costa (Ed.), *Developing minds: A resource book for teaching and thinking.* Alexandria, VA: Association for the Supervision and Curriculum Development.

On the Teaching for Understanding model: Blythe, T., & Associates. (1998). *The teaching for understanding guide.* San Francisco, CA: Jossey-Bass. Perkins, D. N., & Unger, C. (1999). Teaching and learning for understanding. In C. Reigeluth (Ed.), *Instructional design theories and models: Volume II* (pp. 91–114). Mahwah, NJ: Lawrence Erlbaum. Wiske, op. cit. Wiske, M. S., with Franz, K. R., & Breit, L. (2005). *Teaching for understanding with technology.* San Francisco: Jossey-Bass.

The WIDE World online professional development program: This large-scale program was founded by Martha Stone Wiske and myself. David Zarowin is its executive director. See http://wideworld.pz.harvard.edu/.

Students' response to teaching for understanding: Perkins & Unger, op. cit. Wiske, op. cit., Chapter 9.

Making the Most of Expectations (pp. 67–70)

The original "Pygmalion" study: Rosenthal, R., & Jacobson, L. (1968). *Pygmalion in the classroom*. New York: Holt, Rinehart, & Winston.

Challenges to Rosenthal and Jacobson: Spitz, H. H. (1999). Beleaguered *Pygmalion*: A history of the controversy over claims that teacher expectancy raises intelligence. *Intelligence, 27*(3), 199–234.

The four-factor framework of influence: Rosenthal, R. (1974). *On the social psychology of the self-fulfilling prophecy: Further evidence for Pygmalion effects and their mediating mechanisms*. New York: MSS Modular.

Incremental and entity learners: Dweck, C. S. (2000). *Self-theories: Their role in motivation, personality, and development*. Philadelphia: Psychology Press.

Entity learners' response to front-end confusion: Licht, B. G., & Dweck, C. S. (1984). Determinants of academic achievement: The interaction of children's achievement orientations with skill area. *Developmental Psychology, 20*(4), 628–636.

Making the Most of Choice (pp. 71–74)

Reactance: Brehm, J. (1966). *A theory of psychological reactance*. New York: Academic Press.

Graffiti experiment: Pennebaker, J., & Sanders, D. (1976). American graffiti: effects of authority and reactance arousal. *Personality and Social Psychology Bulletin, 2*, 264–267.

Extrinsic motivation undermines intrinsic motivation: Lepper, M. R., & Greene, D. (Eds.). (1978). *The hidden costs of reward: New perspectives on the psychology of human motivation*. Mahwah: NJ: Lawrence Erlbaum.

The haiku experiment: Amabile, T. M. (1983). *The social psychology of creativity*. New York: Springer-Verlag, pp. 153–157.

Conditional instruction: Langer, E., & Piper, A. (1987). The prevention of mindlessness. *Journal of Personality and Social Psychology, 53*, 280–287. Langer, E. J. (1997). *The power of mindful learning*. Reading, MA: Addison-Wesley.

Cultural differences in the motivating effects of choice: Iyengar, S., & Lepper, M. (1999). Rethinking the value of choice: A cultural perspective on intrinsic motivation. *Journal of Personality and Social Psychology, 76*(3), 349–366.

Too much choice: Iyengar, S., & Lepper, M. (2000). When choice is demotivating: Can one desire too much of a good thing? *Journal of Personality and Social Psychology, 79*(6), 995–1006.

Challenge, Imagination, and More (pp. 74–76)

On flow: Csikszentmihalyi, M. (1990). *Flow*. New York: Harper & Row.

Video games and level of challenge: Schaffer, D. (2006). *How computer games help children learn*. New York: Palgrave Macmillan.

Egan, K. (2005). *An imaginative approach to teaching*. San Francisco: Jossey-Bass. Industrial revolution example: pp. 112–120.

3. Work on the Hard Parts

Expertise and deliberate practice: Ericsson, K. A., & Charness, N. (1994). Expert performance: Its structure and acquisition. *American Psychologist, 49*(8), 725–747. Ericsson, K. A., & Smith, J. (Eds.). (1991). *Toward a general theory of expertise: Prospects and limits.* Cambridge: Cambridge University Press.

Slighting the Hard Parts (pp. 80–83)

Students interpreting their algebra errors: Kendall, W. (1991). *Imbedding metacognition in the math problem solving curriculum: An intervention leading students to analyze their own errors.* Unpublished doctoral dissertation, Harvard Graduate School of Education, Cambridge, MA. "Didn't seem to know enough . . .": p. 65.

Embracing the Hard Parts (pp. 83–89)

On colleagues' and my work with organizational learning: see Wilson, D., Perkins, D., Bonnet, D., Miani, C., & Unger, C. (2005). *Learning at work: Research lessons on leading learning in the workplace.* Cambridge, MA: Project Zero, Harvard Graduate School of Education. Perkins, D. N. (2003). *King Arthur's Round Table: How collaborative conversations create smart organizations.* Hoboken, NJ: John Wiley & Sons. Both of these sources discuss communicative feedback. See Chapter 3 in Perkins, op. cit. See the "ladder of feedback" in Wilson & others, op. cit.

Anticipating the Hard Parts (pp. 89–100)

On troublesome knowledge: Perkins, D. N. (1999). The many faces of constructivism. *Educational Leadership, 57*(3), 6–11. Perkins, D. N. (2006). Constructivism and troublesome knowledge. In J.H.F. Meyer & R. Land (Eds.), *Overcoming barriers to student understanding: Threshold concepts and troublesome knowledge* (pp. 33–47). London: Routledge.

"I know what to do . . .": Taba, H., & Elzey, F. (1964). Teaching strategies and thought processes. *Teachers College Record, 65,* 524–534.

The private universe film: Schneps, M. H. (1989). *A private universe.* Santa Monica, CA: Pyramid Film & Video.

Inert knowledge experiment: Bransford, J. D., Franks, J. J., Vye, N. J., & Sherwood, R. D. (1989). New approaches to instruction: Because wisdom can't be told. In S. Vosniadou & A. Ortony (Eds.), *Similarity and analogical reasoning* (pp. 470–497). New York: Cambridge University Press.

Centrisms: Kegan, R. (2001). Competencies as working epistemologies: Ways we want adults to know. In D. Rychen & L. Salganik (Eds.), *Defining and selecting key competencies* (pp. 92–204). Seattle: Hogrefe & Huber.

"Objects in motion . . .": Linn, M. (2002). The role of customization of innovative science curricula: Implications for design, practice, and professional development. Symposium at the annual meeting of the National Association for Research in Science Teaching, New Orleans, LA.

Anchoring intuitions: Clement, J. (1993). Using bridging analogies and anchoring intuitions to deal with students' preconceptions in physics. *Journal of Research in Science Teaching, 30*(10), 1241–1257.

Advanced knowledge acquisition: Feltovich, P. J., Spiro, R. J., & Coulson, R. L. (1993). Learning, teaching, and testing for complex conceptual understanding. In N. Frederiksen & I. Bejar (Eds.), *Test theory for a new generation of tests* (pp. 181–217). Mahwah, NJ: Lawrence Erlbaum.

Building a Theory of Difficulty (pp. 100–105)

On theories of difficulty: Perkins, D. N. (2007). Theories of difficulty. In N. Entwistle & P. Tomlinson (Eds.), *Student learning and university teaching*, British Journal of Educational Psychology Monograph Series II: Psychological Aspects of Education—Current Trends (pp. 31–48). Leicester, UK: British Psychological Society.

4. Play Out of Town

The Meaning of Transfer (pp. 111–115)

Coding in terms of surface characteristics: for example, Chi, M.T.H., Feltovich, P., & Glaser, R. (1981). Categorization and representation of physics problems by experts and novices. *Cognitive Science, 5*, 121–152. Larkin, J. H. (1983). The role of problem representation in physics. In D. Gentner & A. L. Stevens (Eds.), *Mental models*. Mahwah, NJ: Lawrence Erlbaum. Larkin, J. H., McDermott, J., Simon, D. P., & Simon, H. A. (1980). Modes of competence in solving physics problems. *Cognitive Science, 4*, 317–345. Schoenfeld, A. H., & Herrmann, D. J. (1982). Problem perception and knowledge structure in expert and novice mathematical problem solvers. *Journal of Experimental Psychology: Learning, Memory, and Cognition, 8*, 484–494.

For a review of controversies about transfer: see Lobato, J. (2006). Alternative perspectives on the transfer of learning: History, issues, and challenges for future research. *The Journal of the Learning Sciences, 15*(4), 431–449.

The Trouble with Transfer (pp. 115–119)

The Bo Peep, Lost Sheep, and Good Shepherd theories: I first used this metaphor in Chapter 5 of Perkins, D. N. (1992). *Smart schools: From training memories to educating minds*. New York: The Free Press.

The idea of affordances: Gibson, J. J. (1986). *The ecological approach to visual perception*. Mahwah, NJ: Lawrence Erlbaum.

Thorndike's investigations: Thorndike, E. L. (1923). The influence of first year Latin upon the ability to read English. *School Sociology, 17*, 165–168. Thorndike, E. L., & Woodworth, R. S. (1901). The influence of improvement in one mental function upon the efficiency of other functions. *Psychological Review, 8*, 247–261.

On computer programming and transfer: Salomon, G., & Perkins, D. N. (1987). Transfer of cognitive skills from programming: When and how? *Journal of Educational Computing Research, 3*, 149–169.

Luria's results on literacy: Luria, A. R. (1976). *Cognitive development: Its cultural and social foundations*. Cambridge, MA: Harvard University Press.

The Vai and literacy: Scribner, S., & Cole, M. (1981). *The psychology of literacy*. Cambridge, MA: Harvard University Press.

Olson's view of the stance toward text developed by literacy: Olson, D. R. (1994). *The world on paper: The conceptual and cognitive implications of writing and reading*. Cambridge, UK: Cambridge University Press.

Discussions of situated learning and the decontextualized character of much of education: for example, Brown, J. S., Collins, A., & Duguid, P. (1989). Situated cognition and the culture of learning. *Educational Researcher, 18*(1), 32–42. Kishner, D., & Whitson, J. A. (Eds.). (1997). *Situated cognition: Social, semiotic, and psychological perspectives*. Mahwah, NJ: Lawrence Erlbaum. Lave, J., & Wenger, E. (1991). *Situated learning: Legitimate peripheral participation*. New York: Cambridge University Press.

The Hope for Transfer (pp. 119–123)

The high road/low road model and the prospects of transfer: Perkins, D. N., & Salomon, G. (1989). Are cognitive skills context bound? *Educational Researcher, 18*(1), 16–25. Salomon, G., & Perkins, D. N. (1989). Rocky roads to transfer: Rethinking mechanisms of a neglected phenomenon. *Educational Psychologist, 24*(2), 113–142.

Transfer and the CASE program: Adey, P., & Shayer, M. (1993). An exploration of long-term far-transfer effects following an extended intervention program in the high school science curriculum. *Cognition and Instruction, 11*(1), 1–29. Adey, P., & Shayer, M. (1994). *Really raising standards: Cognitive intervention and academic achievement*. London: Routledge.

Preparation for future learning: Bransford, J. D., & Schwartz, D. L. (1999). Rethinking transfer: A simple proposal with interesting implications. In A. Iran-Nejad & P. D. Pearson (Eds.), *Review of research in education* (Vol. 24, pp. 61–101). Washington, DC: American Educational Research Association.

Preparation for future learning applied: Schwartz, D., & Martin, T. (2004). Inventing to prepare for future learning: The hidden efficiency of encouraging original student production in statistics instruction. *Cognition and Instruction, 22*(2), 129–184.

Transfer as Importing (pp. 127–128)

Transferring in understandings from a remote context: Lustig, I. (2002). *The effects of studying distal conflicts on the perception of a proximal one.* University of Haifa: Unpublished MA thesis, as cited in Salomon, G. (2004). Does peace education make a difference? *Peace and Conflict: Journal of Peace Psychology, 10,* 257–274.

5. Uncover the Hidden Game

Baseball's hidden game of statistics: Thorn, J., & Palmer, P. (1984). *The hidden game of baseball: A revolutionary approach to baseball and its statistics.* New York: Doubleday Books.

The Hidden Game of Strategy (pp. 136–140)

Polya's treatment of heuristics: Polya, G. (1954). *Mathematics and plausible reasoning* (2 vols.). Princeton, NJ: Princeton University Press. Polya, G. (1957). *How to solve it: A new aspect of mathematical method* (2nd ed.). Garden City, New York: Doubleday.

Teaching heuristics: Schoenfeld, A. H. (1982). Measures of problem-solving performance and of problem-solving instruction. *Journal for Research in Mathematics Education, 13*(1), 31–49. Schoenfeld, A. H., & Herrmann, D. J. (1982). Problem perception and knowledge structure in expert and novice mathematical problem solvers. *Journal of Experimental Psychology: Learning, Memory, and Cognition, 8,* 484–494.

Reading improvement through reciprocal teaching: Palincsar, A. S., & Brown, A. L. (1984). Reciprocal teaching of comprehension-fostering and comprehension-monitoring activities. *Cognition and Instruction, 1,* 117–175.

On self-explanation: for example, Chi, M., & Bassok, M. (1989). Learning from examples via self-explanations. In L. Resnick (Ed.), *Knowing, learning and instruction* (pp. 251–282). Mahwah, NJ: Lawrence Erlbaum. Chi, M.T.H., deLeeuw, N., Chiu, M-H., & LaVancher, C. (1994). Eliciting self-explanations improves understanding. *Cognitive Science, 18,* 439–477.

Review of the impact of reading strategies: Haller, E. P., Child, D. A., & Walberg, H. J. (1988). Can comprehension be taught? A quantitative synthesis of "metacognitive" studies. *Educational Researcher, 17*(5), 5–8.

Students' attitudes toward reading strategies: Simmons, M. R. (1992). *The role of prospective memory in students' sustained use of reading strategies.* Unpublished dissertation, Harvard Graduate School of Education, Cambridge, Massachusetts.

The Hidden Game of Causal Thinking (pp. 140–146)

The traffic jam systems thinking question: Sweeney, L. B. (2001). *Learning to understand the dynamics of a complex world: A theoretical review of three frameworks for systems-based inquiry.* Unpublished doctoral dissertation, Harvard Graduate School of Education, Cambridge, Massachusetts. Also see Sweeney, L. B. (2001). *When a butterfly sneezes: A guide for helping kids explore interconnections in our world through favorite stories.* Waltham, MA: Pegasus Communications.

How electrons flow: for example, Grotzer, T. A., & Sudbury, M. (2000, April). *Moving beyond underlying linear causal models of electrical circuits.* Paper presented at the Annual Conference of the National Association for Research in Science Teaching, New Orleans. See review in Grotzer, T. A. (2003). Learning to understand the forms of causality implicit in scientific explanations. *Studies in Science Education,* 39, 1–74.

On complex causality: see Grotzer, op. cit. Grotzer, T. A. (in press). *Understandings of consequence: Educating students for the world of today and tomorrow.* Lanham, MD: Rowman & Littlefield. Perkins, D. N., & Grotzer, T. A. (2005). Dimensions of causal understanding: The role of complex causal models in students' understanding of science. *Studies in Science Education,* 41, 117–166.

The candle RECAST activity—a description appears in: Grotzer, T. A. (2004, October). Putting science within reach: Addressing patterns of thinking that limit science learning. *Principal Leadership,* pp. 217–221.

The Hidden Game of Inquiry (pp. 146–153)

On the thinking about thinking course and its epistemic games: Perkins, D. N. (1994). The hidden order of open-ended thinking. In J. Edwards (Ed.), *Thinking: Interdisciplinary perspectives.* Victoria, Australia: Hawker Brownlow Education.

On epistemic games: Collins, A., & Ferguson, W. (1993). Epistemic forms and epistemic games: Structures and strategies to guide inquiry. *Educational Psychologist,* 28(1), 25–42. Perkins, D. N. (1997). Epistemic games. *International Journal of Educational Research,* 27(1), 49–61.

Students' sense of proof in geometry: Chazen, D. (1989). *Ways of knowing: High school students' conceptions of mathematical proof.* Unpublished doctoral dissertation, Harvard Graduate School of Education, Cambridge, MA.

Visible Thinking: Perkins, D. N., & Ritchhart, R. (2004). When is good thinking? In D. Y. Dai & R. J. Sternberg (Eds.), *Motivation, emotion, and cognition: Integrative perspectives on intellectual functioning and development* (pp. 351–384). Mahwah, NJ: Lawrence Erlbaum. Tishman, S., Perkins, D. N., & Jay, E. (1995). *The thinking classroom.* Boston: Allyn & Bacon. Web site: http://www.pz.harvard.edu/vt/.

Artful thinking: http://www.pz.harvard.edu/tc/. Tishman, S., & Palmer, P. (2006). Artful thinking: Final report. Accessed December 2006 from Artful Thinking Web site at http://www.pz.harvard.edu/at/index.cfm.

Cultures of thinking: Ritchhart, R., & Perkins, D. N. (2008). Making thinking visible. *Educational Leadership,* 65(5), 57–61.

The explanation game example: in the *Visible Thinking* DVD (2005), produced by Project Zero, Harvard Graduate School of Education, Cambridge, MA: President and Fellows of Harvard College.

The explanation game in looking at art: Housen, A. (1996). *Studies on aesthetic development*. Minneapolis: American Association of Museums Sourcebook. Housen, A., Yenawine, P., & Arenas, A. (1991). *Visual thinking curriculum*. (Unpublished but used for research purposes.) New York: Museum of Modern Art.

The Hidden Game of Power (pp. 153–156)

The school chair-desk: Luttrell, W. (2004). Finding and using culture. Cambridge, MA: Class guest lecture at the Harvard Graduate School of Education.

"I became painfully aware . . ." : Luttrell, op. cit.

Critical pedagogy: Freire, P. (1970). *Pedagogy of the oppressed*. New York: Continuum.

How Games Hide (pp. 156–163)

The different levels of science education: this general scheme can be found in Perkins, D. N., & Grotzer, T. A. (2005). Dimensions of causal understanding: The role of complex causal models in students' understanding of science. *Studies in Science Education, 41,* 117–166.

Richards, I. A. (1929). *Practical criticism: A study of literary judgment*. New York: Harcourt, Brace.

Peripheral awareness: Polanyi, M. (1958). *Personal knowledge: Toward a post-critical philosophy*. Chicago: The University of Chicago Press.

The power of intuitive thinking that taps tacit knowledge: Claxton, G. (1999). *Hare brain, tortoise mind: How intelligence increases when you think less*. New York: HarperCollins. Gladwell, M. (2005). *Blink: The power of thinking without thinking*. New York: Little, Brown.

Beyond the Horizon of Readiness (pp. 163–166)

Zone of proximal development: Vygotsky, L. S. (1978). *Mind in society: The development of higher psychological processes*. Cambridge, MA: Harvard University Press.

Subject-object theory: Kegan, R. (1994). *In over our heads: The mental demands of modern life*. Cambridge, MA: Harvard University Press.

6. Learn from the Team

A Social View of Learning (pp. 172–174)

Social scaffolding: Vygotsky, L. S. (1978). *Mind in society: The development of higher psychological processes*. Cambridge, MA: Harvard University Press.

On activity theory: for example, Engeström, Y., Miettinen, R., & Punamäki, R. (Eds.). (1999). *Perspectives on activity theory*. Cambridge, UK: Cambridge University Press.

On situated cognition and situated learning: for example, Brown, J. S., Collins, A., & Duguid, P. (1989). Situated cognition and the culture of learning. *Educational Researcher, 18*(1), 32–42. Kishner, D., & Whitson, J. A. (Eds.). (1997). *Situated cognition: Social, semiotic, and psychological perspectives.* Mahwah, NJ: Lawrence Erlbaum. Lave, J. (1988). *Cognition in practice: Mind, mathematics and culture in everyday life.* Cambridge, UK: Cambridge University Press. Lave, J., & Wenger, E. (1991). *Situated learning: Legitimate peripheral participation.* New York: Cambridge University Press.

The cottage cheese story: Lave, op. cit., p. 165.

Pair Problem Solving (pp. 175–177)

Source of the Bill, Judy, and Sally problem: Lochhead, J. (2000) *Thinkback: A user's guide to minding the mind.* Mahwah, NJ: Lawrence Erlbaum, p. 15.

Think aloud pair problem solving: for example, Lochhead, op. cit., and Whimbey, A., & Lochhead, J. (1999). *Problem solving and comprehension, 6th ed.* Mahwah, NJ: Lawrence Erlbaum.

Perkins, D. N. (1986). *Knowledge as design.* Mahwah, NJ: Lawrence Erlbaum.

"With the added vision of video playback": Lochhead, op. cit., p. 20.

Studio Learning (pp. 177–181)

Hetland, L., Winner, E., Veenema, S., & Sheridan, K. (2007). *Studio thinking: The real benefits of arts education.* NY: Teachers College Press.

Communities of Practice (pp. 181–185)

Study of Xerox technical representatives: Orr, J. (1990). Sharing knowledge, celebrating identity: Community memory in a service culture. In D. Middleton & D. Edwards (Eds.), *Collective remembering: Memory in society.* Beverly Hills, CA: Sage Publications.

On learning by sharing stories: see Brown, J. S., & Duguid, P. (2000). Balancing act: How to capture knowledge without killing it. *Harvard Business Review, 78*(3), 73–79.

Legitimate peripheral participation: Lave & Wenger, op. cit.

Blythe, T., Allen, D., & Powell, B. (2008). *Looking together at student work, 2nd edition.* New York: Teachers College Press.

On the Visible Thinking program: Please find full references under Chapter 5, "The Hidden Game of Inquiry."

Cross-Age Tutoring (pp. 185–189)

Cross-age tutoring discussion and example: Briggs, D. (1998). *A class of their own: When children teach children.* Westport, CT: Bergin & Garvey. Excerpt from page 35.

Lepper and colleagues' research on tutoring: for example, Lepper, M. R., Drake, M. F., & O'Donnell-Johnson, T. (1997). Scaffolding techniques of expert human tutors. In M. Pressley & K. Hogan (Eds.), *Advances in teaching and learning* (pp. 108–144). New York: Brokkline Press. Lepper, M. R., Woolverton, M., Mumme, D. L., & Gurtner, J. (1993). Motivational techniques of expert human tutors: Lessons for the design of computer-based tutors. In S. P. Lajoie & S. J. Derry (Eds.), *Computers as cognitive tools*. Mahwah, N. J.: Lawrence Erlbaum. Lepper, M., Aspinwall, L., Mumme, D., & Chabay, R. (1990). Self-perception and social perception processes in tutoring: Subtle social control strategies of expert tutors. In J. M. Olson & M. P. Zanna (Eds.), *Self-inference processes: The Ontario symposium, Vol. 6* (pp. 217–237). Mahwah, NJ: Lawrence Erlbaum.

7. Learn the Game of Learning

The Passenger's Seat (pp. 197–200)

University students' different approaches to learning: Säljö, R. (1979). *Learning in the learner's perspective. I. Some common-sense conceptions.* (Report 76). Gothenburg: University of Gothenburg, Department of Education. Marton, F., & Säljö, R. (1976). On qualitative differences in learning. I. Outcome and process. *British Journal of Educational Psychology,* 46, 4–11. Marton, F., Hounsell, D. J., and Entwistle, N. J. (Eds.). (1997). *The experience of learning, 2nd Edition.* Edinburgh: Scottish Academic Press. Entwistle, N. J., & Ramsden, P. (1983). *Understanding student learning.* London: Croom Helm. Entwistle, N. J. (2003). Enhancing teaching-learning environments to encourage deep learning. In E. De Corte (Ed.), *Excellence in higher education* (pp. 83–96). London: Portland Press.

Performance versus mastery orientation: for example, Pintrich, P. (2000). Multiple goals, multiple pathways: The role of goal orientation in learning and achievement. *Journal of Educational Psychology,* 92(3), 544–555.

The work of Carol Dweck: for example, Dweck, C. S. (2000). *Self-theories: Their role in motivation, personality, and development.* Philadelphia: Psychology Press.

Students' conceptions of learning: Hadar, L. (2006). *Ideal learning and school learning: Are we talking about the same thing? Analyzing Israeli high school learners' perceptions of learning.* Unpublished paper.

On cognitive apprenticeship: Collins, A., Brown, J. S., & Newman, S. E. (1989). Cognitive apprenticeship: Teaching the craft of reading, writing, and mathematics. In L. B. Resnick (Ed.), *Knowing, learning, and instruction: Essays in honor of Robert Glaser* (pp. 453–494). Mahwah, NJ: Lawrence Erlbaum.

Learning logs: for example, Sanford, B. (1988). Writing reflectively. *Language Arts,* 65, 652–657.

Children's capacity to raise generative questions: Scardamalia, M., & Bereiter, C. (1992). Text-based and knowledge-based questioning by children. *Cognition and Instruction,* 9, 177–199.

Driver Education (pp. 205–210)

On the infusion versus the stand-alone approach: Swartz, R. J., & Perkins, D. N. (1989). *Teaching thinking: Issues and approaches.* Pacific Grove, CA: Midwest Publications. Perkins, D. N. (1995). *Outsmarting IQ: The emerging science of learnable intelligence.* New York: The Free Press.

Explicitness in heuristics instruction: Schoenfeld, A. H. (1979). Explicit heuristic training as a variable in problem solving performance. *Journal for Research in Mathematics Education, 10*(3), 173–187. Schoenfeld, A. H. (1980). Teaching problem-solving skills. *American Mathematical Monthly, 87,* 794–805.

Afterword: The Future of Learning

Five ways to engage emerging challenges: Gardner, H. (2006). *Five minds for the future.* Boston: Harvard Business School Press.

Challenges of preparing for the world of work: Eraut, M. (1994). *Developing professional knowledge and competence.* London: Falmer Press.

Neomillennial learning styles: Dede, C. (2005). Planning for "neomillennial" learning styles: Implications for investments in technology and faculty. In J. Oblinger & D. Oblinger (Eds.), *Educating the net generation* (pp. 226–247). Boulder, CO: Educause Publishers. Dede, C., Dieterle, E., Clarke, J., Ketelhut, D. J., & Nelson, B. (2007). Media-based learning styles: Implications for distance education. In M. Moore (Ed.), *Handbook of distance education* (Second ed., pp. 339–352). Mahwah, NJ: Lawrence Erlbaum. Also see the Educause Web site at http://www.educause.edu/content.asp?page_id=6069&bhcp=1.

The cognitive needs of the contemporary workplace: Murnane, R. J., & Levy, F. (1996). *Teaching the new basic skills: Principles for educating children to thrive in a changing economy.* New York: The Free Press. Quote from p. 9.

Levy, F., & Murnane, R. (2004). *The new division of labor: How computers are creating the new job market.* Princeton, NJ: Princeton University Press.

The ignorance map: From the PDF document (no author, no date) *Q-Cubed: Questions, questioning, and questioners.* Tucson, AZ: The University of Arizona College of Medicine. See the Web site at http://www.ignorance.medicine.arizona.edu/pdfs/SIMIBRO3.PDF.

INDEX